Gender, Race, Ethnicity, and Power in Maritime America

Papers from the Conference Held at Mystic Seaport

September 2006

Edited by Glenn S. Gordinier

Mystic Seaport
75 Greenmanville Ave., P.O. Box 6000
Mystic, CT 06355-0990

www.mysticseaport.org

Printed in the United States of America

First edition

Designed by Trish LaPointe, LaPointe Design, Old Mystic, CT

ISBN 978-0-939511-27-3

Contents

Introduction

Mystic Seaport was founded as the Mystic Marine Historical Association in a time of increasing difficulty for the nation, December of 1929. In spite of the tenor of the times, the founders sought to preserve the threatened heritage of Mystic, Connecticut and its maritime legacy. At the outset, however those involved were also thinking much more broadly than one might expect of a locally inspired historical society. The mission of the young organization was always seen to have regional and national importance. In the years that followed, with the acquisition of the whaleship *Charles W. Morgan*, the growth of the outdoor museum as well as the vessel, object, and manuscript collections, the institution grew in stature. Along with the augmentation of collections came the growth in programming including exhibit interpretation, school outreach, skills classes, and higher education. By the late 1970s Mystic Seaport was the leading institution in maritime preservation and the only museum in the nation with accredited residential higher education programs, the graduate level Frank C. Munson Institute, and the undergraduate Williams College-Mystic Seaport Program in Maritime Studies. Additionally, the Museum had a long history of publications, symposia, and conferences.

In 1993, then Mystic Seaport President J. Revell Carr led the effort to gather scholars, educators, museum professionals, and the general public to discuss issues of race and ethnicity in the maritime setting. As a result the first National Conference on Race, Ethnicity and Power in Maritime America was convened in the fall 1995. Speakers from across the country gathered to examine how the dynamics of race, ethnicity, and power had played out in America's maritime communities at home, abroad, afloat, ashore, on the coasts, and in the hinterland. The energy, scholarship, and goodwill fostered by that gathering resulted in a second, like-named conference, in 2000. Once again, leading scholars and educators found that the unique setting and programming offered at Mystic Seaport served to augment their discussions, inspiring open and direct communication about the thorny issues that intertwine with race, identity, and human interaction. Happily, the funding for this second conference also supported the publication of select papers from the event. Published by Mystic Seaport in 2005, *Perspectives on Race, Ethnicity, and Power in Maritime America* offered a wide array of analysis covering topics stretching from the eighteenth-century factories in Guangzhou (Canton) to the Mississippi steamboats of the jazz age, and from early byways of Martha's Vineyard to the offices of Marcus Garvey's Black Star Line.

At the closing session of each of the first two conferences on race and ethnicity, a panel discussion sought to reflect on the new understandings sparked by the presenters and to identify new areas of interest worthy of study. In both cases, the conversation identified one field that had been touched upon; an area that had, indeed, often been embedded in the topics at hand, but had not been explicitly included. That topic was gender. Thus it was determined that when a third conference was convened it would include gender in its purpose. The call for papers for the conference to be held in 2006 stated that Mystic Seaport was seeking to "engage a wide community . . . in an inclusive conversation about issues of gender, race, ethnicity, authority, and power in American maritime history very broadly defined, in local, national, and global contexts." The third in this series of conferences, then cast its net wide, and the resultant multidisciplinary discussion of gender, race, and ethnicity in the maritime world reflected that wider mission.

The expanded mission of the National Conference on Gender, Race, Ethnicity, and Power in Maritime America, organized by the Museum's Frank C. Munson Institute of American Maritime Studies and held at Mystic Seaport in the fall of 2006, was evident in the programming of the event. The keynote speaker was Professor Martha Hodes of New York University, whose presentation was based on her important book, *A Sea Captain's Wife: A True Story of Love, Race and War in the Nineteenth Century*. The attendees were also privileged to view *Shipping Out, The Story of America's Seafaring Women*, Maria Brooks's striking and informative educational video about contemporary women in the merchant marine flying the stars and stripes. A third program element that enjoined the place of gender in maritime America was the Saturday evening performance titled "Wade in the Water," created and performed by inspiring soprano Alicia Hall Moran, accompanied by her husband, acclaimed jazz pianist Jason Moran.

The essays that make up this volume are representative of those offered at the conference in 2006. As such, they reflect the goals of that gathering, an inclusive conversation about gender, race, ethnicity, and power wherever Americans may have engaged in maritime activity from the early years of the Atlantic market to the twentieth century.

1

The Middle Passage has been infamous for its cruelties and inhumanity since its earliest days. The descriptions penned by Ottobah Cugano and Olaudah Equiano over two centuries ago confronted English society with its horrors. Since that time, antislavery activists, government officials, and scholars have described and analyzed the scope and character of the carriage of enslaved Africans to the shores of the Americas. Embedded in those volumes, as it is embedded in the communal memory of many millions today, is the record of unrestrained violence visited by one human upon another. Accounts of sanctioned assaults, mutilation, torture, drownings, beatings and more have been part and parcel of the record of the trade. In chapter one, "'Make Haste & Let Me See You With a Good Cargo of Negroes': Gender, Power, and the Centrality of Violence Within the Eighteenth-Century Atlantic Slave Trade," Sowande' Mustakeem presents an unflinching examination of the darkest elements of the Middle Passage, particularly as they relate to female slaves and the additional terrors they confronted while crossing the broad Atlantic.

This paper examines the place of gender, race, resistance, and corporal punishment within the broader narrative of maritime history and the Atlantic slave trade. While on one hand drawing from the accounts of eighteenth-century merchants, government records, and surgeons' and seamen's journals, Mustakeem also turns to histories of gender and slavery as well as recent scholarship in the study of violence. Her multi-layered examination of bondpeople afloat and their captors considers these relationships through three phases: the entrance of those in bondage into the slave trade, the rape of African women aboard ship, and the role of bondwomen and bondmen in slaveship rebellions. As informative as it is jarring, Mustakeem's examination of gender and violence further lifts a veil that long has hidden some of the most tragic aspects of the Middle Passage.

2

Herman Melville took care to include a Gay Head Indian among his select cadre of boatsteerers aboard the *Pequod* in *Moby-Dick*, yet he also asserted that the Pequot tribe that inspired the name of Ahab's ship was "extinct as the ancient Medes." Melville's assertion that Native Americans could be found handling harpoons in the Yankee whaling fleet, ironically, matches his miss-assertion that the Pequot people had vanished from the scene. Scholars have been aware of the presence of Indians aboard American whalers since the nineteenth century, but success in identifying them, quantifying their numbers and analyzing the impact of their participation in the fishery has proven to be illusive.

Anthropologist Jason Mancini's research into the maritime activities of the Indian men who shipped out of the port of New London has uncovered a wealth of new and valuable information. In his chapter, "Beyond Reservation: Indians, Maritime Labor, and Communities of Color from Eastern Long Island Sound, 1713-1861," Mancini has linked their seafaring lives to the landed communities from whence they came, and by so doing sheds light on both environments, aqueous and terrestrial. Mancini explores how the long absences of mariners from the tribal lands near the eastern end of Long Island Sound impacted their lives and the lives of the communities they left behind. As seafarers, these generations of men became part of a larger, Euro-dominated social network that took them far from their natal communities. As a result, the native communities ashore were seen to be vanishing. As their peripatetic sons traveled far in New London's extensive whaling and shipping fleets, these communities became increasingly a part of the larger social geography and thus difficult to identify. This piece will help the reader "find" again a people that seemed to have vanished, and in doing so will make clear relationships that were, in fact, maintained in and through a maritime world that largely reshaped an ancient heritage.

3

In the eighteenth century, escaped slaves from British North America often turned to the "Black Atlantic" as a vast, and complex environment in which to secure their freedom. In chapter three, "Possibilities and Limits for Freedom: Maritime Fugitives in British North America, ca. 1713-1783," Charles Foy examines the promise the Atlantic World held for the fugitive, as well as the limits that world set on that promise. By examining the records of over 7,500 mariners of color, Foy has been able to identify the vessels, seaports, and travels of the "maritime maroons" of the Atlantic.

There were a variety of vessels in which a maroon could ship, including merchant carriers, navy ships, privateers, and pirate ships. The littoral havens also offered a multiplicity of options for those bondmen hoping to live in freedom. Ports in Great Britain, the West Indies, and North America were a part of the extended maritime web and presented an array of settings in which to avoid identification. Just as the escaped bondman networked and learned to identify literal harbors of refuge, so too did the slave master. Slaveholders' agents who sought escaped mariners were active in those same communities and impinged on the boundaries of freedom. This work examines the opportunities, the challenges, and the dynamics of mobility that swung the door to freedom open or slammed it closed for maritime maroons.

4

During the twentieth century, racial stereotypes held that African Americans and whites often recreated in different ways. Whites, according to these stereotypes, were swimmers, while blacks essentially were not. In his "Enslaved Underwater Divers in the Atlantic World," Kevin Dawson concludes that these racial markers in the eighteenth and nineteenth centuries, were, in fact, reversed. He found, rather, that Africans carried their advanced swimming and underwater diving skills with them from Africa to the Americas. This cultural retention, though long overlooked by scholars, influenced the lives of those involved and the character of the slave institution in which they operated.

This study begins by comparing the swimming abilities of Africans and Europeans. White observers regularly reported on the comfort of Africans in the water. Letters and journals consistently noted Africans' extraordinary ability to perform feats of speed and endurance, both on the surface and below when they took to the water. Play and competition in the water was a commonplace in western Africa, and swimming methods of the native people were far more efficient and complex than those of Western observers. Even the long-held belief that surfing originated in the islands of the Pacific is proven to be a misconception; it was also practiced along coast of Senegal, the Ivory Coast, and beyond.

The widespread use of swimming skills armed those who survived the Middle Passage to apply their expertise on the far side of the Atlantic. Slaveowners then put those talents to work for their own benefit by demanding that their bondmen do such tasks as pearl-diving, sponge-diving, and underwater salvage. Even while suffering the exploitation of their skills and dexterity, enslaved divers then leveraged their talents to gain limited privileges from their overseers in another example of maritime settings creating seams in the slave institution.

5

In 1846 the American reading public was offered another selection in the growing body of "true" sea literature. George Little's *Life on the Ocean* told of his travels around the watery world. Part of his travels, naturally, included encounters with the "other" as he moved across ocean barriers, from nation to nation and region to region.

Historian Brian Rouleau's chapter, "Ambassador in the Forecastle: The Reflections of an American Seaman Abroad," uses Little's *Life* as a mechanism to examine one American mariner's sense of self and sense of national identity in response to a wide and multifaceted maritime environment. The observations and sensibilities of Little are examined in order to inform the reader about issues of national identity, race and racial boundaries, cultural assumptions and intercultural contact, as well as the influence of shipboard life on these elements.

As a representative of his native land, its people, and its institutions, American mariner George Little was very self-conscious about his place in the maritime world. He was also acutely aware of the demeanor of those with whom he interacted. Thus, when reporting on those interactions, Little is a particularly valuable informant, and one who speaks from the forecastle, the haunt of working-class men who got wet.

Little's travels began in 1807 and took him to such places as Chile, Mexico, and Hawai'i. As he traveled the eastern reaches of the Pacific rim and beyond, Little's interpretations of, and notions about, native peoples were informed by a sense of national identity that was as certain and heartfelt as it was simplistic and chauvinistic. Challenging scholarship that asserts that the seafaring experience informed international associations based on class and a shared experience, the words of American sailor George Little remind us of countervailing influences. Racial stereotyping, incipient nationalism, and a belief in America's exceptional role in the world informed the observations of George Little, and the assumptions of his readers alike.

6

Beginning with first National Conference on Race, Ethnicity and Power in Maritime America in 1995, Mystic Seaport sought to bring together scholars, museum professionals, and the general public. As part of that effort, public history and programming were included in the conference agenda. Tours, gallery talks, and dramatic and musical presentations have always had a place in the ensuing conferences. The 2006 conference included a panel put together by the staff of the Constitution Museum in Charlestown, Massachusetts. Panel members included co-authors Lauren McCormack, Kristin Gallas, and Anne Grimes Rand, as well as living-history interpreter Rashaun Martin. Martin's stirring and thought-provoking performance was a high point of the three-day conference.

The paper presented by the panel, "'I never had any better fighters': Exploring USS *Constitution* and Black Sailors in the United Sates Navy During the War of 1812," combined their research into the experience of free black sailors in the United States Navy during the War of 1812, and an explanation of the programming that evolved from it. The research was based upon extensive naval records documenting the lives of the 7-15 percent of seamen in wartime naval service who were of color. The nature of that naval experience was the focus of the panel's documentation, scripting, and program efforts.

The panel also addressed how the research served as the foundation for exhibitry, outreach, and public programming designed to build a bridge between the museum, and the local black community. The innovative experiential exhibits, audio representations of voices from the past, and live performance were all received with great enthusiasm. Formative evaluation of museum visitors proved the research and delivery methods to be effective as the Constitution Museum engaged visitors in learning about a compelling past in equally compelling ways.

7

Just as the series of social history conferences at Mystic Seaport in 1995, 2000, and 2006 sought to engage nonacademics along with scholars, it also welcomed papers from a variety of disciplines. Chapter seven, "Citizens, Sailors, and Slaves," comes from the pen of Bryan Sinche, a professor of English who looked to the writings of Frederick Douglass in order to examine how race and identity intersected for American mariners in the nineteenth century.

Dr. Sinche probed Frederick Douglass's 1853 novella, "The Heroic Slave," and his 1881 memoir, *Life and Times of Frederick Douglass*, to examine how Douglass used the sea both as a setting and as a metaphor in these two separate works. The author's escape from slavery disguised as a sailor is widely known and is directly attributable to the commonality of mariners of color in the early nineteenth century. That escape also connected Douglass to the liminal existence of American mariners, whose protection certificates allowed them, whatever their color, some of the protections of citizenship. And yet, the wording of those very documents was challenged, as was the safety and welfare of a seafarer, simply by the nature of his work.

An important image in the world of the Yankee sailor was the American eagle. It appeared, for instance, on the protection document that Douglass referenced in both his tale about Madison Washington and in his own true experience. Sinche examines how that American icon, which was explicitly associated with freedom, also reflected the complex interrelations between race, identity, and seafaring. After all, the eagle also represented the young nation state and its mariners, some of whom were white and free but subject to strict authority, and some of whom sailed the open sea even while being held in bondage. Through an examination of Douglass's literary imagery and artistic renderings of symbol, the relationships between citizens, sailors, and slaves become more clear.

8

Between the spring of 1849 and the early days of 1850, approximately 40,000 people arrived in San Francisco in search of their fortune. Most sought gold in the valley of the Sacramento, while others realized that profits were to be had in the burgeoning port town on the bay. These adventurers came from across the globe, but those who immigrated from the eastern rim of the great Pacific had an early advantage due to their relative proximity. Among some of those advantaged settlers were the first of the 8,000 Chileans who would sail through the Golden Gate in mid-century.

Edward Melillo's essay, "Feeding 'La Boca del Puerto': Chileans and the Maritime Origins of San Francisco," deals with the contributions Chilean immigrants made to the ever growing and dynamic port of San Francisco. The city rapidly grew out over Yerba Buena Cove, encompassing a number of ships that had been abandoned by their crews. One of the most famous of these hulks was the merchant ship *Niantic*, which had arrived flying the Chilean flag. As a part of "a Venice built of pine instead of marble," as one émigré from Chile described the waterside city, the *Niantic* played her role in the expansion, but was eventually lost beneath the sands of time. So too did those thousands of Chilean adventurers play an important role in San Francisco's growth. They worked on the docks and in the stores, whorehouses, and watering holes of the city. As the title suggests, they also imported flour and other important foodstuffs in the years before California was able to feed itself. In these roles and others, Chileans helped shape the economic and cultural life in America's most dynamic city. Using a transnational framework, this paper examines the myriad, lost roles of Chileans in San Francisco and the transpacific relationships they embodied.

9

As early as the 1830s, Richard Henry Dana Jr. had declared that San Francisco afforded "the best anchoring-grounds in the whole western coast of America" and promised to be the center of California's prosperity . . . "a place of great importance." Thus, when the gold fever finally broke, the port city continued to grow, attracting thousands to its shores, including the diverse crews of whaleships. Timothy Lynch, of the California Maritime Academy, offers here an examination of one of the better known of San Francisco's whaling captains in the paper titled "Black Ahab of the Bay: William T. Shorey and the San Francisco Whale Fishery."

William Thomas Shorey was a son of Barbados who had learned his craft from an old Yankee whaling master out of Provincetown, Massachusetts. By the time he sailed through the Golden Gate at the age of 24, he was a first mate in the whaling trade. His arrival at the city was not without note however, as he was charged with the beating of one of the vessel's crew. Pleading guilty, Shorey soon found himself shipping out as an officer of the very same vessel, his reputation as a "hard case" firmly established. He soon rose to command and continued to sail out of San Francisco Bay for 25 turbulent years.

Shorey's career included commanding some of the most famous whalers out of San Francisco, associating with notorious shanghaiiers, marrying into a prominent Bay area family, and accomplishing feats of seamanship that were noteworthy even in his time. The life of William Shorey, the only black captain on the Pacific coast, provides a view of the interplay of race and power in maritime America and the seeming paradox embodied in a person of color who rose to a position of prominence and respect in his community.

10

As American whalemen, missionaries, merchants, naval crews, and adventurers spread outward, the Pacific-American experience covered nearly the whole of that 64,000,000-square-mile basin. Interaction between Americans and other Pacific peoples were equally widespread, but they were more common, obvious, and influential the closer they came to North American soil. This was the case regarding interactions with Chinese maritime workers in the late nineteenth and early twentieth centuries. By examining case studies of American-Chinese interactions during that period, professor Joshua Smith's contribution, "'Hands full with the Chinese': Maritime Dimensions of the Chinese-America Experience, 1870-1943," sheds light on the racism endured by the Chinese maritime community on the American west coast.

The first case study deals with the Chinese fishermen on the West Coast. Government reports from the 1880s targeted Chinese fishermen for a variety of unacceptable practices, many of which are familiar to those studying fishery issues today. At that time, however, issues of over-fishing, risk-taking, and the use of destructive fishing gear were all cast in the light of racism. Ultimately, legislation relative to the fisheries as well as immigration drove "inassimilable" Chinese fishermen from the fishing grounds of San Pablo Bay and the Columbia River.

Another example of anti-Chinese campaigning is found in the efforts of Andrew Furuseth and the International Seamen's Union. For decades, Furuseth and the union attacked Chinese seafarers through the press, in the halls of government, and via regulations. Their view of Chinese mariners as inferior and docile, yet prone to uncontrollable violence, was reinforced by the reporting of the "mutiny" aboard the SS *City of Peking* in 1900. In this short-lived incident, Chinese crewmembers organized to defend what sailors for centuries had identified as their "rights." For white officers and observers, however, the actions of the Asian crewmen were laden racial markers and reinforced their fears and distrust. These examples of racism in the maritime environment serve to highlight and clarify similar developments in the larger American experience, and once again suggest the value of maritime studies in informing the past.

11

The seafood-canning industry came to Biloxi, Mississippi in 1881, and oysters and shrimp were packed by hand in that Gulf South town for the next 128 years. Deanne Nuwer, of the University of Southern Mississippi, wrote about the various racial and ethnic groups involved in that town's seafood industries for the race and ethnicity conference in 2000. In 2006, she was welcomed to the dais again to speak about gender in her "Sharing the Work: Biloxi Women in the Seafood Industry."

From the earliest days of canning in Biloxi, and even beyond its near total destruction in Hurricane Katrina, the gendered division of labor has been the norm. This division meant the men worked on the oyster and shrimp boats while the women worked in the canneries to shuck or peel the catch and then pack the cans. The work of these women was physically demanding as they stood at their wet benches hour upon hour in the winter cold or summer heat, their toughened hands rapidly working for maximum profit as the detritus rose around their feet. Pay by the piece was standard in the canneries of Biloxi. It was standard practice as well for children to accompany their mothers, including those youngsters who were hidden when government inspectors passed through in the vain attempt to enforce child labor laws.

Nuwer's sources include a variety of period publications and secondary sources, but one truly senses the lives of the women of Biloxi when reading their own words. Several informants in personal interviews offer telling personal accounts of their days in the cannery houses. Child-rearing, seasonality, and the blast of the cannery whistle proscribed the lives of the women of Biloxi's seafood industry. They worked generation after generation, creating tight-knit communities of mutual support as they filled a vital role in the economy of the home and the economy of the port of Biloxi.

12

The polyglot nature of the communities along the California coast brought various nationalities in constant contact with the dominant American culture. By the 1930s, the margin of Los Angeles's San Pedro Bay supported Anglo, Filipino, Italian, Mexican, Yugoslavian and Japanese families. Immigrant Japanese Issei, and first-generation Nisei, were heavily represented on Terminal Island, where they were central to the fishing industry. There, the men worked aboard the boats, the women processed fish in the canneries, and family members ran the neighborhood restaurants and stores that serviced those who lived at Fish Harbor. The Japanese community dominated Terminal Island and evolved as a successful ethnic enclave within greater Los Angeles.

Karen Jenks's study, "The Junior Outing Club, Nisei Identity, and the Terminal Island Fishing Community," concerns American-born daughters of Japanese immigrants. A number of these junior-high-school Nisei girls belonged to the Junior Outing Club, and the minutes of club meetings and oral histories are central to Jenks's investigation of their lives. The chapter begins by setting the Japanese-American community on Terminal Island within the context of the region's fisheries industries. Gender roles and racial negotiations during the years before the Second World War are then examined. Building on the work of Valerie Matsumoto, this study identifies how these young Nisei women created their own identities from the confluence of their ethnic Japanese roots and the mainstream culture within which they were situated. Subsequently, their self-conscious Nisei identity supported these young women through the whirlwind that engulfed and destroyed their community in the months following December 7, 1941.

Acknowledgments

Members of the administration of Mystic Seaport—most particularly Susan Funk, Vice President of Education and Public Programs—deserve credit for making possible the National Conference on Gender, Race, Ethnicity, and Power in Maritime America, 2006. Planning Committee members James Horton, Lisa Norling, Earl Mulderink, Dwayne Williams, J. Revell Carr, Bill Pinkney, and Elysa Engelman also deserve our thanks, as does Andrea Potochick, whose creativity, reliability, and uplifting spirit were so vital to making the event a success. Thanks is also owed to Trish LaPointe who designed this volume of papers, and to Andrew German, who provided editorial, illustration, and indexing support, and more. Thank you all.

Glenn S. Gordinier, Editor

This publication is made possible by a grant from the Connecticut Humanities Council.

Contributors

Kevin Dawson, Ph.D., is an associate professor of history at the University of Nevada, Las Vegas. He specializes in the Atlantic world and African Diaspora and is completing a book titled *Enslaved Watermen in the Atlantic World, 1444-1888*. His article, "Enslaved Swimmers and Divers in the Atlantic World," was published in *The Journal of American History* (March 2006).

Charles R. Foy, Ph.D., is an assistant professor of Early American and Atlantic History at Eastern Illinois University. His articles on freedom in the Black Atlantic have appeared, or will be published shortly, in *Early American Studies: An Interdisciplinary Journal,* and *New Interpretations in Naval History: Selected Papers from the 2007 Naval History Symposium* (Annapolis, 2009).

Kristin L. Gallas is the North Shore outreach manager for Boston Ballet. Formerly of the USS Constitution Museum and the Montana Historical Society, she earned her M.A. in Museum Education from The George Washington University. She is the author of "A Foil for the Good Guys," in Jon Axline et al., *Speaking Ill of the Dead: Jerks in Montana History*, vol. 2 (Helena, MT: TwoDot, 2000).

Karen Jenks is a Ph.D. candidate in History at the University of California, Irvine, and a 2008-09 W. M. Keck Foundation Fellow at the Huntington Library. Her interests include the significance of the coast and the intersection of coastal and transpacific networks in the history of the American West and world history.

Timothy G. Lynch, Ph.D., is an assistant professor of History at the California Maritime Academy, a specialized campus of the California State University. He is a graduate of Mystic Seaport's Frank C. Munson Institute of American Maritime Studies. His current project, *Beyond the Golden Gate: A Maritime History of California*, focuses on the maritime heritage of the Golden State.

Jason R. Mancini is a doctoral candidate in the University of Connecticut's Department of Anthropology and senior researcher at the Mashantucket Pequot Museum and Research Center. His dissertation addresses how the Indians of southern New England negotiated race, ethnicity, and identity, their varied responses to land dispossession, and their maintenance of social and kinship networks during the eighteenth and nineteenth centuries.

Lauren McCormack is the coordinator of program development at the outdoor history museum, Old Sturbridge Village. Prior to this she was the research coordinator at the USS Constitution Museum, where she studied the lives of the sailors who served aboard USS *Constitution* during the War of 1812.

Edward D. Melillo, Ph.D., earned his doctorate in History at Yale University. He is currently serving as a visiting assistant professor in the Department of Earth and Environment at Franklin and Marshall College and is completing a book titled *Strangers on Familiar Soil: Chile and the Making of California, 1848-1930.*

Sowande' Mustakeem, Ph.D., is an Andrew Mellon Post-Doctoral Fellow in History at Washington University in St. Louis. Much of her work interrogates the social history of the Middle Passage during the legal era of slaving. She is currently revising her book manuscript and is also authoring a forthcoming article that explores disease and mortality among bondmen and bondwomen aboard slaveships.

Deanne Stephens Nuwer, Ph.D., is an assistant professor of history at the University of Southern Mississippi. She has had several articles and chapters published on various aspects of Mississippi's history, including yellow fever and seafood strikes along the Gulf Coast. Currently, she is researching Electric Mills, a Progressive-era lumbering town in northeast Mississippi.

Anne Grimes Rand is the executive vice president of the USS Constitution Museum, responsible for the visitor experience. She received her MA in American Studies from Brown University. Her work focuses on hands-on history exhibits rooted in rich scholarship, where all ages can have an enjoyable, educational experience.

Brian J. Rouleau is a Ph.D. candidate in the History Department at the University of Pennsylvania. He is currently working on a dissertation that addresses the varieties of intercultural contact between American sailors and foreign peoples overseas. He also authored "Dead Men Do Tell Tales: Folklore, Fraternity, and the Forecastle," in *Early American Studies: An Interdisciplinary Journal*, published by the University of Pennsylvania Press.

Bryan Sinche, Ph.D., is assistant professor of English at the University of Hartford, where he teaches American and African-American literature of the nineteenth and twentieth centuries. He has published on Hannah Crafts, Frederick Douglass, and various aspects of nineteenth-century maritime literature, and he is at work on a monograph exploring literary imaginings of American sailors.

Joshua M. Smith, Ph.D., is an associate professor of humanities at the United States Merchant Marine Academy, Kings Point, New York. He is author of *Borderland Smuggling: Patriots, Loyalists, and Illicit Trade in the Northeast, 1783-1820*, which won the John Lyman Award in American Maritime History in 2007, and *Voyages: Documents in American Maritime History, 1492-Present*, both published by the University Press of Florida.

Glenn S. Gordinier, Ph.D., is the Robert G. Albion Historian at Mystic Seaport, where he co-directs the Frank C. Munson Institute of American Maritime Studies. He teaches for Williams-Mystic, the Maritime Studies Program of Williams College and Mystic Seaport, and for the University of Connecticut. He edited this book's companion volume of papers from the 2000 conference, *Perspectives on Race, Ethnicity, and Power in Maritime America*.

Gender, Race, Ethnicity, and Power in Maritime America

Papers from the Conference Held at Mystic Seaport

September 2006

BRANDING A NEGRESS.

"Branding a Negress" symbolizes the culture of violence experienced by bondwomen in the Middle Passage.
(Capt. Canot, *Twenty Years of an African Slaver (1854),* G.W. Blunt White Library, Mystic Seaport)

1

"Make Haste & Let Me See You With a Good Cargo of Negroes": Gender, Power, and the Centrality of Violence within the Eighteenth-Century Atlantic Slave Trade

Sowande' Mustakeem

On December 23, 1773, the *Virginia Gazette* contained a brief letter extract from West Africa at Fort James reporting,

> The Snow Britannia, Captain Deane, being in the River Gambia, with 230 Slaves on Board, they got Possession of the Guns, &c, rose up and fought the white People for upwards of one Hour, when many were killed on both Sides; and finding they were likely to be overpowered, the Blacks set Fire to the Magazine and blew up the Ship, whereby 300 Souls perished. Most of the Officers were killed, among which were the two Doctors; the Mate escaped, by being on Shore; the Captain was wounded, but soon recovered.[1]

Critical to the above testimony is the graphic narrative of violence circumscribing the interaction of enslaved Africans and seamen while traveling aboard a slaveship. Instances of violence within the slave trade were commonly sensationalized in early newspaper reports, often helping to further characterize African people as highly volatile in nature even as they fought for freedom. Accounts of ship rebellions, similar to the one above, commonly filtered across pages of eighteenth-century British, New England, and Southern newspapers, offering their readership close insight into the state of international slave trading affairs.[2]

The transtlantic slave trade brought together diverse populations of people—merchants, seamen, surgeons, and African captives—amidst the rapid expansion of markets in pursuit of laborers for the development of

Atlantic plantation systems. As virtual human commodities, bondpeople were critical to this emerging Atlantic economy. Yet, in order for slave-owners to effectively exploit the labor of countless black bodies, the oceanic transport of bondmen and women was salient to their economic needs. Representing the largest forced migration of a people in world history, the Middle Passage became an important symbol of slavery, migration, and mercantilism. Amid the movement of slave vessels charting the often dangerous Atlantic waters between West Africa, the Caribbean, and much of the Americas, they helped to bridge people, ports, and ideas.

Unraveling the entangled lives of bondpeople and their captors, this study interrogates the human relations contained in the day-to-day interactions of the slaveship experience. In so doing, it closely analyzes the *culture of violence* shaping the procurement, sale, and forcible movement of African people through the Middle Passage. "Violence" here is conceptualized as those behaviors and acts that resulted in psychological torment, the spilling of blood and/or subsequent death stemming from calamitous interactions common between bondpeople and seamen. The analysis offered within this project intersects conversations concerning labor, migration, and gender.[3] Yet, the mitigation of resistance often waged through violent means aboard slaveships also positions these discussions within the growing field of violence studies.[4] This essay bridges studies of the slave trade with scholarship concerning maritime history, recognizing that the movement of people *as* goods came to shape seafaring culture and the industry of eighteenth century shipping and trade. In drawing upon and further expanding these respective bodies of literature, this project examines the interrelated factors of gender, power, and violence.

Employing a comparative and gendered analysis, this study explores enslavement in the British and the American slave trade systems during the legal slave trading period of the eighteenth century. It proposes that as a result of the constant outpouring of violence waged by both seamen and bondpeople, slave ships came to function as "mobile battlefields," being shaped by warfare and bloodshed. As declarations of power manifested through widespread ship rebellions and the disciplinary measures seamen used to overcome insurgent captives, the invisible battle lines aboard slave vessels were inscribed akin to an unending war zone. Amidst this evolution, however, personal battles also ensued, where the vulnerable bodies of black females became the human terrain upon which sailors sought to assert control and domination.

Considering these realities, this essay analyzes power and violence through three primary modes of outplay: the violent entrance of bondpeople into the slave trade, the rape perpetuated against black female captives, and role of bondwomen and bondmen in slaveship rebellions along with the attendant punishments they both received. Several questions will guide this inquiry. First, where do black women fit within the discourse regarding the Middle Passage? What were the conditions that particularly affected black females who were caught up in the trade? How did they respond to their bondage? And, lastly, how did ships' crew punish women who resisted?

Scholars interested in the slave trade have often conflated the dynamics bondmen and women faced aboard slaveships through their employment of the generic term, "slaves." In uncovering the complexities of slaveship rebellions, black men are often designated as the primary insurgents as their tactics and strategies in many cases are preferenced in analysis. As a result, black females have become historically invisible as the varied circumstances shaping their bondage at sea have been largely unexplored. This study departs from the traditional narrative by inserting black women at the center of the transatlantic slave trade scholarship.

During their oceanic crossing, bondwomen faced challenges that were quite different from their male counterparts. Facets of bondwomen's Middle Passage experience, including rape, motherhood, and resistance can be made more clear by acknowledging their place within the slave trade as black, female, and a valuable laborer. These factors all offer further insight into the varied ways gender structured life aboard slaveships.

MERCANTILISM THROUGH THE ATLANTIC SLAVE TRADE

The primary instigators of the transatlantic slave trade were merchants located across much of the Atlantic. As entrepreneurs, many of these men held certain expectations regarding the procurement, transport, and sale of their African "cargo." Their financial investments were founded on the success of vessels traveling to the western part of Africa. As a result, the merchants were forced to rely on the labor and seafaring expertise of shipmasters and crews within the evolving eighteenth-century shipping trades.[5] Distance, localized exigencies, and a specialized skill set forced sedentary entrepreneurs to trust their slaveship operators. For example, owners of the vessel *Corsican Hero* expressed to the captain, "you have been so often at Affrica its needless to Recommend particular care in the treatment & usage of your Slaves as its as much your Interest as Ours to bring a good & healthy Cargo—to Markett."[6]

In order to outline the seamen's conduct, many merchants penned letters specifying procedures to be followed in trade for bondpeople. For some, unity among the ship's crew was of primary concern. Rhode Island merchants Samuel and William Vernon warned ship captain John Duncan, "be carefull to keep up good harmony & agreement amongst your officers & crew."[7] Success within the West African trade was largely contingent upon the crew, not only to expedite coastal trading and safely operate and maintain the ship, but even more to attend to the vessel's security following the transfer of bondpeople aboard. Yet, the acquisition of wealth through the exchange and sale of African captives remained the dominant factor among many merchants' correspondence. Slave trader James D'Wolfe wrote to his brother and ship captain, Levi D'Wolfe, on August 8, 1792, expressing concerns regarding his vessel, and Levi's command, the sloop *Sally*. While detailing the process of business negotiations to Levi, he expressed his eagerness in seeing him in less than two months time with "a fine cargo of slaves." Upon ending, James emphasized, "I know nothing more to say to you only make haste & let me see you with a good cargo of negroes."[8]

Despite the expectations merchants held regarding the West African trade, the realities of securing and transporting bondpeople were daunting. Life at sea, often for months at a time, was fraught with difficulties for ships' crews.[9] Yet, while engaged in daily slave trading activities, the dangers inherent within this Atlantic system posed an even greater risk. In 1708, while trading along the coast of Africa, the brigantine *Mary* endured "a Riseing on Board. . . . In which were Drowned 30 Men & 3 Women Slaves & 3 Dead of their wounds, occasioned by the Carlessness of y'e Men And the Brigantine not being provided for Defence ag't Such a Cargoe of Negros."[10] The safety of slave vessels was always in jeopardy following the conclusion of purchases, especially while in close proximity to the African shoreline.[11] Captive insurgency was a permanent fixture of the slave trade, underscoring the often-dangerous sphere of violence many seamen were expected to chart in the pursuit of profit for their distant financers. According to Winston McGowan, "the act of resistance most feared by white slave traders" was the violent rising of bondpeople seeking liberation.[12]

To better understand the centrality of violence within the Middle Passage, attention must be extended toward the process of how some Africans entered the trade. The capture of bondpeople did not occur in a peaceful manner. Instead, they were often carried off in a seemingly haphazard and unexpected fashion, while engaged in a variety of activities—within towns, while at work in fields, and sometimes even in the midst of battle.[13] James Towne attests to the forceful methods used in pursuit of potential captives, explaining that when a ship arrived on the African coast, seamen would send for coastal African traders and often offer presents to encourage them to bring people to sell as slaves. Towne described one case on the Galenas River in which an African man was met by a group of four blacks who, "took and plundered him of what he had, stripped him naked, brought him on board . . . and sold him."[14] In another instance, two black women, taken by surprise one evening while asleep in their beds, were suddenly dragged out of their houses, confronted by several "war-men" who then tied them up and transported them in a coffle bound for the coast.[15] A similar example of extreme violence took place on the coast of Bonny Point, when a young woman came out of the woods one morning to bathe. Two men grabbed her, "secured her hands behind her back, beat her, and ill-used her, on account of the resistance she made."[16] Although the methods of capture differed, these stories expose the often wanton brutality used to force African people into the growing system of Atlantic slavery. It is also clear that the initial procurement of men and women demonstrates that the Atlantic slave trade created fertile ground for the perpetuation of violent cycles of kidnapping and the forcible procurement of people as commodities offered for later sale.

SEXUAL VIOLENCE AS A MECHANISM FOR CONTROL

Upon boarding a slaveship, the dynamics of enslavement for female captives began to coalesce. Slave trade participant William Littleton pointed out that once aboard ship bondmen were placed in chains and transferred immediately beneath deck while "the women, girls, and children are all at liberty . . . except when we put them below at night, and lock them down."[17] Despite the illusion of "freedom" that Littleton's comment suggests, the ability to move freely about the ship was predicated upon the perceived docility of black women. Yet, this did not shield them from the cycle of sexual violence set into motion following their boarding the slaveship.[18] To further maintain these gendered separations throughout their Atlantic passages, some vessels constructed a high barricade "as strongly put together as wood and iron can make it" to ensure that, "the women cannot see the men, nor the men the women."[19] These separate locations were typically maintained to quell any collaboration from occurring among captives.

Enslaved women confronted the double oppression of bondage once set at sea. Deborah Gray White argues that being both black and female, enslaved women were the most vulnerable group within antebellum slave communities.[20] This same analysis can be extended to the Middle Passage, considering that aboard one Dutch slaveship the quarters where women were held was commonly referred to by the ship crew as "the whore hole."[21] Although respective to the Dutch slave trade, this labeling—both literally and figuratively—provides a context for comprehending the function female captives served in the minds of some seamen. It was largely within the spaces of slaveships that the bodies of African women became sexualized. This understanding offers greater insight into how they were perceived, along with how they were treated by members of a ship's crew. One ship's log contained evidence stating, "[t]his morning found our women Slave apartments had been opened before by some of the ship's crew, the locks being spoiled and sundered."[22] Although liberated from the weight of irons upon their bodies, this report confirms that enslaved women were instead bound both physically and psychologically within a sphere of sexual violence.

As captives, bondwomen were forced to abide by the social order of slaveships, which in many cases governed and permitted the free use of their bodies by sailors. Violence was often utilized by seamen to force sexual relationships with black women. Yet, belief in their hypersexuality also played a role, demonstrated through the point that "those of Africa," particularly the women "have the superiority over those of Europe, in the real passions they have for the men who purchase them."[23] This assumption is suggestive of inherent powers black women held over their captors. While relieving the perpetrator of guilt, these beliefs further justified the use of sexual violence against African women. As Nell Irvin Painter noted, "submission and obedience [operated as] the core values of slavery" by which all bondpeople, especially bondwomen, were held.[24] In recognition of these conditions of bondage, it is therefore conceivable that many females traveled the Atlantic waters tormented with unending fears of seamen's invasion of both their quarters and their captive bodies, with neither prior warning nor the possibility of protection.

The duality of enslavement many black females faced aboard slaveships owed largely to misconceptions in circulation regarding their sexuality. Evelyn Brooks Higginbotham offers the point that, "the social constructions and representation of black sexuality reinforced violence," permitting the continual use of rape instigated against black women.[25] Although stereotypical ideas concerning the sexual prowess of black men abounded, for black females, their existence, culture, and ultimately their bodies became viewed through a dual prism of both promiscuity and savagery. This is evidenced through the declaration, "African women are Negroes, savages, who have no idea of the nicer sensations which obtain among civilized people."[26] Creating a general yet debased understanding of women of African descent, these racialized and yet gendered ideals further permitted the use of rape as a mechanism for "civilizing" African women. As a result, "the most challenging task confronting black women under slavery was how to maintain a healthy opinion of themselves as sexual beings."[27] These psychological difficulties stemmed not only from slave owners' overdependence upon their bodies for their reproductive value, but even more from the consistent use of violence against them through sexual aggression.

Belief in black women's promiscuous nature often played out in the violent mistreatment they endured. These forceful measures typically occurred through the private means of rape, which can be difficult to document by those seeking to fully recount the widespread nature of their exploitation within the slave trade. Yet, a few sources have been identified that permit scholars to begin to ascertain the environment of sexual dominance used to threaten female captives. For instance, during the 1753 voyage of the *African*, sailor William Cooney felt free during the ship's passage to seduce a female captive referred to as number 83, who was described as "big with child." This seaman became sexually aggressive, forcing the pregnant bondwoman "into the room and lay with her brute like in view of the whole quarter deck."[28] For his actions, the captain "put him in irons." Yet, his unashamed exploitation and rape of this captive's body indicates that even pregnant females were not free from assault by slaveship sailors.[29] This incident also attests that the violent misuse of enslaved people, including that of bondwomen, was a public practice and thus never a secret within slavery.[30]

Violent force was also used to hold dominion over captive females, regardless of age. In one report, a ship captain "mistreated a very pretty Negress, broke two of her teeth, and put her in such a state of languish that she could only be sold for a very low price at Saint Domingue, where she died two weeks later." Still unsatisfied, he "pushed his brutality to the point of violating a little girl of eight to ten years, whose mouth he closed to prevent her from screaming. This he did on three nights and put her in a deathly state."[31] These graphic accounts reveal the lengths to which some seamen would go in the rape of black females, both young and old, even to the point of causing mortal injury.[32]

Such aggressive behaviors commonly shaped the contours of females' enslavement. The close confinement aboard slave vessels further magnified the conditions of bondage African women endured as they traveled in close proximity and within constant access of seamen throughout their oceanic passage. Beyond their time aboard ship, however, the long-term effects these physically and psychologically violent acts could have had on these women lie imbedded in the permanent scars of both fear and anger etched in their future dealings with men, regardless of whether they were white or black.[33]

For many seamen, raping black women provided a semblance of temporary ownership over their bodies. Although the African female body came to be viewed as "[a] body both desirable and repulsive, available and untouchable, productive and reproductive, and beautiful and black," this did not hinder seamen from the exploitation of bondwomen.[34] Surgeon Alexander Falconbridge referred to these particular practices noting that on the vessels he serviced, "the common sailors are allowed to have intercourse with such [*sic*] of the black women whose consent they can procure." Additionally, the ships' officers, as he disclosed, were "permitted to indulge their passions among them at pleasure."[35] The power dynamics in place between seamen and female captives, as "slaves," deemed bondwomen voiceless, forcing their demands to go disregarded. Yet, seamen in many cases were not held accountable for the resulting implications—injury, pregnancy, or venereal diseases—that could result from the sexual relationships they forced upon black females.[36] Therefore, it is probable that bondwomen became virtual "sexual hostages," often to more than one seaman, prior to their arrival in the Americas and subsequent sale within the domestic slave market.[37] These realities underscore the dual "rite" in place for bondwomen and their captors. For white seamen, the bonded status of black women gave them the "right" to violate their captive bodies. Quobna Ottobah Cugoano attests to these perceived freedoms felt by seamen through his observation as a captive aboard a slave vessel, where "it was common for the dirty filthy sailors to take the African women and lie upon their bodies."[38] While it can be argued that some women used sexual relationships with their captors for personal gain, rape within the Middle Passage for female captives became akin to a violent "rite of passage." These introductions foreshadowed the cycle of sexual aggression many of these women would have to endure or bear witness to once bought and sold within the Atlantic plantation community.[39]

During times of warfare, behaviors hinging on sexually aggressive motives are often seen as *by-products* of war. This idea suggests that their occurrence resulted as a consequence of physical engagements of violence. Elaine Scarry offers a salient point that, "the language of 'by-product' denotes 'accidental,' 'unwanted,' 'unsought,' 'unanticipated,' and 'useless.'"[40] Considering that rape and the threat of sexual violence were used on several occasions as tools of terror and power against black women, these measures were not undesired or devoid of intent. Slave trader John Newton attests to these calculated practices owing to the fact that "when the women and girls are taken on board a ship, naked, trembling, terrified . . . they are often exposed to the wanton rudeness of white savages." As a result of this, as Newton indicated, "the poor creatures cannot understand the language they hear, but the looks and manner of the speakers are sufficiently intelligible" resulting in the fact "the prey is divided upon the spot, and only reserved till opportunity offers."[41] These *opportunities* stemmed from the accessibility seamen had to bondwomen's bodies without the threat of interference, owing largely to the initial separation of females from captive males. Therefore, as slave-ships became the spatial battlefield upon which captives and sailors positioned themselves in defense of their respective interests, for seamen these battle lines extended even further onto the bodies of enslaved women.

Along with rape, specialized roles were sometimes used to manipulate black women's allegiance on slave vessels. Ties of loyalty to the crew were presumed to be much easier to forge among bondwomen. This is demonstrated through the assertion that, "the happy discovery and prevention of conspiracies that would have destroyed all their oppressors by the hands of their slaves, hath been owing to the faithful attachment of these negro women."[42] Although acknowledging a contradictory and rather vindictive role that some African women willingly held, this presumption embraces the view of black women as the "weaker sex."[43] On several occasions, roles were distributed to female captives in exchange for their presumed loyalty. Thomas Trotter recounted the role of interpreter being given to one black woman whose primary duty was to provide the officers with information concerning the melancholic disposition of captives stowed aboard.[44] A similar case involved a black woman aboard the ship *Nightingale.* As Henry Ellison described it, this bondwoman, "whom we called the boatswain of the rest, used to keep them [captives] quiet when in the rooms, and when they were on deck likewise." Her duties were, however, short lived when she "one day disobliged the second mate." As a result of her defiance, "he gave her a cut or two with a cat he had in his hand. She flew at him with great rage, but he pushed her away from him, and struck her three or four times with the cat very smartly." Yet, upon recognition that "she could not have her revenge of him, she sprung two or three feet on deck, and dropped down dead. She was thrown overboard in about half an hour after, and tore to pieces by the sharks."[45]

These duties may have shielded select bondwomen from the threat of violence. It is clear, however, that if these "trusted" female captives displayed any behaviors counter to the crew's expectations, they were subjected to immediate disciplinary actions. The punishments used against these unyielding females reinforced the dynamics in place as captive and captor. However, the allocation of these "special" roles set into motion prescribed social boundaries, dictated by seamen, within which these women were expected to operate.

The promise of material reward was also used to secure bondwomen's obedience to seamen. In one example, a female captive, captured and stowed aboard ship, was considered "prey of the ship's officers, in danger of being flogged to death if she resisted." If she acquiesced to the seamen's demands, however, her reward "was a handful of beads or a sailor's kerchief to tie around her waist."[46] In this case, material objects were used to secure the woman's loyalty, suggesting the use of psychological violence. Yet, there were dangers attendant to the distribution of these types of trinkets. In some cases, material items fostered hierarchal division among captives. One participant in the trade noted female captives who were "furnished with beads for the purpose of affording them some diversion." In some cases, this practice led to internal squabbles among bondwomen.[47] Although this evidence bolsters the idea that black women were easily manipulated by materialism, there was much more at stake within their condition of bondage. Stripped of virtually everything following their initial capture, their receipt of such tokens may have fanned a desire to hold dear certain items, especially those believed to be from their former homelands. On the other hand, these gifts may have also offered relative safety for these females by indicating symbolic ownership. That is, the mere display of these material items during their ocean passage could have implied total possession of these women by seamen, thus deterring other interested parties.

THE INTERPLAY OF VIOLENCE ABOARD SLAVESHIPS

In addition to the challenge of protecting themselves against the threat of sexual violence, some bondwomen also bore the responsibilities of motherhood during the Middle Passage. Birth for many African women was attended with feelings of joy and accomplishment through the creation of new life. However, for the mother of an infant cramped within the hold of a slaver, this newfound excitement was likely replaced with feelings of fear, anger, and vulnerability. One scholar argues that slavery did not allow bondwomen to express much compassion regarding their children for fear of being perceived as weak.[48] Yet, despite their bondage, many women held dear to their children and their parental duties.

Yet, these emotional ties were often challenged by the violent nature of bondage. In 1789, William Rotch Jr. addressed a letter to Moses Brown of Rhode Island, "endeavouring to find what instances of barbarity could be substantiated" that occurred aboard New England slave vessels. Within his inquiry he highlighted a case involving a seaman who had "thrown a child overboard." To his understanding, this seaman, "succeeded to the Command . . . by the death of the Cap'n & Mate," and after assuming command he "was so inhuman as to take a child by the feet whose crying afflicted him & repeatedly whipd it before its mother & once made an attempt to burn it by thrusting it into the Caboose."[49] Although further details concerning the fate of this enslaved mother and her young child go unrecorded, this account attests to the additional burden of violence some bondwomen faced through the mistreatment of their offspring. While traveling the Atlantic, many females held to their parental responsibilities, offering their children what meager care bondage could permit. However, as evidenced, these mothers were often unable to protect their young from the violence that could erupt at any point during their passage. Even more, bearing the pain and anguish of witnessing brutality committed upon the bodies of their children at the hands of another likely caused them great psychological tormented. If a child died, this would have created psychological damage.

Considering that the trauma of sexualized violence could couple with the demands of motherhood some bondwomen experienced while being transported, the question lingers, how did they respond to their captivity? One response was resistance. There was a range of resistive measures that bondpeople, regardless of gender, drew upon to maintain their autonomy. These expressions of individual agency often occurred through nonviolent methods of suicide: self-starvation, hanging, and jumping overboard. Meanwhile, much more drastic and violent measures were also used to deny the status of "slave" that was being forced upon them.

From the moment of their sale and transfer aboard ship, the resistance bondpeople exerted became problematical for seamen. An American seaman on the sloop *Dolphin* in 1796 reported that an enslaved female and male were able to "fetch some poison" in order "to put into some rice that was on the fire." Although the crewmembers chained and "whipt them [both] severely," this attempted plot exemplifies the premeditated and coercive measures some Africans resorted to for their liberation.[50] John Newton described a similar use of poison on his slaver, *Duke of Argyle,* recounting, "we were alarmed with a report that some of the Men Slaves had found means to poison the water in the scuttle casks upon deck, but upon enquiry found they had only conveyed some of their Country fetishes, . . . which they had the credulity to suppose must inevitably kill all who drank of it."[51] While this declaration highlights the carryover of Africans' cultural knowledge—albeit for deadly purposes—it also testifies to the myriad forms of resistance employed against their captors. Yet, Newton's dismissal of these weapons as mere "country fetishes" does not diminish the ongoing threat to seamen's lives that attended the carriage of enslaved Africans.

Outside the use of toxins, the two primary modes of violence bondwomen drew upon were gynecological resistance and collaboration in shipboard revolts.[52] Commonly recognized as a plantation phenomenon, and rare within historical records of the slave trade, some black women held aboard slaveships asserted reproductive control through the use of abortion. In so doing, their behaviors demonstrated an unwillingness to permit their unborn children to bear the pain of enslavement. In 1765 a bondwoman was taken and transferred aboard the ship *Sane.* Several weeks into the passage she came to a difficult decision regarding the fate of her unborn child. It is unclear whether this woman entered the trade pregnant, or the child was conceived on the African coast, or perhaps was conceived while on board ship. Whichever was the case, it is likely that the possibility of bearing a child within enslavement inflicted further trauma upon this female. In order to protect herself and the child within her womb from facing the psychological burden of separation once placed for sale, she elected to take its life. In committing this drastic yet silent act of defiance, this woman reclaimed reproductive agency, ensuring that her child did not enter the world of captivity to which she had been subjected. The tragedy was further compounded when complications arose and this defiant woman also died.

African women were often known for possessing knowledge of herbs and even serving in various spiritual roles, which may have granted this bondwoman knowledge of how to terminate an unwanted pregnancy.[53] Further details that would illuminate how this woman succeeded in her resistive efforts were not reported. Therefore, it is unknown whether she somehow ingested an herbal remedy, or if she perhaps got hold of a piece of wood or a rusted tool that she may have forced into her body, taking the life of her child, and likely causing her to hemorrhage severely. In view of this bondwoman's subsequent death as a result of her own actions, it is probable that she purposefully chose death to free herself along with her child. One can also speculate that in recognition of the jeopardy she posed the life of her unborn child, depression may have ensued in her final days aboard ship where she virtually permitted herself to die.[54]

Much like assertions of power through reproductive agency, ship rebellions also illustrated the unending quest for freedom bondpeople sought over their lives. John Bell, physician aboard the slaveship *Thames,* remarked on the devastation of these risings. Following an insurrection that took place before the vessel's departure from the African coast in 1776, he reported, "the Voyage has been attended with nothing but losses & disappointments." He described how, following their passage up the coast from Accra, "on Friday the 8th Inst' we had the misfortune to lose 36 of the best slaves we had by an Insurrection, . . . when there was only the Boatswain, Carpenter, and 3 White People & myself on board." The revolt ensued because, according to Bell, "we had 160 Slaves on board & were that day lett out of the Deck Chains in order to wash, [where] advantaged by this They began by rising." As the outbreak of violence spread, many of the captives gained access to tools lying in proximity which they then used as weapons. The battle carried on "for upwards of 40 Minutes, when," according to Bell, the captives "f[ound] they could not effect it all [and] the Fantee & Most of the Accra Men Slaves jumped overboard" in an attempt to escape to the nearby coastline. During their effort to suppress the revolt, crewmen discovered "34 Men & boys w't 2 women a rising." In order to thwart their efforts to join in the rebellion, several seamen "fired 2 magnets amongst them." Though doing so was quite uncommon, Bell offered further explanation regarding the female captives relative to the revolt. He stated,

> had the woman assisted them in all probability your property here at this time would have been but small, The woman having no hand in it was owing to their having no time to consult about it, as their riseing at that time was entirely owing to there being so many white people out of the vessel, /which they said themselves/ though they had 2 or 3 times before been going to attempt it, The only reason we can give for their attempting any thing of the kind, is, their being wearied at staying so long on board the ship, those left will give no reason for their riseing, but lay the blame entirely on those thats lost.[55]

Recognizing the rebellious intent among these bondpeople, his report counters prevailing views of bondwomen as being obedient. For it was believed by many, "from the women, there is no danger of insurrection."[56] The inclusion of these women in the affair aboard the *Thames* verifies that on some occasions they, like their male counterparts, contemplated open and violent resistance. In this case too, the slave traders inability to fully grasp the impact of enslavement placed upon the captives led them to characterize the rebellion as owing to fatigue or anxiousness.

Another incident of open warfare thath crossing gender lines, occurred in 1721 aboard the slaver *Robert*. Departing the coast of what was later to become Sierra Leone, this ship set sail across the Atlantic carrying 30 Africans. Five of the captives, including an enslaved woman, planned to overthrow the ship's crew in an effort to steer the ship back to the shores of their homelands. As part of the effort, the female, being unbound on the main deck, served as a spy. Much like plantation owners, seamen traveling aboard slave ships "were never . . . in control as fully as they would have liked."[57] This is evident in the fact that once the crew was deemed to be asleep, this insurgent bondwoman successfully brought, "a Hammer at the same time (all the Weapons that she could find) to execute the Treachery."[58] In the end, only the female and two other men elected to follow through with the surprise attack. The ship's crew quickly suppressed the attempt at freedom by the small cadre. The efforts of the bondwoman in this case confirms the vital role they often played in slaveship rebellions. At the same time, her liberty to roam the ship also attests to the presumed docility of women and children.[59] Yet, some African women were willing to take advantage of being quartered near the ship's storage room, and in doing so perhaps sacrifice their lives in hopes of freeing their enslaved cohorts.

Perhaps most compelling to this case is the "counter-resistance" waged by the ship's crew against all the insurgents involved in the uprising. The ship captain, listed as Harding, ordered the seamen to "whip and scarify . . . only" two bondmen who were involved. Interestingly, three other captives accused of serving as "Abettors, but not Actors" were sentenced to death. Before their final execution, they were made to "first eat the Heart and Liver of one of them killed." The sentence the bondwoman received was equally as severe. In fact, the punitive measures used against her affirms the frequent use of public displays of brutality aboard slave ships as she was, "hoisted up by the Thumbs, whipp'd, slashed . . .

with Knives, before the other Slaves till she died."[60] This operated much like a triple punishment for the bondwoman's role in the attempted revolt. Whipped, slashed, and murdered in view of the entire ship, her death was likely used as deterrence for others. Yet, the scars and the ultimate destruction of her body this female endured reinforces the idea that "torture usually mimes the killing of people by inflicting pain, the sensory equivalent of death, substituting prolonged mock execution for execution."[61] It is probable that the willing role of this bondwoman was unanticipated by the ship's crew. However, because she stepped outside the boundaries of social order of the ship, as she engaged in seditious efforts along with her male compatriots, they all were subjected to severe disciplinary measures imposed by the attending seamen, even at the risk of losing profits.

Another revolt that further demonstrates the centrality of violence through ship revolts took place in 1729 aboard the English ship *Industry.* In this instance, an African woman was discovered smuggling gunpowder and ammunition through a hole leading down to the hold where the men were held. Following suppression of the revolt, it was determined that because the woman had been so badly scarred drring the fighting, she was deemed unfit for sale. As a consequence, they "hoisted her up to the Fore-Yard-Arm in view of the other slaves . . . and fired half a Dozen Balls tho' her Body, the last shot that was fired cut the Rope which she was strung by, [and she] tumbled amain into the sea."[62] Thus, rather than try and restore the woman and her economic value, the ship's master sought instead to use her as a sacrificial example for future insurrectionists. As demonstrated, public spectacles of violence often served as the tools seamen used to reinforce their power against African captives. This owed to the belief that, "when correction, or punishment for great offences becomes necessary. . . . The stroke of the whip does not materially injury [sic] a negro by the laceration of his body. It operates by the effect it has on his mind."[63] Therefore, it is plausible that these public exhibitions of violence functioned as both warnings and celebrations.[64] However, while these ritualized punishments served to fracture any semblance of African unity, they also brought seamen together, creating a sense of strength, protection, and communal identity among the various members of the ship's crew.

The social space of slaveships permitted violence to become the unifying basis of collectivity. In solidifying the lines of respective loyalty, the entire ship—both the top deck and the hold beneath—saw battle lines drawn. On one side, the enslaved might formulate the beginnings of community, while on the other, seamen also came together as they sought to penalize African conspirators. Hence, within both groups, sailors and bondpeople boarded slave ships as strangers, yet in the case of rebellion they coalesced as temporary units to defend and protect their collective interests—albeit for profit or ultimate liberation.

Moving beyond lines of both gender and ethnicity, ship revolts encapsulated a collective language of resistance. In order to quell potential attempts of the ship, many seamen sought to prevent "chaining those together who speak the same language."[65] As previously noted, these strategies often failed to thwart collectivism among captives. It is clear that those who elected to resist were "unorganized, undisciplined, and united only in their insatiable desire for liberty."[66] Yet, although isolated on a borderless and unfamiliar sea, both bondmen and women actively drew upon the terrain of the ship in their efforts to reclaim power and freedom.

One scholar of the slave trade argues, "the voices of those who were its victims are rarely heard when one looks for evidence or explanations of shipboard slave revolts."[67] If resistance is perhaps viewed to include the nonverbal modes of communication carried out through illicit activity, then the scornful voices of the captive can be interpreted through the incessant rumblings of rebellion that were widespread throughout the Middle Passage. Critical to this discussion is that these behavioral languages often extended beyond racial lines, permitting seamen the ability to interpret the cultural meanings of these insurrectionary motives. While some whites held to the belief that "civilized or not, Negroes . . . [were] cowards all their life-time and heroes for an instant," many slave-ship sailors understood Africans' violent motives and responded with a language of counter-resistance manifested in the unrestrained discipline they utilized against any rebellious bondpeople.[68]

CONCLUSION

The evolution of the transatlantic slave trade transcended lines of race, ethnicity, gender, and age, forcibly placing varied populations of people in close interaction. As the web of global economic networks solidified, black bodies were bartered, sold, and ultimately transported aboard slaveships owned by traders from various nations around the Atlantic world. The Middle Passage can therefore be conceived of as a pivotal theatrical stage whose principal actors were seaman and their African "cargo," who influenced the contours of Atlantic history. Yet, these concepts further push the boundaries of maritime history and culture suggesting that alongside white seamen and free black sailors, captive Africans make up yet another viable presence within eighteenth-century seafaring culture.[69]

As this essay has demonstrated, these oceanic passages were far from fixed and prescribed. Instead, "every stage in the Negro traffic was marked by slave behavior which was uncooperative and belligerent," critically hampering all intentions of trade.[70] The unbridled measures of violence bondpeople and seamen engaged in aboard slaveships further demonstrates the contentious struggle that was carried on for control of the black body. For slave traders, this aggressive defense served to protect not only their lives, but more importantly, to insure the possibility of profit awaiting the successful conclusion of a voyage. For enslaved Africans, these engagements in violent combat served as the openly confrontational means upon which they asserted control and ownership of their own lives.

A primary intention of this project has been to illuminate the experience of bondwomen aboard slave vessels in an effort to reveal the varied circumstances of bondage they confronted. This essay seeks to rectify historian David Richardson's observation that, "the role of women in supporting and encouraging revolts has perhaps not been fully appreciated."[71] As previously revealed, along with gynecological means of resistance, much like their enslaved male shipmates, bondwomen also conceived of and immersed themselves in the hazards attendant to ship rebellions. Through this they affirmed not only their humanity, but took their fate out of the hands of the slave traders and moved it into their own. Bondwomen "did not participate in the trade as fully as men"; however, beyond statistical understandings, testimonies of their social experiences within the Middle Passage are deserving of further historical inquiry.[72] Far from suggesting female captives' experiences of bondage were worse than their male counterparts, these gendered discussions seek to facilitate the examination of the conditions African women faced within the slave trade, conditions that often paralleled their later lives within plantation communities.

In 1944, historian Lorenzo Greene stressed the importance of ship revolts in the history of the slave trade, suggesting that they served as "a single scene in the first act of a mighty drama for freedom."[73] Building upon this history of violent human interface, this discussion revealed that slave vessels operated as mobile battlefields even as they traversed the waters of the Atlantic. Kali Gross notes that "the precise effects of violence are difficult to qualify."[74] Attempts to interrogate the multiple layers of violent action common within the slave trade—sexual violence, plots of rebellion, and the punitive measures employed against insurgents—are important windows to better comprehend gender, sexuality, power, and resistance. With these interrelated factors at play slaveships became the floating coffins within which both seamen and bondpeople fought and in many cases drew their last breath championing their respective causes.

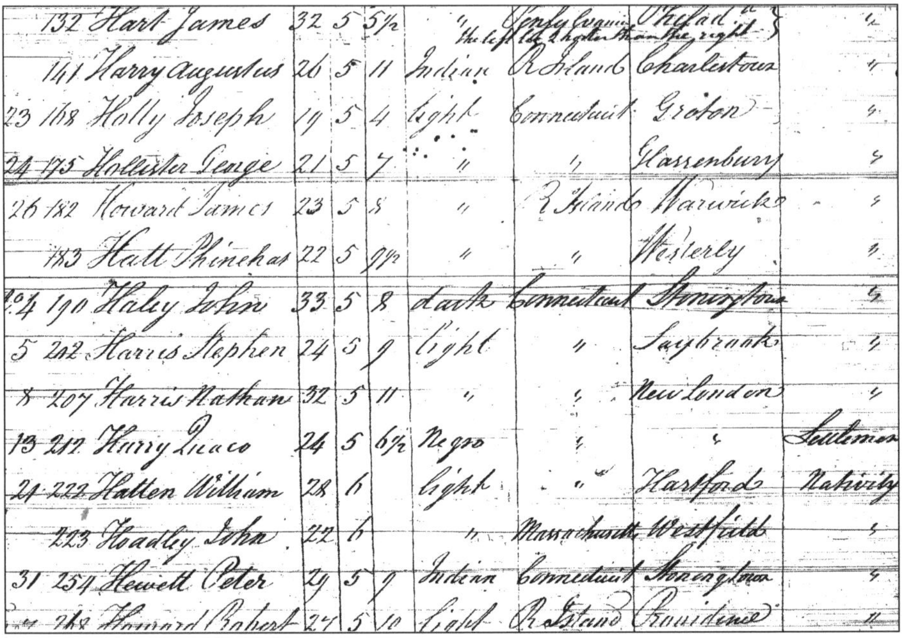

	132	Hart James	32	5	5½	" the left leg 2 inches shorter than the right	Pennsylvania	Philad.a	"
	141	Harry Augustus	26	5	11	Indian	R Island	Charlestown	"
23	168	Holly Joseph	19	5	4	light	Connecticut	Groton	"
24	175	Hollister George	21	5	7	"	"	Glassenbury	"
26	182	Howard James	23	5	8	"	R Island	Warwick	"
	183	Hatt Phinehas	22	5	9½	"	"	Westerly	"
[illegible]4	190	Haley John	33	5	8	dark	Connecticut	Stonington	"
5	202	Harris Stephen	24	5	9	light	"	Saybrook	"
8	207	Harris Nathan	32	5	11	"	"	New London	"
13	217	Harry Quaco	24	5	6½	Negro	"	"	Settlement
21	222	Hatten William	28	6		light	"	Hartford	Nativity
	223	Hoadley John	22	6		"	Massachusetts	Westfield	"
31	254	Hewett Peter	29	5	9	Indian	Connecticut	Stonington	"
[illegible]	[illegible]	Howard Robert	27	5	10	light	R Island	Providence	"

Indian seamen can be identified in the register of seaman's protection certificates issued by the New London, Connecticut, customhouse, as shown in this microfilm printout.
(National Archives and Records Administration, Waltham, Massachusetts; microfilm at G.W. Blunt White Library, Mystic Seaport)

2

Beyond Reservation: Indians, Maritime Labor, and Communities of Color from Eastern Long Island Sound, 1713-1861

Jason R. Mancini

On July 17, 1710, Peter Wayamayhue, a Pequot Indian "Whoe Served Aprentesship with Leu^{tt}: John Faning of Grotton," indentured himself with the permission of his mother and her husband, "Onest Will," to Major John Merrett and Mrs. Mercy Raymond of Fishers Island for a period of two years. The terms of the agreement stipulated that Peter would be permitted two weeks out of the year to "wisiett [sic, visit] his mouther and other relations" on the mainland. On his return to Fishers Island early in his second year of service, he encountered a man-of-war sloop entering Long Island Sound under the command of Lieutenant Daniel Allyn. The crew of the vessel beckoned him to come onboard, which he did. One of the men then "turned his canoo adrift" and they continued on their voyage, effectively terminating Peter's indenture.[1]

Two and a half years later, on January 1, 1713, while in Boston, Peter Faning, "an Indian man late of New London," in the company of several seamen, became very drunk on "Slip and punch" and indentured himself as a mariner's apprentice to Daniel Allyn Jr. for a period of three years. Shortly thereafter "in May 1713 he did Run away and absent himself from his s^{d} master . . . & his service." His whereabouts were unknown for nearly three years, at which time he appeared in Groton on March 27, 1716, and provided a sworn statement before a local Justice of the Peace. This occurred only after the sheriff of New London was "required to attach ye goods or Estate . . . and for want y^{r} of to take ye body of ye s^{d} Peter Fannen and him Safely to keep so y^{t} you may have him before ye County Court."[2]

These narratives bear a strong resemblance to one another and they should. Peter Wayamayhue and Peter Faning were the same person. As the defendant in both lawsuits, it might be easy to cast Peter as a victim of a harsh, indifferent, and discriminatory labor market and accompanying colonial legal system. But Peter had three things working in his favor: an alias, an apparent willingness to violate his contractual obligations, and a seaman's knowledge and mobility.

The experience of Peter Wayamayhue, alias Peter Faning, provides insight to the ways Indians and other people of color were adapting to and resisting a power structure that attempted to place them near the margins of Anglo-American society. This article draws from W. Jeffrey Bolster's examination of the presence, experiences, and lives of black mariners, and Marcus Rediker's insights into the development of maritime labor systems and social world of mariners. This study also builds upon Daniel Vickers's social history of mariners as they seamlessly moved between the land and sea interacting with family and friends, but focuses on the Indian communities of eastern Long Island Sound and the customs district for the port of New London, Connecticut.[3] It is here that a new model for maritime ethnohistory emerges.

This paper examines important ways that Indian people "forged" their existence and community structure on land, in port, and at sea.[4] First, arguing that in an era of dispossession and diminishing autonomy on the land, Indian mariners, as a class of transient laborers, rapidly learned to use Anglo-American structures and institutions to establish for themselves a degree of power and personal freedom. Second, by the end of the eighteenth century as the number of Indian mariners increased, military and customs records indicate that they had articulated maritime-based social networks that included other men of color. Through most of the nineteenth century, this allowed Indians both to maintain and to adapt traditional inter-community dynamics. Third, as Indian men moved more fluidly between the land and sea and between the region's land-based indigenous enclaves, they were often gone from their homes for years at a time. In their absence, Indian women, who anchored these communities to the land, formed relationships and families with Indian and non-Indian mariners alike. The elaboration of these social networks at sea facilitated and contributed to the development of multiracial, multiethnic communities of color on the land. These groups appeared on Indian reservations and, increasingly, in surrounding areas off of the reservations as mariners or their female relatives were now capable of acquiring freeholds with a seaman's earnings.

NEGOTIATING POWER AND LABOR – EARLY ACCOUNTS OF INDIAN MARINERS

Some of the earliest accounts documenting the Indian experience of the maritime world emerge in the court records and runaway advertisements during the eighteenth century. These are among the very few records available to highlight the ways in which Indians began to both adapt to and resist English institutions. The Treaty of Utrecht, which ended Queen Anne's War in 1713 and terminated inter-colonial conflicts between the French and English, also transformed the power structure between the English and Indians in the region. As Indian people were increasingly alienated from their lands and subjected to English law, they actively renegotiated their existence within Anglo political, economic, and religious structures in order to maintain the connections to family and community that had existed unrestricted only a little more than a generation earlier.[5]

As the century progressed and their depth of experience increased, Indians developed a clearer understanding of English legal and economic systems. With this, Indians began to gain some control over their lives and livelihoods. Indians throughout the region were engaged in numerous court cases involving land loss and encroachment and trials for theft, murder, and breach of service (runaways). In the first quarter of the eighteenth century, they also participated in the colonial legal system by appearing periodically as jurors of inquest.[6] Consequently, Indians became better equipped on their own or with the assistance of white overseers to take matters into their own hands.

Twenty years after Peter Wayamayhue was defending his actions in court, George Jobe, an Indian mariner from New London, was exercising his rights as a plaintiff. Demonstrating his experience with English law, in 1733 Jobe sued the master of the brigantine *London*, Naboth Graves, after he refused to pay the agreed-upon wage of 55 shillings per month. As a foremast man on a 12-month and 14-day voyage, Jobe was part of a crew that sailed to "Ireland, Madeira, Cape deVerd Island, Soranam Boston and New London" between July 11, 1732, and July 25, 1733. A writ attaching "the goods or Estate" of Graves suggests that his complaint was not quickly brushed aside. The case was later adjudicated in favor of Jobe and settled when Graves's father-in-law "John Prentice gave special bail £68 for abiding judg.^{mt}."[7]

In addition to economic motivations, efforts to avoid certain types of servitude also drew Indian men to maritime work. Having learned that their labor was central to the wealth and success of their white "masters," Indians began to exercise control over this. Empowered, Indians found themselves in the middle of some labor disputes (accidentally or purposefully) between masters. One such case involved an Indian boy of Lyme named Tantipinant, alias Philip. In 1732, Tantipinant was bound to the service of John Lay 2nd, also of Lyme, for a term of six years and one month. At some point in December 1734, Lay and Tantipinant were on board Capt. John Sears's sloop *Elisabeth* and Lay apparently "Considering yt his Indian had so Great a Desire to Go to Sea he Thought it would be more for his Profitt to Let him go Than to keep him att home." From that point, Tantipinant continued on as one of Sears's hands to the West Indies islands of Antigua and St. Christophers.[8]

During his service to Sears, when their sloop was "providentially frozen in att Rocky Hill [along the Connecticut River]," Tantipinant was released with two other sailors "to go home until ye vessel was thawed out and he [Sears] would take them on board att Saybrook."[9] It is not clear from these records if Tantipinant went home to the Indian community in Lyme or if he returned to the service of John Lay. It might appear from the legal proceedings that Tantipinant did not return to Lay's service, which was likely the source of the dispute between Lay and Sears. Tantipinant had selfish motivations to go to sea, and he must have recognized that placing himself in a situation between "masters" confirmed certain power on himself. He also knew that the power of his two masters was situational and could not extend to both land and sea.[10]

There were, of course, more numerous and less formal disputes between masters on land and masters at sea. As the number of Indian men (and other men of color) in the maritime industry continued to increase, patterns of resistance emerged in the form of runaways and deserters.[11] Marcus Rediker notes that "the tactic of desertion was used in complex and ingenious ways," and as Indians grew more familiar with how English institutions worked, they began to use them more extensively to their advantage.[12] By the mid-eighteenth century, it is clear that they were doing their best to redefine the nature of labor relations. In the *Providence Gazette* between 1763 and 1798, 168 runaway or deserter advertisements attest to the frequent abandonment of all terms of service by persons of color.[13]

Of these departures, 54 (32 percent) appear to be connected to the maritime industry: 28 "negro," 7 "Indian," 13 "mulatto," and 6 "mustee."[14] Though these individuals were often not identified specifically as sailors or mariners, the frequent descriptions of their clothing including sailor's trousers, pea coats, and blue sailor jackets, as well as admonitions to "masters of vessels" not to "harbor" or "carry away" these men, are testaments to their maritime affinity. For these men, the sea offered a place of escape or refuge from oppressive and unfair treatment on the land. This is somewhat ironic, since conditions on board ship could be worse than on land. For mariners, though, the ability to abscond was close at hand.[15]

With some Indians, the maritime life was the only thing they knew. Aliases and a familiarity with potential exits from unwelcome or unwanted situations at sea contributed to the mobility and disappearance of Indians.[16] David Pompey, for example, "a light complexioned Indian . . . was bro't up to the sea." At 22 years old, he had an alias (Thomas Ginnings) and on March 5, 1760, he had deserted from the schooner *Three Sisters*. The captain, Simon Rodes, knowing that Pompey would head to sea, used particularly harsh language in warning his fellow "masters of vessels . . . against harbouring, concealing or carrying off said indian on the utmost penalty of the Law."[17] Tracking down runaways and deserters may have been next to impossible as it had "become very fashionable for Sailors to assume some fictitious name by which they ship and are known before they sail."[18] That Pompey easily disappeared at sea suggests that there may have been many others that looked like him. In these ways, Indian mariners, like others, were able to make use of the anonymity associated with the vastness of the sea. For every mariner, as Rediker argues, "the greatest source of power, at least in the early eighteenth century, was his mobility, and desertion was a crucial part of the self-activity of maritime working people."[19]

Mobility and the intimate knowledge of transportation systems and routes, both maritime and terrestrial, were important not just for disappearing but for returning home. Joseph Johnson, a Mohegan Indian, left on a whaling voyage from Providence, Rhode Island, sometime after the spring of 1769 and returned in early October 1771. "To Enquiring friends, or to strangers," he wrote, "Some of my time, I have Spent upon the Ocean wide. I have been down Eastward, as far as to the Western Islands twice. Curvo, & Florus, I have Seen, and to the Southward I have been as far, to the West Indies. Seen also the Islands between Antigua and Granades, and again from Antigua I have Sailed down leeward Sailed by the Virgin Islands, also by Sandy Cruize, Portireco, down as far as to Mona."[20] Upon his return to Providence, and longing for family and home, Johnson immediately began to search for a vessel that would take him home. Finding a vessel bound for New London, he entrusted his belongings to the captain, who evidently departed without him. Over the course of the next 10 days and "museing with myself" about why this had happened to him, he tracked down his possessions over 70 miles away, moving along both land and coastal shipping routes. By October 30, Johnson remarked "I brought my things [to] Shore here once more on Mohegan land."[21]

FORGING A MARITIME NETWORK – INDIANS OF THE LITTORAL

Thus far, these accounts, as they reflect individual experiences, have not spoken to group or community-level interaction. Whether the growing number of Indian men may have provided opportunities to form durable social networks or communities of color at sea is not yet clear from these records. But, by the American Revolution opportunities for men to aggregate in military oriented companies began to emerge both on land and at sea.[22]

Among the earliest documented community-level presence and involvement of Indians in New London's maritime industry appeared during the construction of the Continental frigate *Confederacy* along the Thames River in Preston. A number of these workers were associated with the Mohegan community that resided directly across the river. Many of these men, including Peter Neshoe, Thomas Mosset, Turtle Hunter, Gurden Wyaugs, Ebenezer Tanner, Daniel Uncas, Dennis Mohegan, Simeon Ashbow, and James Jeffrey, were almost exclusively employed as ships' riggers between October 1778 and February 1779.[23] The nature of this work, which involved detailed knowledge of ship engineering and operation, suggests that these men were all by this time experienced mariners and recognized as such.

Furthermore, men from various Indian communities, including some of those involved in the construction of the *Confederacy*, later sailed as crew members, including Simeon Ashbow and Daniel Uncas as marines,

Ebenezer Tanner as a cook's mate, and William Fagins, Jonas Peege, and Turtle Hunter as seamen. Other vessels, such as the Continental frigate *Trumbull*, Connecticut frigate *Oliver Cromwell*, Connecticut galley *Shark*, and Connecticut brigantines *Defence* and *Marshall,* had groups of Indian mariners such as Gurden Wyaugs, John Wampy, Abimelech Uncas, John Jeffords (alias Jacob Sowwas), Benjamin Cinamon, and Indian Peter serving on them in various capacities.[24] The growing presence of Indians working in the maritime industry, and their demonstrated ability to perform well in difficult circumstances, impressed their white superiors. Thus, with a reputation for hard work and the need for employment and opportunity in a place where race mattered less, Indians and other men of color were becoming an important part of New London's maritime labor force.[25]

For Indians, New London also became a place where they could revive and adapt their social networks. The port of New London was located within 22 miles (as the crow flies) of six Indian reservations: four in Connecticut—Mohegan, Western Niantic, Mashantucket Pequot, and Lantern Hill Pequot; one in Rhode Island—Narragansett; and one in New York—Montauk (see map, page 30).[26] Arguably, this consortium represents and anchors one of the densest concentrations of Indian people in the Northeast. Living not just on reservations, but throughout the surrounding towns of southern New England and eastern Long Island, many Indian men gravitated towards New London's waterfront and developing urban economy.

The extent to which Indians were drawn to New London's maritime industry was never directly mentioned in historical records; rather it was, in part, reflected by the absence of Indians living on reservations. Commenting on the current state of Pequot Indians at Mashantucket in May 1804, Colonel Edward Mott of Preston noted in a letter to William Hillhouse, a member of the Connecticut General Assembly, that "a Considerable Number of Aged & a Number of Females & some Males (sic) Invalids" remained on the Indian reservation and "a great part of their able & Smart Men are gone."[27] This account and others like it during the eighteenth and nineteenth centuries have left an indelible impression in the historical record that highlight both the perceived decline of the region's Indian population and the insular nature of their communities.

With the drastic reduction of Indian lands in the mid-eighteenth

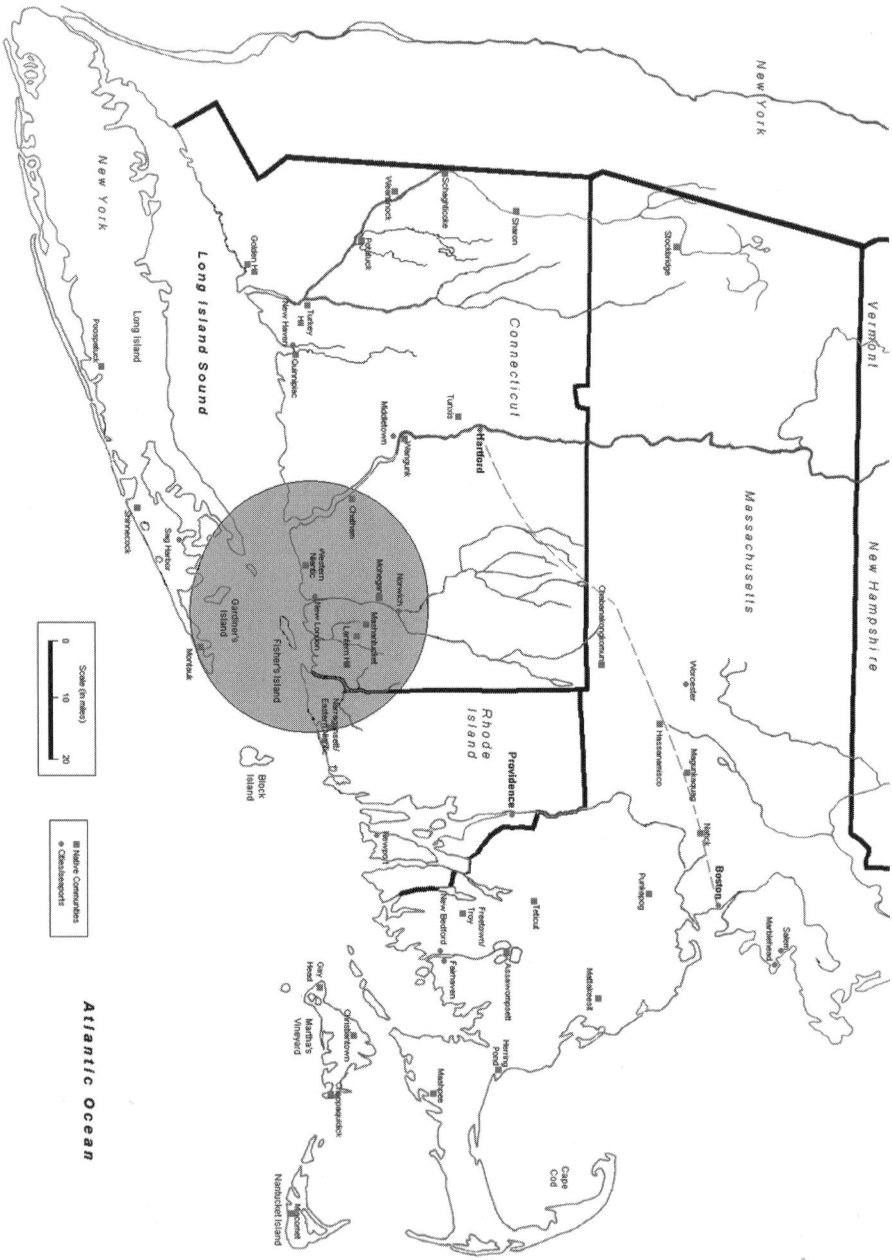
New York
Vermont
New Hampshire
Massachusetts
Connecticut
Rhode Island
New York
Long Island Sound
Long Island
Atlantic Ocean
Block Island
Fisher's Island
Gardiner's Island
Martha's Vineyard
Nantucket Island
Cape Cod
Hartford
Providence
Boston
Scale (in miles)
0
10
20
Native Communities
Cities/seaports

century, so many Indians had dispersed that the English began to misunderstand and misrepresent both reservation life and the social networks that were developing to keep Indian people connected.[28] Consequently, little is known about the Indian experience beyond the borders of their reservations.[29] Recent work with the Records of the Collector of Customs for the Collection District of New London, Connecticut has begun to illuminate some of this off-reservation activity. Between August 1796 and the date of Mott's letter, nearly 80 Indian men from across the region had registered for a seaman's protection certificate or appeared on a vessel crew list arriving at or departing from New London. Hundreds more would follow.

On May 28, 1796, the Fourth Congress of the United States passed "An Act for the relief and protection of American Seamen." This act was drafted in response to the impressment of American merchant seamen by the British Royal Navy. Impressment, which involved forced service of British-born (including American) citizens on British Royal Navy ships, was considered by Americans to be tantamount to kidnapping. The quality of life for the average sailor in the Royal Navy was at best harsh, offering little in the way of comforts or compensation. The practice of impressment, considered unjust and oppressive, was undertaken during the Napoleonic Wars in order to supply crews for the growing number of warships and to offset the high rate of desertion.[30] The registers of seamen and surrendered crew lists that were mandated by Congress and created at individual ports contain valuable information on individual seamen and also provide an opportunity to better understand broader community dynamics. The register of seamen from the New London, Connecticut, Customs District includes information on individuals, such as their name, date of registration, certificate number, age, height, complexion, nativity, and distinguishing characteristics such as scars, missing digits, and severe pock marks. Beginning in 1815, hair color (or texture) and eye color were also recorded. For many of these men of color, the customs records at various ports represent the only evidence that they ever existed.

As the customs records indicate, the Indian population moving into and out of New London appears to be significant when compared to other regional ports of commerce and when considering the anecdotal reports of languishing Indian populations living on the region's tribal reservations (see Table 1).[31] Preliminary statistics are further complicated by the language of race used through most of the eighteenth and nineteenth centuries to describe people of color. In the customs records, the category of "complexion" encompassed diverse terms to describe gradations of color or race, and the specific term "Indian" was only one of several used to describe men of Indian descent. For the maritime world and for Indian

Table 1 • **A Comparison of Some "Complexions" in Regional Customs Records, 1796-1860***

	Salem Crew Lists (Database contains 76,000 records, all complexions)	**New London Crew Lists** (Database contains 14,500 records, only people of color)	**Marblehead Crew Lists (Partial)** (Database contains 3,900 records, all complexions)	**New Bedford Crew Lists (Partial)**** (Database contains 62,000 records, all complexions)
"Indian"	2	163	0	40
"Mulatto"	123	419	2	29
"Colored"	110	302	10	39
"Copper"	30	626+ ***	0	12
"Yellow"	382	316	12	44
Total	647	1826+	24	164

	New London Seaman Protection Certificates (Database contains 910 records, only people of color)	**Providence Seaman Protection Certificates** (Database contains about 10,200 records; 1,480 are people of color)
"Indian"	111	11
"Mulatto"	88	129
"Colored"	120	1
"Copper"	2	4
"Yellow"	7	261
Total	328	406

* Figures corresponding with different "complexions" reflect total individuals, not total records (individuals often have multiple records documenting their presence in the maritime industry).

** Not all crew lists and complexions have been entered in the New Bedford database; people of color may be grossly underreported.

*** After 1850, could not distinguish names and enumerate all Hawai'ians and Pacific Islanders; approximately 350 names not interpreted, representing an unknown number of individuals.

history, this has contributed to a perception that Indians were numerically insignificant. In New London, approximately one-third of the men of color issued a seaman's protection certificate or who appear on vessel crew lists were identified by more racially ambiguous terms, such as "copper," "yellow," "colored," "mustee," "mulatto," "darkish," or "dark." These classifications complicate the racial "landscape" and have resulted in scholarship that has both polarized and essentialized these complexions as "white" or "African."[32]

A comparison of customs records with tribal documents and federal census records indicate that of 224 individuals specifically identified as "Indian" in the customs records between 1796 and 1860, only 28 appear on tribal lists, records, or petitions. Restated, 88 percent of New London's seafaring Indians never appear on tribal documents, but nonetheless were born in or resided in the towns surrounding these Indian reservations. Although it is difficult to establish how people of color identified themselves by using customs records alone, many of Indian mariners declared their tribal affiliation in other sources, such as tribal petitions, census records, and legal proceedings. In the customs records, men of Indian descent were often placed in categories associated with African ancestry, such as "black" or "Negro," and in categories typically associated with European ancestry, such as "fair" and "light." Some of these Indian men included, for example, Joshua Poheague, Gideon Tokus, Jonathan Brushell, James Bunn (Shinnecock), and George Cottrell (Mashantucket Pequot), who were considered "mulatto." Isaac Fagins (Lantern Hill Pequot), Robert Fagins, Joseph Shantup (Mohegan), Crawford Cheets, Paul Baker, Cyrus Shelly (Lantern Hill Pequot), John Skeesucks (Mashantucket Pequot), and Leonard Mazzeen (Mohegan) were labeled as "of color" or "colored." Isaac Hazzard was labeled "copper," Titus Cinnamon was identified as "Negro," Peter Nocake (Narragansett) and William Cheats were listed as "black," Peter Cinnamon, Thomas Aaron, and Gurden Nookey were called "dark," Charles Cooper (Mohegan) and Moses Brushel (Lantern Hill Pequot) were described as "yellow," Leonard Apes was "fair," and John Nedson (Mashantucket Pequot) was called "light."[33] Further complicating this picture is the inconsistency with which many individuals were perceived and labeled. Between 1810 and 1818, Henry Fagins of Bozrah was labeled on various crew lists as "negro," "of color," "mulatto," and "dark." Similarly, in the period between 1819 and

1834, David Rogers of New London was listed as "Indian," "colored," "dark," "mulatto," and "yellow."[34]

At the turn of the nineteenth century, the port of New London, Connecticut, was one of the largest ports located in Long Island Sound. Like many other ports in the Early Republic, New London rapidly expanded its Atlantic commerce. This growth increasingly relied on young men who became the labor force. For the first time, Indians and men of color, who continued to be tempted by the lure of the sea, can be seen actively manifesting and forming social networks in port and at sea. It appears that, for these men, personal relationships and inter-community connections were an important part of the recruitment process drawing men of color to New London through at least the 1860s.

Though Indian voices were strangely silent during this time, their actions were not. Beginning in 1796, with the initiation of the New London customs records, family and community connections can be observed and documented in the maritime industry. While the registration lists were maintained in alphabetical order over a period of decades, each mariner (often with an alphabetically different surname) received a numbered protection certificate on a certain date. By reorganizing the protection certificates sequentially and by date, a startling pattern emerges where it has become clear that many of these men were enlisting together (Table 2).

Most of these men never appear on tribal lists, rolls, or petitions, but their consecutive appearance in the Registers of Seamen is interpreted to represent individuals who registered together and were socially connected through their family, community, or "colored" classifications or status. These records begin to elucidate both local and regional interactions among the Indian populations of Connecticut, Rhode Island, Massachusetts, and coastal New York. In the years following the creation of the seaman's protection certificate, family ties are demonstrated with brothers Peter and Benjamin George of Groton (Mashantucket), who registered in New London on November 21, 1796, and received seamen's protection certificate numbers (SPC#) 309 and 310, respectively. Indians from the same town, such as Robert Fagins (SPC#253), Peter Hewitt (SPC# 254), and George Skeesucks (SPC#255) of Stonington registered on October 31, 1796. On September 6, 1796, Indians from different towns and/or states, including Joseph West (SPC #138) of Warwick, Rhode Island,

Table 2 • **Examples of Social Connections in the Register of Seamen**

Date	SPC #	Name	Age	Height	Complexion	Other Traits	Town	State
9/6/1796	138	West, Joseph	26	6′	Indian		Warwick	RI
9/6/1796	139	Pomps, George	26	5′6″	Indian		Groton	CT
9/6/1796	141	Harry, Augustus	26	5′11″	Indian		Charlestown	RI
10/31/1796	253	Fagens, Robert	28	5′11″	Indian		Stonington	CT
10/31/1796	254	Hewett, Peter	29	5′9″	Indian		Stonington	CT
10/31/1796	255	Keesocks, George	23	6′	Indian		Stonington	CT
11/21/1796	309	George, Peter	25	5′ 6-1/2″	Indian		Groton	CT
11/21/1796	310	George, Ben	30	5′9″	Indian		Groton	CT
12/21/1796	408	Pain, James	20	5′7″	Negro		New Shoreham	RI
12/21/1796	409	Brewster, Joseph	28	5′11″	Negro		Lebanon	CT
12/21/1796	411	West, Timothy	34	5′10″	Indian		Warwick	RI
12/21/1796	412	Lord, George	23	5′8″	Indian		Berwick	MA
12/21/1796	416	Doughly, Henry	23	5′ 8-1/2″	Indian		Branford	CT
8/6/1799	1325	Ambrose, John	22	5′8-1/2″	Mulatto		Boston	MA
8/6/1799	1326	Huntington, Pomp	35	5′9″	Negro		Norwich	CT
8/6/1799	1327	Will, Peter	18	5′6″	Negro	Pckmarked	Norwich	CT
8/6/1799	1328	Wormsley, Joseph	19	5′8″	Indian		Glastonbury	CT
8/6/1799	1329	Hicks, Morris	26	5′10-1/2″	Mulatto		New York	NY
8/6/1799	1330	Forcastle, James	21	5′7-1/2″	Mulatto		Jamaica	NY

George Pompey (SPC #139) of Groton, Connecticut, and Augustus Harry (SPC #141), a Narragansett of Charlestown, Rhode Island, all registered as well.[35]

In the first half of the nineteenth century, as the port of New London became a regional center of racial and ethnic diversity, international communities of color were developing in the Atlantic and Pacific worlds. In addition to the presence of ethnic Mohegan, Mashantucket Pequot, Lantern Hill Pequot, Niantic, Narragansett, Montauk, Shinnecock, non-reservation Indians, and other people of mixed heritage from the southern New England region, people of color from around the world appeared in New London. Customs records reported many men born in Africa, Barbados, Jamaica, Bermuda, Cuba, Brazil, Cape Verde Islands, Sandwich Islands (Hawai'i), Western Islands (Azores), Calcutta (India), and the Philippines. On May 25, 1804, some of these Atlantic world interactions were represented by five men, including Sylvester Alvords

(SPC #2954), negro, from Cape Verde, Portugal, Samuel Shantup (SPC #2956), Indian, of Stonington, Samuel Prince (SPC #2957), mulatto, of Stonington, Jonathan Brushell (SPC #2959), mulatto, of Labrador, Canada, and Samuel Peters (SPC #2960), mulatto, of Stonington. The importance of these connections will be addressed later in this paper.

In New London, an important regional community of color began to take shape. Men of varying racial and ethnic backgrounds and birthplaces may reflect the development of a brotherhood or fraternity among people of color, forged at sea or in port and evidenced when registering together at the customs house. One of the larger and more "racially" diverse examples of this clustering occurred on August 6, 1799, with the registration of John Ambrose (SPC #1325) a "mulatto" of Boston, Massachusetts; Pomp Huntington (SPC#1326) and Peter Will (SPC#1327), both "negro" men of Norwich; Joseph Walmsley (SPC #1328), an "Indian" of Glastonbury, Connecticut; Morris Hicks (SPC #1329) a "mulatto" of New York, New York; and James Forcastle (SPC #1330), a "mulatto" of Jamaica, New York.[36] These race-based groupings may have been a form of protection against discrimination and violence as conflicts between white and non-white mariners were well documented occurrences in the industry.[37] This cohesion can be seen in the crews of merchant vessels reported in the New London customs records between 1796 and 1822, and principally on whaling vessels after 1821. Like the registers of seamen, men of color appeared on these vessels in groups of three to six men. On board, they filled a variety of roles such as able seaman, ordinary seaman, cook, steward, boy, and occasionally cooper or mate.[38] But, as these fraternities were forming, they were also being obscured by the arbitrary classification of race or "complexion" by white customs officials.

An analysis of surrendered crew lists provides evidence for how these interactions may have adapted and manifested themselves. As the recruitment of seamen was often based on long-standing relationships, men commonly signed articles of agreement at the same time as friends, relatives, and townsmen.[39] By examining the crew lists for individual vessels over time, one can determine if groups of men continued on or dispersed to work on other vessels, though "some captains went out of their way to reward men for enlisting or reenlisting."[40] On the Ship *Connecticut* for example, and among a broader crew of color, men associated with several Indian communities, including Mohegan in Montville, Pequot at Mashantucket, and possibly Nipmuc at Brimfield, Massachusetts, appear on crew lists between 1825 and 1837. Jacob Fowler and Leonard Mazzeen of Montville and Christopher Quam of Brimfield appear on the earliest crew list in June 1826. Mazzeen appeared again in September of 1827 with Peleg George of Mashantucket. Several Mohegan men are present in June of 1830, including Jacob Shillett, Edward Uncas, and Thomas Williams. The next voyage was crewed by Benjamin Uncas (a male relation to Edward) of Montville and Elisha Apes, Joseph Fagins, and Charles Brayton, all of whom were living at, or connected to, the Indian community at Mashantucket. Charles Fagins, a brother of Joseph, appears in May of 1833, and Peleg George in May of 1834, as the lone Indian men in these crews. In May 1836, Peleg George appears with Peter Potter, a "black" man who also sailed with him on the 1827 voyage.[41] The smaller ratio of people of color to whites on these whaling vessels, compared to merchant vessels, may have also contributed to a perception that the population was diminishing. But this series of intra- and inter-community connections strongly suggests that while there was an appearance of a vanishing or disintegrating community on land, these men were actively maintaining and/or forming social networks at sea. These patterns are evident on several vessels, including ship *Commodore Perry*, brig *Catherina*, ship *Ann Maria*, ship *Stonington*, and ship *Flora*.[42]

On a more subtle level, the interaction of Indian men at sea transcended colonial and state geopolitical boundaries. The sea also served to unite reservation and non-reservation Indians as well as other people of color living throughout the region. As an aggregation and departure point, the port of New London became an essential meeting place where Indian men, including those of Mashantucket, Lantern Hill, Mohegan, Niantic, Narragansett, Shinnecock, and Montauk, could assemble. While at sea they found opportunities to interact, share experiences, and bring news of other Indian groups when they returned to their own communities. On the brig *Antelope* in 1807, for example, Josiah Fowler, an "Indian" born on Long Island and residing in Preston and Norwich, and Reuben Aaron, an "Indian" of Preston, were shipmates bound for the West Indies. Likewise, Charles Cooper and Luther Cooper, both Mohegan and "Indians" of Montville, and John Brown, an "Indian" of Charlestown, Rhode Island, were on the ship *Stabrock* in 1807 headed for Demerara. John Harry, a Narragansett identified as "mulatto" and "Indian" of Charlestown, Rhode Island, and James Simons, "Indian" of Stonington, sailed together on the brig *Albatross* of Stonington, bound for the South Seas in July 1826. Hundreds of men of color from outside New London County also appear in New London customs records, including Augustus Harry, a Narragansett Indian of Charlestown, Rhode Island; John Caujock, an "Indian" of Long Island; and Reuben Rives, "mulatto" of Montogue [Montauk], New York, in 1803.[43] Other "Indian" mariners included Timothy Treat (SPC #413) of Derby, Connecticut, Elisha Way (SPC #1338) of Farmington, Connecticut, James Courageous (SPC #528) of South Hampton, New York, Zacheus Pocknet (SPC #5857) of Sandwich, Massachusetts, and Daniel Tickens (SPC #1538 and 5788) of Westerly, Rhode Island.

Once at sea, either as individuals or groups, these men were not as isolated as one might think. They continued to interact with the crew members of other vessels and, when anchored in ports around the world, had an opportunity to encounter family, friends, and acquaintances. On September 25, 1835, as the ship *Acasta* of Stonington approached the harbor at Tova Island (off the coast of Venezuela) looking for recruits, many ships were present from New London's customs district, including ship *Jones*, ship *Friends*, ship *Mercury*, brig *Uxor*, brig *Henry*, schooner *Francis*, schooner *Ann Howard*, as well as the bark *Hesper* from New York, New York.[44] Here, men from an expanded maritime community of color could congregate and make decisions whether to continue on with their current captain, abandon their articles of agreement and join a different vessel, or blend in with the local port community or indigenous population. Beyond the congregation of "jacks in port," "the turnover of personnel from ship to ship brought the sailor into association with an exceptionally large number of his fellow tars."[45]

MEN OF THE SEA AND WOMEN OF THE LAND – EMERGING COMMUNITIES OF COLOR

As Indian mariners were maintaining, developing, and adapting social networks at sea, they were also negotiating their place on the land. Even when home, as Lisa Norling describes, "reunion held the potential for confusion and struggles over authority" and mariners may have felt out of place, unwanted, or unneeded.[46] This may have been even more punctuated within Indian communities. Indian seamen, who returned from a hyper-masculine maritime environment, were confronted with a home environment where women traditionally maintained more authority and autonomy than their counterparts in white society. Perhaps unwelcome and maybe out of place on the land, many Indian men did not stay as customs records point to their consistent return to the sea.

Highlighting the primacy of maritime labor among the Indians of eastern Long Island Sound, two mid-nineteenth-century tribal rolls, in 1833 and 1858, which document the entire "Pequot Tribe which belong and reside in Groton [Mashantucket],"[47] indicate that, with few exceptions, the men between ages 15 and 40 were mariners. While difficult to establish for the regional Indian population, if the patterns present at Mashantucket were reflective of a regional population, it would appear that nearly all Indian men (reservation and non-reservation) who were young and able, chose to go to sea. Though some men engaged in periodic or seasonal farm labor work, comparatively few elected a life on the farm.[48]

Such heavy participation in the maritime economy by Indians inevitably led to tension within their communities between men and women and between permanent residents and transient laborers. Often gone for years at a time, mariners were not present for the daily subsistence, labor, and protection needs of their families and communities. Consequently, family relations were often tested by the lure of the sea as women and children were left to fend for themselves. In a February 12, 1743, confession, Samuel Ashbow of Mohegan acknowledged some of the problems that arose from a seaman's long absence. He reported that "Sometime ago I went to Sea and was Gone 14 months When I Came home I understood by Common Publick Report which had Gaind Credit with Many and So far as I know a General belief y^{t} my wife had before a Sufficient Evidence been Guilty of Gross adultery In my absence."[49] Court records indicate that this was not an isolated event, but since many Indians maintained "flexible" relationships, adultery may be somewhat underreported in the colonial and state court records.[50]

Over time, as Indian men continued to follow the sea, two dominant patterns emerged. Many mariners never returned from the sea, and

Indian women became more visible representatives of their communities at home.[51] As Edward Kendall noted in an 1807 visit to Mohegan, the community was populated "for the most part [by] very aged persons, widows, and fatherless children. The young men go to sea and die."[52] While this statement may be overly fatalistic, it does address the root of important changes that Anglo-Americans perceived to be occurring within the Indian community. The sea offered Indian men a different type of freedom and high potential for reward and advancement, but a seaman's work was dangerous and the ocean was arbitrary. Half a century later, John Milton Earle observed among one Massachusetts Indian community what was all too common in eastern Long Island Sound: "Nearly all their young men, heretofore, have gone to sea, and many of them never return; some dying at sea, and others finding new homes in distant lands. The places of these [men] are supplied by others, chiefly sailors, from abroad, who, getting acquainted with the Gay Head men at sea, come here, and marry Gay Head women, and settle here for life."[53] Some men, like Manuel Sebastian of Brazil, found their way into and became part of New England's Indian communities.[54] Thus, Indian women and male outsiders, whether of Indian, European, or African ancestry, gave rise to a growing multiracial and multiethnic population that identified as Indians.

These multiethnic and multiracial communities developing on the land mirrored those emerging at sea. On the land, Indians and other mariners of color had families or communities both on and off the reservations to which they returned when they reached port. Though many sailors were known to spend recklessly their hard-earned lays at grogshops, brothels, and boardinghouses, some did not and invested their income in ways that benefited their families and communities.[55]

One strategy people of color developed to ensure their individual and/or collective survival and autonomy was the acquisition of private land.[56] During this time a number of individuals purchased a land base on which several extended family networks or communities of color emerged. This acquisition of land provides some of the earliest evidence of the true connection between the mariners of color and their families and communities on the land. Two of the smaller reservation enclaves at Niantic (300 acres) and Lantern Hill (280 acres) had experienced the pressures of population growth, both internally and externally. Consequently, Indian men associated with both of these communities began to purchase adjacent lands privately and in the "English manner." Nathan Hill purchased his first parcel of land with a dwelling house and buildings in 1798 in Stonington. In two subsequent purchases in 1813 and 1817, he added a total of 18 acres abutting Richard Nedson, a Pequot mariner, and York Noyes, a man of color, in an area immediately north of the Stonington Pequot community at Lantern Hill.[57] Hill's initial land acquisitions coincided with his presence in the custom's records in New London in 1800 and his ability to accumulate land may have been associated with his lump sum earnings for his time at sea. Similarly Philip Occuish, in three transactions between 1764 and 1773, acquired about 46 acres of land adjacent to the Niantic reservation at Black Point in present day East Lyme, Connecticut.[58] Little is known about Philip, but he was a mariner on the Connecticut frigate *Oliver Cromwell* with Joseph Squib, Benjamin Uncas, Abimelech Uncas, and Gurden Wyaugs when it was captured in June 1779 by the British during the American Revolution. He later appeared as a prisoner of war aboard the infamous prison ship *Jersey* in New York.[59]

Similar purchase power appears among non-reservation Indians as well. Their success and careful management of finances enabled them, for a period of time, to contribute (directly or indirectly) to the viability of their communities. Extended family networks or communities were more dispersed on the regional landscape, but their origins and persistence appear to connect them to the maritime world. For example, the Cinnamon and Orchard families formed the core of one non-reservation community of color that emerged by 1790 and continued to appear in records through the 1820s. This group, located immediately in the Old Mystic area of Stonington, grew rapidly after widow Lydia Orchard purchased six acres with "a house hut or cell." Her ability to purchase and sustain this land-base may be derived from a number of mariners associated with this community including Peter Cinnamon, Titus Cinnamon, Titus Almon (possibly an alias for Titus Cinnamon), Gideon Tokus, Joshua Cuff(ee), and David Orchard.[60] All were mariners identified in the New London customs records during this time.

Having successfully developed strategies to work within and around Anglo-American society, Indian communities once again began to see their autonomy challenged during the years prior to the Civil War. In their shore-side communities, Indian women increasingly took on public leadership roles. At Mashantucket, Hannah Miller Fagins, who was the mother of four mariners, was the principal petitioner in 1856 against an effort by the State of Connecticut to sell (at public auction) 800 acres of the tribe's land.[61] This move by the state was initiated largely because of the decline of "clear blood" tribal members and the perception that the tribe "will soon become extinct."[62] Similar efforts were underway at Niantic in 1855, and the Indian communities of Massachusetts became the subject of an extended debate on citizenship and enfranchisement during this time. These efforts were reflected in state-sponsored "investigations of the number and circumstances" of resident Indians in the 1849 Bird Report and the 1861 Earle Report.[63] In spite of these efforts and the never-ending challenges to their identity, their autonomy, and their very existence, many of these communities did adjust and persist, albeit in new, creative, and often unrecognized ways.

CONCLUSION

At a time when the Indian population was perceived by Europeans to be vanishing, these individuals and groups were adapting and redefining themselves in ways not recognized or documented in contemporary historical accounts. The nature and extent of these connections are only realized by considering Indian reservation populations as part of a larger regional network of Indians and people of color.

During the 1740s and 1750s, a number of Indian boys (and some girls) were groomed in Eleazer Wheelock's Indian school as Christian missionaries. These individuals would become important to maintaining some intercommunity connections in the last quarter of the eighteenth century. Though highly educated, their numbers were few and their support from Church sponsors was often tepid. As a result, the overall influence and appeal of these Indian missionaries appears to have paled in comparison to the influence of maritime life in maintaining social connections. It is important to acknowledge that the Christian Indians, who were literate, commonly kept diaries and updated their English patrons on their successes and failures through frequent correspondence (much of which has survived). While these accounts have served to inform past authorities and present historians about various Indian activities, it may be of greater significance that the English appear to have been completely unaware that these types of broad connections and social interactions among the Indian population were going on "undocumented" at sea.

Seafaring men of Indian descent may be one of the most elusive demographic groups in the historical record. But, by reassessing the broader population of color in the southern New England region through a multidimensional and cross-disciplinary approach, scholars are providing a new framework with which to develop and refine our understanding of the cultural landscape during the eighteenth and nineteenth centuries. As demonstrated above, Indian presence on the landscape has been obscured by our inability to recognize individuals as "Indians." By considering various biases, including those of race, identity, and mobility, and framing them in a study of population and community, the rich and detailed histories of Indian individuals emerge.

The customs records of New London provide detail about minority communities that heretofore have not been seen in other land-based documents. With the synthesis of these record groups, patterns of community interaction, connectedness, and mobility can be observed between the land and the sea to a degree that has not yet been identified in ethnohistorical studies. Though the registers of seamen and crew lists were initiated rather late in the eighteenth century, additional records provide necessary detail to suggest a much earlier presence of Indians (if not community structure) in the maritime world. This material contributes significantly to our understanding of land-based Indian communities and their ongoing efforts to maintain social connections beyond their shrinking reservations. Through this study, one thing has become clear: to understand Indian presence in the maritime world, scholars must understand the flaws present in systems of racial labeling, the persistence of ethnic identity, and the adaptation of community.

POSTSCRIPT

Maritime historians have written about sailors' distinct behavior and tendencies, their motivations, their resistance to, and rejection of, authority, mobility, acceptance or accommodation of diversity, and their social world.[64] Discovering not only vast numbers but also community structure and organization among men of color in the maritime world raises new questions about these people and begins to inform us about a larger and more dynamic social landscape. How did the experiences of Indians and men of color on the land influence their behaviors and actions at sea and vice versa? And to what extent did these experiences affect or contribute to our understanding of the common seaman? By expanding our understanding of diversity at sea and contextualizing community relationships, scholars can reconsider the origins of, and changes to, this class of laborers and examine the broader roots of maritime life.[65]

ACKNOWLEDGMENTS

I am particularly indebted to the past and present staff and interns in the Research Department at the Mashantucket Pequot Museum and Research Center for their assistance, support, and database management: Debra Jones, David Naumec, Laurie Pasteryak, Sara Schneider (also for the map), Candyce Wallingford, and Brenda Hill. Helen Rozwadowski, Matt McKenzie, Kevin McBride, Nancy Shoemaker, Nina Dayton, Francoise Dussart, Lisa Wilson, David Silverman, Colin Calloway, Danny Vickers, and Russ Handsman have provided valuable insight, comments, and advice on the organization and content of this work. Fellow UConn graduate student Chris Thee reviewed and commented on earlier incarnations of this work. The staff, faculty, and librarians at Mystic Seaport have been tremendously helpful on a number of levels, and I am grateful to Elysa Engelman, Glenn Gordinier, Mary K Bercaw-Edwards, Kelly Drake, and Leigh Fought for sharing their knowledge. Faith Davison, Mohegan Tribal Archivist, and Michael Spellmon of the Indian and Colonial Research Center in Mystic willingly shared their extensive knowledge and information with me. Marguerite Capone provided much-needed editorial guidance. Financial support for this research has been provided through the Paul Cuffe Memorial Fellowship at Mystic Seaport's Munson Institute. This and other research projects have been supported by the vision and long-term support of the Mashantucket Pequot Tribal Nation and mandated through the mission of the Mashantucket Pequot Museum and Research Center.

"A View of New York from the North West," showing a British frigate anchored off the Battery, ca. 1776, depicts one of the principal ports of opportunity for maritime fugitives. The aftermost oarsman in the frigate's longboat appears to be black. (Joseph F.W. Des Barres, *The Atlantic Neptune* (London, 1777-81), G.W. Blunt White Library, Mystic Seaport)

3

Possibilities and Limits for Freedom: Maritime Fugitives in British North America, ca. 1713-1783

Charles R. Foy

In 1724, Pompey fled his New England slave master. Found stowed away on a ship sailing to Portugal, the slave's maritime flight resulted in Boston ship captain Moffat being fined £50 for transporting a slave on a vessel without the consent of the slave's master. Unlike the three 16-year-old slaves who had been "carried up the Delaware River" the prior year, Pompey did not find employment as a mariner. Nor did his voyage result in Pompey finding freedom in the Iberian Peninsula. Instead, Pompey was returned to enslavement in New England.[1]

Near the end of the period this essay discusses, Robert, a slave, fled his Port Royal, Virginia, master. Robert hoped to obtain his freedom by reaching the British army. Prior to doing so he reached the Chesapeake Bay. There, along with some other fugitives in 1781, Robert boarded a French ship stationed in the bay bound for Rhode Island. It is unknown why the Virginian bondsman entered the French vessel. He mistakenly may have thought it to be a British man of war or entered based on a belief that freedom was more likely in Rhode Island. When the warship reached Newport, Robert and his companions found themselves sold back into slavery in clear violation of Rhode Island's 1774 act outlawing slave imports. Within a week of the sale, a contract was drafted between Robert and his new owner, Newport baker Gregory Wainwood. The contract provided that Robert would be freed after nine years of service. Not willing to wait the nine-year term, Robert found freedom in 1789 by running away, obtaining the assistance of the Providence Abolition Society and suing Wainwood.[2]

These stories evidence the diversity and commonality of slave maritime employment in British North America and the mobility of mariners of color in the eighteenth-century Atlantic. They also evidence the opportunities for freedom British North American maritime fugitives could expect to find via the sea, while highlighting the importance that contingency, place, and the British Royal Navy played in shaping opportunities for freedom.[3]

This essay describes how slaves in Britain's Northern colonies in North America attempted to obtain freedom and "competence in life" in the Black Atlantic via the sea. It considers their efforts to find the "content & ease" that many mariners, both white and colored, found difficult to obtain, and where they were able to "anchor" themselves after they escaped enslavement.[4] It also is the story of how, during the eighteenth century, enslaved Northern mariners were—as black watermen in Southern colonies would be in the nineteenth century—at the center of slave resistance.[5] And in telling the stories of these men's lives, this essay demonstrates that blacks' "relationship to the sea" was, as Paul Gilroy has observed, "especially important." These maritime fugitives were part of "movements of black peoples" across the Atlantic in which individuals crossed "borders in modern machines that were themselves micro-systems of linguistic and political hybridity." For most blacks, their experience with European ocean-faring vessels was the horrific Middle Passage. For others, ships represented both "slavery and exploitation." And for numerous Northern slaves, maritime employment offered freedom of movement and the opportunity to escape the brutality of slavery ashore.[6]

During the eighteenth century, the sea served as a magnet for hundreds of fugitive slaves. Slaves who wore the striped osnaburg clothing that marked them as bondmen understood that a ship berth offered the possibility of permanent escape. Ships disappearing over the horizon provided strong visual images of escape that drew many slaves to Northern wharves seeking berths. Slaves who sought to flee via the sea, individuals whom I classify as "maritime fugitives," comprised approximately one-fifth of known Northern runaways.[7] Who were these maritime fugitives? What factors led these individuals to believe flight by sea offered opportunities for freedom? Where did they flee? Were they able to find freedom? And what were their lives at sea like?

Maritime fugitives were young, tall, healthy males who often had prior maritime experience and possessed linguistic capabilities, attributes that made them attractive to ship captains. The average age of maritime fugitives from 1713 to 1783 was 23 years of age, younger than any other group of Atlantic seamen studied.[8] Most Northern masters had small slave holdings, did not value slave children, and opposed slave marriages. With Northern ports having imbalanced gender ratios, many maritime fugitives had limited family connections in Northern ports, making fleeing via the sea an enticing option for those lacking with such ties.[9]

Fugitive slave advertisements indicate that most maritime fugitives had strong linguistic skills. For example, more than 70 percent of advertisements in which New York City maritime fugitives' linguistic abilities were noted characterized the slave as speaking English. In addition, many maritime fugitives also spoke a second European language. Such linguistic abilities enabled fugitive slaves to forge passes, obtain berths, and fit in among multinational crews sailing from Northern ports.[10]

These young Northern maritime fugitives were also taller, stronger, and in better health than other Northern slaves. In an era when the average American was 5 feet, 7 inches, numerous maritime fugitives who were 5 feet, 10 inches, or taller could be found on Northern waterways. Men such as Levi Hollingsworth's "remarkably strong" 22-year-old, six-foot slave, who worked on a Delaware River shallop, were commonly found lurking about shipyards, fleeing in stolen boats, and working on privateers, British men of war, and merchant ships. Healthy slaves with maritime experience were particularly valued. Slave want and sale advertisements regularly highlighted the health of slave mariners. Over half of the Pennsylvania want advertisements indicating the physical traits sought in slaves listed "healthy" as a required characteristic. New York and Newport owners were only slightly less insistent on needing "healthy" slaves. Advertisements seeking strong young mariners, such as the one a New Yorker placed in 1769 seeking "6 or 8 stout . . . Negroes, that have been used to the Sea," were common in Northern newspapers.[11]

Many young slaves fled via the sea due to a lack of other good alternatives to obtain permanent freedom. Runaways seeking permanent freedom in Southern and West Indian colonies often sought shelter in maroon colonies, such as in Virginia's Great Dismal Swamp, where they led what whites considered a "wild and savage freedom." The geography of populated areas in Northern colonies—flat with few hills—provided only limited areas in which fugitives slaves could find permanent refuge from their masters. Frontier areas north and west of Northern port cities attracted some slave runaways.[12] Fugitives like the New Yorker Robin, who in 1765 fled northward believing freedom could be found in the northern frontier, were exceptions, not the rule, among Northern runaways. Slaves who did escape to frontier areas tended to be Native Americans or mixed-race men who sought haven in remnant tribal structures, or like the Mulatto named Tom, attempted "to pass for an Indian."[13]

Four factors led maritime fugitives to believe that freedom could be obtained by transforming themselves from wearers of striped osnaburg clothing to Black Tars of the Atlantic: their prior maritime experiences; the nature of slavery in Northern ports; ship captains' labor needs, especially during wartime; and the permanent freedom that flight onto a ship offered.

Many slaves came to Northern ports experienced in maritime matters, having been mariners or worked in land-based maritime trades in the West Indies or Africa. Masters on Antigua, St. Croix, Bermuda, and Jamaica, from which considerable numbers of slaves were regularly sent to Northern ports, frequently used slaves as seamen, with one-third of Antigua's mariners being black crew members.[14] Many other West Indian slaves were employed as fishermen and were often considered critical in providing island residents with sufficient sustenance.[15] The prevalence of West Indian-born slave seamen in Northern ports is illustrated by New York Captain Robert Gibb regularly employing West Indies-born slave seamen. When Gibb made West Indies voyages during the 1760s and 1770s, his West Indian-born slave, Falmouth, regularly worked as a crew member. In 1779 Captain Gibb had "three Negroe and one Mulatto sailors" flee his sloop, at least one of whom, 30-year-old George, was described as a Negro Bermuda-born seaman.[16]

The West Indies was not the only region with rich maritime traditions from which slaves were imported into Northern ports.[17] During the last quarter of the seventeenth and the first decades of the eighteenth century, English and French pirates sought Madagascar men as mariners due to their well-known seafaring skills. At the same time, New York merchants established a trading post in Madagascar from which they provisioned pirates and imported significant numbers of Madagascar slaves. Elias Neau observed that large numbers of Madagascar slaves were brought to New York, which Jacobus Van Cortlandt believed had been the cause for "the very slow" state of the slave trade at the end of the seventeenth century. Despite Parliament enacting legislation in the 1720s clearly barring private slave trade from Madagascar, slaves from the island continued to be regularly observed in Northern ports during the first half of the eighteenth century.[1]

Malagasy slaves were not the only enslaved Africans with maritime skills imported to the Northern colonies. The skills of West African fishermen had been long noted by European travelers. In the 1750s, at a time when a considerable number of Senegambian men had seafaring experience, both as Atlantic fishermen and on sailing boats with Portuguese sails and rigging, groups of Senegambian slaves with maritime experience were transported to New York, Philadelphia, and Newport. Of the African slaves imported to Pennsylvania whose origins are known, 57.7 percent were from Senegambia. Senegambian slaves also comprised 53.5 percent of African slaves imported to New York. The Upper Guinea coast was known for its skilled African seamen. Europeans employed *grumetes* (Portuguese reference to an apprentice mariner or cabin boy) or *laptos* (derived from the Wolof word for sailor) from Africans familiar with maritime labor. These men included both free Africans and enslaved individuals who typically who gave half their wages to their masters or mistresses. By the end of the eighteenth century, large numbers of *grumetes* were working for the British along the Guinea Coast.[19] It is likely that some of the Senegambian and Madagascar mariners transported to North America would have gained exposure to European sailing practices during the Middle Passage. While the numbers of Madagascar and Senegambian slaves with maritime experience who were transported to North America cannot be stated with certainty, during the eighteenth century such men were regularly observed in Northern ports. Prince, a man "of a Madagascar colour" who had "been much used to the sea," and other African "saylor[s]," regularly were subjects of fugitive and sale advertisements.[20]

When slaves disembarked in Philadelphia, New York, and Newport, they entered cities in which hundreds of blacks, free and enslaved, worked on the wharves and docks. These maritime workers were part of a larger Black Atlantic maritime community with thousands of mariners of color and maritime fugitives. This extensive Black Atlantic maritime community attracted fugitive slaves from both Northern ports and distant rural communities.[21]

Mobility was central to the operation of Northern ports. Immigrants, ships, refugees, and goods continually entered and left these cities. So did many slaves. Numerous slaves imported into Northern colonies came with considerable knowledge of the larger Atlantic world. They included Muslims from Senegambia, mariners from the Dutch and Danish West Indies, and considerable numbers of Spanish Negroes. Men like Robert and London from St. Christopher, who were brought to Northern ports on trips with their masters, came with an understanding of the larger Atlantic world. Slaves' lives in Northern colonies, despite strict social and legal controls, involved regular movement around and between those cities.[22] As one master observed, Northern bondmen often "never staid long in one place" and were said to have more free time than their Northern rural counterparts. Their movements brought slaves in frequent contact with peoples from throughout the Atlantic world providing them with knowledge of the opportunities available elsewhere. Slaves' mobility in northern cities can be seen in newspaper dispatches concerning slaves finding lost watches on docks, shooting bears in the outlying marshes, bringing goods to market, and drowning while at sea.[23] The daily routines of slaves such as William Chancellor's three sailmakers required them to purchase needles and other supplies throughout the Philadelphia's Southwark and Center City districts, work in Chancellor's sail loft, and make deliveries of sails to ships docked at wharves along the Delaware River. They and other slaves were often unsupervised by their masters for extended periods of time. Slaves' movement was also a function of their masters frequently hiring them out to other whites for temporary employment. Often hired out over time to a number of different employers, slaves gained familiarity with a variety of neighborhoods, including maritime quarters of various cities. Slave masters also were willing to hire their slaves out to distant employers. For example, in 1761 Philadelphian William Masters hired out 12 slaves, some to employers in Wilmington, Delaware. Owners were not hesitant to hire slaves to work on ships. When lacking work for the bondman, Bostonian Samuel Lynde hired his Negro slave out as a ship's cook. Similarly, during the Seven Years War, Dr. Amos Throop of Providence hired out his slave Newport Greene as a mariner.[24]

Slaves' involvement in the Northern maritime industry was not limited to working on wharves and docks. Slaves were employed in maritime-related occupations such as shipmasters, pilots, and ferry crewmembers. They also worked on Northern fishing boats, oyster shallops, whaling vessels, ferries, transatlantic ships, and their master's or others' privateers.[25] Fugitive slave advertisements indicate that a substantial portion of Northern slave runaways were mariners or were familiar with maritime matters. Almost 25 percent of New York City masters and 37 percent of Rhode Island masters believed their slaves to have fled via the sea. Certain maritime sectors, such oyster and whaling ships, attracted significant numbers of fugitive mariners. For example, William West, Gideon Cheat, George Gregory, Titus and Jeffrey, and many others, ran from their Rhode Island masters for service on whalers. Owners understood these men intended "to go to Nantucket . . . to sail on a whaling voyage." Connecticut and Long Island slaves similarly fled to Nantucket to go whaling.[26]

Who provided berths to these runaways? Privateer, merchant, and naval captains all employed these men. Privateer captains found maritime fugitives to be particularly attractive. Requiring large crews to be able to board enemy ships, privateer captains were frequently willing to ignore a dark-skinned man's possible enslaved status to fill out their crews. Men like Quam, Strode, Mingo, the Governor of Maryland's slave, and the 23 blacks on Alexander McDougall's privateer *Tyger* were among the scores of black privateers.[27] Merchant captains similarly were also willing to hire maritime fugitives. As a 1743 census of North American vessels in Jamaica that found 41 black mariners among the ships' 131 sailors demonstrates, colored mariners, free, enslaved and runaways, were commonplace in the eighteenth century Atlantic. Colonial officials complained of their port cities "filling up with foreigners" seeking berths, and the British Admiralty bemoaned the "evil" of "wooly haired" sailors. Despite such attitudes, British privateers, including naval officials manning their privately owned cruizers, used slaves as crew. As the governor of Cuba acknowledged, without mariners of "a broken color" West Indies privateers would have lacked sufficient numbers of mariners.[28]

The havens where Northern maritime fugitives sought freedom included what Jane Landers calls the "Negroid Littoral"—Spanish Florida, Puerto Rico, Cuba, villages on the Central and South American coast, as well as England, especially after the *Somerset* decision provided legal protection for those who could reach England.[29] Maritime fugitives who reached these havens found employment in the French and Spanish navies and privateers, whose vessels had multinational crews and often included slaves or fugitive slaves.[30]

St. Augustine attracted fugitives not merely from Georgia and South Carolina, but as far away as New York. In 1721, John Cannon, the commander of New York's oyster fleet, advertised that six Spanish Indians and several Negroes stole his sloop with the intent of making for the Spanish stronghold. Twelve years later three slaves stole Cannon's sloop and headed south. Like the group of Havana-born slaves who stole a boat in South Carolina and headed to Cuba, Cannon's slaves understood that the Spanish would welcome them and, if the slaves converted to Catholicism, provide them with freedom.[31]

Porto Rico similarly attracted maritime fugitives. By 1770 their numbers became so great that a British naval vessel was sent to the island in a fruitless effort to reclaim fugitive slaves. Treaties between several nations, including Spain and Denmark, specifically dealt with the need for the return of slaves who fled via the sea.[32]

England also served as a haven in the Atlantic world for fugitive slaves long before it formally outlawed slavery. With the British Royal Navy often "regard[ing] a man-of-war as a little piece of British territory in which slavery was improper," slaves coming to England before the American Revolution found naval officers helpful allies in their attempt to become free. For example, in 1751 William Castillo, a slave seamen on a merchant vessel in Boston, suspected he might be sold on shore. Castillo convinced ship Captain James Jones to purchase him, as Castillo preferred life at sea. Captain Jones promised to emancipate Castillo when the sailor's wages equaled his purchase price. Five years later, not wishing to wait any longer, Castillo fled. In 1758, while in Portsmouth, England, Castillo ran into Captain Jones, who had him arrested and put in an iron collar, and threatened to sell the black mariner in the West Indies. Being literate, Castillo was able to write to the Admiralty seeking its intervention. The Admiralty's response was to tell Portsmouth officials "the laws of this country admit of no badges of slavery," and that Castillo should be placed back on the warship's books as a free able-bodied seaman.

Thus, in the years preceding the American Revolution, as English slave ships transported enormous numbers of Africans to slavery in the

Americas, slave mariners from North America had opportunities, albeit slim ones, to find freedom. These opportunities expanded with Justice Mansfield's decision in *Somerset v Stewart*.[33]

In 1772 Justice Mansfield's *Somerset* decision held that slavery could only be supported by "positive law," which England lacked. The decision emphasized that slavery was defined differently within the Atlantic world, not merely as between different nations, but also as between the metropolis and its colonial possessions. Although Justice Mansfield's decision was ambiguous in its reach, slaves throughout the colonies came to believe that if they reached England they would be freed. Slaves throughout the Atlantic shared and acted upon this understanding that England was a land of liberty.[34] British naval officers shared a similar belief. For example, in May 1776 when the Danish sloop *Lawrence,* proceeding from New York to Copenhagen, was forced to dock at Portsmouth to make repairs, naval Captains Cooley and Stiles believed the ship's four slave mariners' presence in England meant they were "*emancipated* from . . . Slavery." The *Lawrence*'s slave mariners (a North American, two West Indians, and an African) apparently believed Justice Mansfield's decision served to free them when they touched English soil, and on that basis they petitioned "not [to] be carried out of the Realm." Their petition evidences that an understanding that the English legal system could serve as the means to make England a "Happy Territory" for themselves and others fleeing slavery in the Americas.[35]

Although maritime fugitives found haven in some Atlantic ports, others were closed to them. Sometimes this was due to maritime labor market dynamics, and other times due to legal and cultural restrictions. For example, in 1748-1749 only seven identifiable colored mariners sailed among the more than 3,000 crewmembers on ships out of Scarborough on Britain's northeast coast. While racist attitudes on the part of Scarborough's mariners and ship captains may have played a part in this, Scarborough's crew lists and seamen hospital's records demonstrates a different reason for the lack of black mariners on the port's vessels. Scarborough's ships were small, with crews of between five and nine men. Scarborough's crews came largely from the local area, with only a sprinkling of foreign seamen in the crews. The crews frequently included multiple family members. Elderly family men often served as cooks on the ships and with the local seaman's hospital lacking financial resources, the hiring of young boys and elderly fathers served as a means of providing for family members. Thus, it was Scarborough's close-knit family culture that limited opportunities for colored sailors.[36]

Flight onto ships did not result in permanent freedom for many fugitives as they often were captured and re-enslaved. British and American captains regularly had captured mariners of color condemned by Admiralty Courts. For example, in the 1730s and 1740s, New York's Captain Lush and Boston's Captain Rouse each had parcels of Spanish colored sailors condemned as prize goods, and in 1780 Stephen Decatur brought a series of Admiralty Court proceedings to condemn captured mariners of color. Even maritime fugitives who reached England and joined the Royal Navy could find themselves re-enslaved. For example, during the Seven Years' War, John Incobs, a New York slave, found his way to England where he entered HMS *Garlands* as an able-bodied seaman. Unfortunately for Incobs, when the *Garlands* docked in New York he found himself discharged for "being a slave," most likely due to his former owner asserting a claim to him.[37]

The varied experiences of eighteenth-century enslaved seamen can be contrasted by the stories of two New England mariners of color, Ben Freebody and Venture Smith. In June 1775, Ben was hired out by his slave owner, Samuel Freebody, a Newport distiller, on a slaving voyage to Guinea with Captain James Brattle. Ben understood that when he was hired to Captain Brattle he would be paid "Sailors Wages," with the wages to be divided between himself and Samuel Freebody. Ben intended to use his share to purchase his freedom.[38] Within a short time of coming on board Captain Brattle's ship, Ben was so severely whipped that his "blood ran down the deck," after which Ben was "pickled with brine." Captain Brattle's harsh treatment led Ben to run away while in the West Indies. Luck was not with Ben, as he was recaptured and brutally lashed by Grenada's Public Whipper. Ben then was compelled to serve on several slaving voyages with Captain Brattle.[39] Despite such abuse, Ben may have believed his fortune turned for the better when Captain Brattle's crew captured two American prizes. As a seaman entitled to "sailors wages," Ben anticipated receiving a share of the prize monies for the captured vessels. While other crew members received £90 in prize monies, Ben was provided some clothes and a dollar to be shared with another slave mariner. Ben's misfortune only got worse. Despite being illegally detained by Captain Brattle and harshly treated, Ben still believed the ship captain would abide by his agreement with Samuel Freebody and allow him to return to Newport. Sadly, Ben was mistaken. After he got aboard another ship bound for Newport, Captain Brattle had him forcibly removed and sent to work on another vessel.

In the ensuing years Ben suffered the loss of an eye due to smallpox. Having little value as a half-blind seaman, Ben was left to "shift for myself" in New York.[40] Having "little remaining part of my cloaths," Ben was "near being sold for payment" of his room rent. He was spared that fate when New York wine merchant Garret Roorback paid his back rent and took him "in out of Charity." In August 1784, Ben was returned to Newport when a Captain Norris brought him "to Rhode Island by [Samuel Freebody's] order." When he returned to Rhode Island, Ben found himself a witness in a proceeding brought by Samuel Freebody against Captain Brattle. While Freebody and Battle contested who was entitled to Ben's wages for his service to the ship captain neither the slave owner nor the ship captain acknowledged Ben's right to wages. The result was that the poor man appears never to have obtained his freedom. Instead, his wealthy master kept him until 1790, at which time he deigned to allow Ben to "look out in the Country for a Person to buy him, as he is discontented with living with me." Discontented! Little wonder; 15 years after first being hired out as a mariner believing his time at sea would provide him with an opportunity to buy his freedom, Ben was forced to sell himself to avoid not having to daily face a man who betrayed him.[41]

Unlike Ben Freebody, Venture Smith found freedom from maritime employment. An African-born slave brought to New England by a steward on a Rhode Island slaver, Smith was employed doing house work and agricultural duties for his master on Fishers Island. He initially attempted to obtain his freedom by fleeing by boat to the Mississippi River. When he returned to his master, Smith found that justice was often denied based on race and was sold three times, a common occurrence among Northern slaves. Thereafter Venture did not, as Ben Freebody and hundreds of other Northern slaves had, seek freedom by serving as a blue-water seaman. Instead, Smith took a slower, but less risky road to independence. Frugally saving money earned from fishing and other ventures, Smith was able to purchase his freedom and the freedom of other members of his family. Thereafter, maritime employment enabled Venture Smith to establish a comfortable life as the owner of a fleet of coasting vessels. Smith's life may have been a rags-to-riches story, but it also illustrates the risks that life at sea posed. His sons Solomon and Cuff followed their father to sea, but did not share their father's fortune. Solomon died of scurvy at sea. Solomon's fate led Venture to bemoan his son's having "walked in the way of [his] father."[42]

In conclusion, the Black Atlantic into which Northern maritime fugitives fled needs to be understood as a dynamic and changing environment in which men of color often found themselves enslaved, freed, and enslaved again. The maritime life fugitives sought was for some a "virtual incarceration," while for others it was "a relatively easy life."[43] Ports in which maritime fugitives at one time found haven over time could prove to be less than welcoming.[44] Moreover, ships changed course, nations declared war, seamen betrayed mates, and captains could not always be trusted. Naval officers often proved to be allies of slaves seeking freedom, but also could prove quite willing to use profit through the condemnation of colored mariners as prize goods. For maritime fugitives such as Romeo who found freedom when captured by the British Royal Navy, the ship they chose took them away from their masters and to freedom. For others, such as the unfortunate John Incobs, life at sea led to re-enslavement. Seeking freedom in the eighteenth-century Anglo-American Atlantic often was a game of roulette in which the ships maritime fugitives entered onto could lead either to freedom or to even harsher enslavement than that they had fled.

Like generations of earlier enslaved divers, this free-born nineteenth-century Bahamian sponge diver practices a skill that conferred special privileges.

(Annie Brassey, *In the Trades, the Tropics, & the Roaring Forties* (London, 1885), G.W. Blunt White Library, Mystic Seaport)

4

Enslaved Underwater Divers in the Atlantic World

Kevin J. Dawson

Long before a single coastal or interior West African was enslaved and cargoed off to toil the length of their days under the skies of the New World, many had become adept swimmers and underwater divers. Sizable numbers of West Africans grew up along riverbanks, near lakes, or close to the ocean. In these waterways, many became proficient swimmers, incorporating this skill into their work and recreational activities. When carried to the Americas, numerous slaves brought this ability with them, where it helped shape generations of bondpeople's occupational and leisure activities.

Up through the nineteenth century, the swimming and underwater diving abilities of people of African descent often surpassed those of Westerners. Indeed, most whites, including sailors, probably could not swim. To reduce drowning deaths, some philanthropists advocated that sailors and others learn to swim as a means of self-preservation. In 1838, *The Sailor's Magazine*, printed in New York by the reformist American Seamen's Friend Society, published the inscription of a city placard titled "Swimming." It read: "For want of knowledge of this noble art thousands are annually sacrificed, and every fresh victim calls more strongly upon . . . such persons as may be likely to require this art, to the simple fact, that there is no difficulty in floating or swimming." Similarly, Theodorus Mason's pamphlet, *The Preservation of Life at Sea*, claimed that "the great majority of people cannot swim, and strange as it may seem to you, there are many who follow the sea as a profession who cannot swim a stroke." Mason then proclaimed that, as part of their instruction, all U.S. Naval Academy cadets should be taught to swim.[1]

This article considers how slaves carried swimming and underwater diving skills to the Americas. It seeks to enhance our understanding of slavery by exploring how this system of labor was shaped by a cultural retention that scholars have heretofore neglected. First, it compares the swimming abilities and techniques of Westerners and Africans in order to demonstrate the African origin of slaves' swimming abilities. Next, it examines how slaves incorporated swimming into their recreational practices. Finally, since slavery was work, this article explores how slave owners used bondpeople's swimming and diving skills in several lucrative occupations. Because occupational diving was dangerous and required exceptional skill, it sometimes influenced white-slave relationships, leading whites to reward slaves' dexterity by granting them limited privileges.[2]

While early-modern accounts indicate that few whites swam, they also reveal that if they did they used variants of the breaststroke, in which both arms are extended forward and pulled back together in a circular motion, while the legs are thrust out and pulled together in circular frog kicks.[3] Until the late nineteenth century, Westerners were averse to the freestyle because it generated more splashing than the breaststroke. According to swimming theorists and practitioners such as Benjamin Franklin, swimming "should be smooth and gentle." Since splashing was deemed unsophisticated, the freestyle was regarded as unrefined when compared to the sedate, harmonious breaststroke. Even though the breaststroke is one of the most rudimentary strokes, many Westerners ironically regarded it as the most refined and graceful.[4]

Conversely, Africans, as well as Native Americans and Asians, used variants of the freestyle, enabling Africans to incorporate swimming into many daily activities.[5] With its alternate over-arm strokes combined with scissor kicks, it is the strongest and swiftest swimming style, enabling Africans to incorporate swimming into many daily activities. Travelers mentioned that considerable numbers of Africans swam, noted that they were better swimmers than most Europeans, and indicated that Westerners tended to use the breaststroke while Africans preferred the freestyle. Significantly, several observers, including Dr. Franklin, referred to the breaststroke as the "ordinary" method of swimming, indicating that whites tended to use the breaststroke.[6]

From 1444 up through 1900, Western travelers to Africa reported that both male and female Africans were sound swimmers, that they were stronger swimmers than Europeans, and that they preferred the freestyle to the breaststroke. In the 1590s, Dutch adventurer Pieter de Marees commented on Gold Coast Africans' freestyle technique, observing "they can swim very fast, generally easily outdoing people of our nation in swimming and diving." In the seventeenth century, Jean Barbot compared the freestyle used by the Fante in present-day Ghana, to the breaststroke employed by Europeans, asserting "the Blacks of Mina out-do all others at the coast in dexterity of swimming, throwing one [arm] after another forward, as if they were paddling, and not extending their arms equally, and striking with them both together, as Europeans do." In 1606, Pieter Van den Broecke noted that many of the Africans at Gorée Island, Senegal, were "extraordinarily strong swimmers." Similarly, Robert Sutherland Rattray noted that Asante men and women, at Lake Bosomtwe, located about a hundred miles inland, used the freestyle. Asante "men are very fine swimmers and some show magnificent muscular development. They swim either the ordinary breast stroke [like Europeans] or a double overarm with a scissor-like kick of the legs." On October 15, 1844, U.S. Navy officer Horatio Bridge revealed that the swimming abilities of Kru from Liberia surpassed those of whites who could swim. Five Europeans and five Kru were aboard a boat that "capsized and sunk. The five Kroomen saved themselves, by swimming, until picked up by a canoe; the five whites were lost."[7]

Sources pertaining to Native American swimming provide further evidence of Westerners' unfamiliarity with the freestyle. While in North Dakota in the late 1830s, George Catlin explained how the Mandans' use of the freestyle made them stronger swimmers than whites. After detailing their overarm technique he stated it "is quite different from that practiced in those parts of the civilized world, which I have had the pleasure yet to visit."[8]

While there is no evidence indicating at what age interior peoples learned to swim, travelers reported that many coastal Africans learned very young, either right after learning to walk, between the ages of 10 and 14 months, or after they were weaned at approximately two to three years of age. "Once the children begin to walk by themselves, they soon go to the water in order to learn how to swim and to walk in the water," wrote Pieter de Marees. William Bosman commented "the Mother gives the Infant suck for two or three Years; which over, and they able to go . . . to the Sea-side to learn to swim."[9]

After parents taught them the fundamentals of swimming, children improved their skills by playing in the water and observing the techniques of stronger swimmers. While at Elmina, Jean Barbot saw "several hundred of boys and girls sporting together before the beach, and in many places among the rolling and breaking waves, learning to swim." He then contended that Africans' strong swimming abilities "proceed from their being brought up, both men and women from their infancy, to swim like fishes; and that, with the constant exercise renders them so dexterous."[10]

Having learned to swim at an early age, many West African men and women incorporated swimming into their recreational and work activities. Canoemen used their swimming skill on a daily basis. As dugout canoes left the beach, watermen often swam alongside them to help keep their bows pointed toward oncoming waves to prevent them from tipping. When a canoe overturned in the surf, canoemen swam to save their lives, and "being excellent swimmers and divers recover goods from the upset canoes."[11] In 1796, Scottish explorer Mungo Park observed a fisherman dive underwater to collect and set fish traps. The fisherman's lung capacity was so great that he was able to remain submerged "for such a length of time, that I thought he had actually drowned himself."[12]

The swimming abilities of several disparate ethnic groups were so strong that they invented surfing independent of Polynesian influence. Africans in Senegal, the Ivory Coast, Ghana, Gabon, and possibly the Congo-Angola region surfed. On November 16, 1834, while at Accra, Ghana, James Edward Alexander wrote that "from the beach, meanwhile, might be seen boys swimming into the sea, with light boards under their stomachs. They waited for a surf; and came rolling like a cloud on top of it."[13]

As Africans were taken to the New World, many carried swimming skills with them. From the early 1500s on, slaveholders realized that slaves' swimming and underwater diving abilities could be profitably exploited. Consequently, some slave traders targeted Africans with swimming skills for capture and sale to New World colonies in need of their skills.[14]

Sports culture historian Richard Mandell wrote, "if there were indigenous sports among the imported Africans, they left no trace." However, many slaves participated in recreational and theatrical swimming activities that were evidently based on skills developed in Africa.[15] Slaves swam for recreation and enjoyment. In the evening, many slipped into the water to cool off, relax, and wash away the day's troubles. North

Carolina slave Bill Crump recalled: "We wucked in the fields from sunup to sundown, but we had a couple of hours at dinner time to swim or lay on de banks of the little crick and sleep."[16]

Slaves' swimming habits extended beyond such impromptu activities. Scholars have discussed bondpeople's competitive sporting activities, including boxing and wrestling matches and foot and horse races. They have contended that such activities could have enhanced slaves' self-esteem, making enslavement more bearable, and that many slaveholders believed sports allowed bondpeople to vent their frustrations without threatening the stability of slavery. Though such activities typically occurred away from white supervision, some slaveholders organized slaves' recreational activities.[17] In the 1770s, John Stedman noted that adolescent slaves in Guiana competed in informal swimming contests, saying they swam "in groups of boys and girls, and both sexes exhibit astonishing feats of courage, strength and activity. I have seen a [slave] girl beat a hardy youth in swimming across the River Comewina."[18]

Slaves also swam in formal, planter-organized contests. Historians have explained that slaveholders occasionally organized boxing matches that pitted the champion fighter of one plantation against that of another.[19] They apparently organized similar swimming contests as well. In the seventeenth century, Richard Ligon observed a planter-organized contest in which slaves from Barbados had to catch a duck placed in a large pond. And the captor was awarded the duck. The proprietor of this contest, Colonel Drax, "call[ed] for some of his best swimming *Negroes,* commanded them to swim and take this Duck; but forbad them to dive, for if they were not bar'd that play, they would rise up under the Duck, and take her as she swome, and so the sport would have too quick an end." Describing the slaves' use of the breaststroke and freestyle, Ligon said "in this chase there was much of pleasure, to see the various swimmings of the [slaves]; some the ordinary wayes, upon their bellies [like Europeans], some by striking out their right leg and left arm, and then turning on the other side, and changing both their leg and arm, which is a stronger and swifter way of swimming, than any of the others." The winner of this contest was a female slave.[20]

Whether organized by slaves or by slaveholders, swimming contests probably offered the winners prestige in the slave community and indicated that female slaves could beat their male counterparts. In addition to providing enslaved participants and observers with entertainment, the communal nature of such contests probably enhanced slaves' sense of community.[21]

Like their African ancestors, accounts indicate that many slaves born in the Americas learned to swim at an early age. Several accounts detail the swimming activities of enslaved children who were between seven and twelve years old. These children seem to have been comfortable in the water, indicating that they probably learned to swim when considerably younger. On February 2, 1773, one of the first sights that greeted John Stedman's eyes as he entered the Surinam River, after crossing the Atlantic, were "groups of naked boys and girls promiscuously playing and flouncing, like many tritons and mermaids, in the water." He then stated that "the scene was new to all," suggesting that European children did not swim. Frederick Douglass recalled that, near the home he lived at when we was approximately seven or eight, "there was a creek to swim in, at the bottom of an open flat space, of twenty acres or more, called 'the Long Green'—a very beautiful play-ground for the children." Enslaved parents, family members, and the entire slave community probably taught children to swim, just as they instructed them in gardening, cooking, sewing, hunting, and enduring bondage.[22]

Though it is impossible to determine the percentage of slaves who swam proficiently, sources suggest that many did. Discussing the abilities of slaves in Barbados, Richard Ligon stated, "Excellent Swimmers and Divers they are both men and women." Even though John Stedman, who was raised in Holland, could swim, he admitted that most Guiana slaves were much better swimmers and divers than he. While Robert Walsh was traversing Brazil in the 1820s, he concluded that most slaves could swim, dubbing them "amphibious." Francis Fedric, who was enslaved in Virginia and Kentucky during the mid-1800s, contended that most bondpeople could swim, saying "unlike most slaves, I never learned to swim."[23]

In *Born in Bondage*, Marie Jenkins Schwartz asserts that slaveholders did not encourage their slaves to learn to swim because they felt swimming did not increase slaves' economic value but could aid them in escaping and could potentially lead to drowning and the loss of valuable human property.[24] Indeed, many slaves did incorporate swimming into their repertoires of resistance.[25] On the other hand, swimming could considerably increase a bondman's usefulness and monetary worth, and some slaveholders encouraged it.

Recognizing that slaves' swimming skills could be used to save lives, some whites advocated their use as lifeguards. While Dr. George Pinckard was in Barbados, he wrote on April 13, 1804, that slaves' swimming expertise "renders the negroes peculiarly useful in moments of distress, such as in cases of accident at sea or in the harbour." When young John Clinkscales of Abbeville County, South Carolina, swam, his parents entrusted his life to a slave named Essex, who was a renowned swimmer.[26] Indeed, throughout the Atlantic world, slaves' swimming proficiencies and whites' inabilities were juxtaposed when maritime accidents compelled blacks to save the lives of drowning whites. In 1805, the Barbadian slaveholder Robert Haynes sent his three sons to a school in Liverpool, along with a slave named Hamlet, who "saved the life of my son George," when he fell "overboard whilst landing at Liverpool." Similarly, a white clerk, "who could only swim a few strokes" slipped off a "ship's gangway" in Baltimore Harbor and was pulled by the current "far out in the harbour." Fortunately for him, his enslaved friend Zamba, who was raised on the "south bank of the river Congo, about two hundred miles from the sea," and had become "quite used to the water in Africa and could swim like a seagull," dove in after him, and "after a few minutes' strenuous exertion made up to my friend, who was just at the moment sinking; having seized him by the coat collar with my left hand, I continued to keep afloat until a boat (several of which were pulling hastily to our assistance) came alongside and hauled us in." After a Brazilian steamer ran aground and began to break apart, a black sailor named Simao "swam through the furious breakers" 13 times to save as many passengers.[27]

While the role of the lifeguard never became widespread, bondmen were employed throughout the Americas as underwater divers. Perhaps as a result of the tradition that barred women from maritime trades, bondwomen apparently were not used as divers, even though many African women on both sides of the Atlantic were proficient swimmers.[28] Or possibly this resulted from the tradition that, unlike males, bondwomen typically could not escape the drudgery of field labor by being placed in specialized occupation.[29]

Slave divers were highly skilled, and their diving abilities were unrivaled. Many could dive ninety-plus feet deep. Since divers descended to great depths, their eardrums sometimes burst. Though not fatal, this was painful and could cause temporary loss of equilibrium. It's unclear how divers acquired their abilities, but the lung capacity and the composure required to work at such depths suggest that they had learned to swim at an early age.[30]

As with masons, seamstresses, Big House cooks, and blacksmiths, divers apparently enjoyed the privileges slaveholders bestowed on skilled slaves. Manipulative slave owners granted privileges to slaves to make them more dependent. Most slaves detested agricultural field labor, and the most important privilege a slave could receive was placement in a skilled occupation. Such a job enabled them to escape the monotony of field work, find some dignity in their labor, enhance their self-esteem, gain the respect of their fellow slaves, and sometimes obtain cash payments, which benefited their lives and those of their families and friends, most of whom were field hands. Skilled slaves were often trusted by their owners, who frequently allowed them to work free of direct white supervision.[31]

Yet, because skilled occupations were privileges, slaves could be stripped of their positions at their owners' whim, for misconduct, or so owners could demonstrate their authority. While plantation production would have quickly ceased without the labors of skilled slaves, such as carpenters and blacksmiths, some slaves could be rotated in and out of skilled positions without disrupting output.[32] Since enslaved divers possessed abilities few other slaves possessed, they may have enjoyed more of an advantage than other skilled bondpeople. Divers and their owners undoubtedly knew how hard it was to replace them. Consequently, as long as divers could execute their duties and there was diving to perform, their positions were relatively safe. So compared to other skilled bondpeople, divers probably faced less danger of being stripped of their positions as a result of minor infractions or their owners' caprice.[33]

Divers differed from other skilled bondpeople in another significant way. Most skilled slaves ascended to privilege by gaining competence in Western artisanry. However, divers' abilities were African-derived. Thus they demonstrated the vitality of African cultural transmissions and their power to shape the New World.

Importantly, the privileges that skilled slaves received were not the fruit of benevolence. Rather, slaveholders bestowed favors to extract more labor, and in turn more wealth, from skilled slaves' limbs and minds.[34] While diving was an arduous, dangerous occupation that taxed divers' health and claimed many lives, enslaved divers gained material reward and respite from field labor. Hence, like other skilled slaves, divers lived existences of privileged exploitation.

Spanish colonists along Venezuela's Pearl Coast were the first Westerners to exploit enslaved African swimmers. Initially, Native Americans were forced to dive for pearls.[35] However, as diseases and overwork depleted their numbers, Spanish colonists looked to Africa for laborers. Commenting on this practice, Pieter de Marees said Gold Coast Africans "are very fast swimmers and can keep themselves underwater for a long time. They can dive amazingly far . . . and can see underwater. Because they are so good at swimming and diving, they are specially kept for that purpose in many Countries and employed in this capacity where there is a need for them, such as [Margarita Island] in the West Indies, where Pearls are found and brought up from the bottom by Divers."[36]

In the morning each pearl canoe "sets sail for the oyster bed or pearl fishery, which generally" lay in waters over 80 feet deep. Divers held rocks to help them rapidly descend. Describing the diving process on Margarita Island, Friar Antonio Vázquez de Espinosa said, "when they dive under water, they carry a little net or reticule, fastened by a rope to the canoe." As they ripped pearl oysters from their rocky fastness, they deposited them into the nets, "and with great speed and skill they come with this to the surface." While catching their breath between dives, they frequently "receiv'd a glass of Wine and a Pipe of Tobacco" as refreshment. Ironically, both would have impaired their diving abilities. While visiting Margarita Island in the late 1500s, after overfishing precipitated its pearl fishery's decline, Richard Hawkins became impressed with the abilities of the island's "expert swimmers, and great deevers," saying "with tract of time, use, and continual practice, having learned to hold their breadth long underwater, for the better atchieving their worke."[37]

These divers were entitled to a portion of the harvested pearls, which frequently they were forced to sell to their owners. Describing these regulated commercial transactions, de Espinosa said, "to this end on certain holidays they lay on a table or elsewhere excellent suits of clothes or other valuable articles of clothing, and the Negroes come out with the clothes, and their masters with riches." Still, some divers accumulated enough wealth to purchase their freedom.[38]

Pearl diving was strenuous, life-threatening work. An oceanic trench near the Pearl Coast channels cold water into the otherwise warm Caribbean waters, causing the year-round ocean temperature to hover in the 60s Fahrenheit. These cool waters induced exposure-related illnesses that sometimes culminated in death. Pearl divers eardrum sometimes burst so that "the blood gushed out of their Mouths and Noses when they came above Water to breath." Sharks attacked divers, some divers drowned, while pirates kidnapped, injured, and killed others. Unlike other types of enslaved swimmers, pearl divers were severely beaten if they could not obtain the desired quantity or quality of pearls.[39]

Before the 1545 discovery of silver deposits in Peru, enslaved divers on the Pearl Coast probably generated more wealth than was produced anywhere else in the Americas.[40] Pearls from the region were an important international commodity. Most were exported to Europe, where some were re-exported to the Middle East, and still others were carried to Africa, where they were exchanged for slaves, ivory, gold, and other goods.[41]

The wealth enslaved pearl divers generated did not lead to reduced workloads or emancipation. Rather, their valuable service encouraged their use in other marine occupations. When Spanish treasure galleons sank, enslaved divers were employed in salvage work. The Spanish began using enslaved African salvage divers after a 28-ship treasure fleet sailed into a hurricane on September 6, 1622, one day after leaving Havana. Aware that enslaved pearl divers dove to great depths, Gaspar de Vargas, who was in charge of the salvage operation, took 20 pearl divers to the wreck area. Freedom was promised to the first slave who found a sunken galleon. One day an excited diver surfaced, shouting that he had located the treasure ship *Santa Margarita*, and as promised, he was granted his freedom.[42]

These Spanish successes set the precedent for employing enslaved salvage divers. When slaveholders in the Bahamas, Bermuda, Cayman Islands, and Florida began "wrecking," or salvaging goods from grounded or sunken ships, around the Florida Straits during the eighteenth century, they typically employed at least one slave who could dive to a depth of at least 70 feet.[43] Many nineteenth-century Connecticut fishermen, especially those from Mystic, wrecked off the Florida coast during the off-season to augment their incomes. Though no evidence could be found, they may have hired enslaved divers.[44]

In the antebellum American South, some bondpeople's swimming abilities were used in clearing fisheries of debris that could ensnare fishing nets. Slaves toiled on two types of fisheries that required clearing. Some worked for their owners on waterways near the owners' property. Others were hired out to commercial fisheries located in coastal estuaries. Charles Ball, who by his own account was an expert swimmer, explained that while he and two other South Carolina field hands were employed as seasonal fishermen by their owner, they also worked to clear the Congaree River of debris. Though the work was cold and hard, it was a welcome escape from field labor.[45]

In the mid-1850s, Frederick Law Olmsted penned a detailed description of North Carolina's substantial intracoastal fisheries that reveals enslaved divers' dexterity. "The shad and herring fisheries upon the sounds and inlets of the North Carolina coast are an important branch of industry, and a source of considerable wealth," he wrote. "The men employed in them are mainly negroes, slave and free."[46]

Work upon this fishery entailed long, dangerous hours. The most hazardous aspect was clearing the fishing grounds, which required the use of "seventy kegs of gunpowder the previous year." In many places, coastal subsidence had completely submerged swamps, leaving the "stumps of great cypress trees, not in the least decayed, yet protrude from the bottom of the sounds." Enslaved divers were key to their removal. After divers had ascertained the debris' position, "two large seine-boats are moored over it." Divers then fastened a chain to the stump or log, which was then hoisted to the surface by a windlass rigged to the boats. When a stump would not yield and the power of the windlass pulled the boats' sides "to the water's edge," a more dramatic technique was employed.[47] With the stump still chained to the boats, a diver placed a long, iron-tipped spike on the stump, which sledgehammer-wielding slaves in the boats drove into it. Once an approximately 10-foot cavity was made, the pole was removed. A diver inserted a cylindrical canister containing several pounds of explosives into the void. The charge was detonated while the stump was still chained to the boats, and the resulting explosion, combined with the upward force of the chains, wrenched the stump free.[48] The scene was described as follows:

> the diver has come up, and is drawn into one of the boats—an iron rod is inserted in the mouth of the tube—all hands crouch low, and hold hard—the rod is let go—crack!—whoo—oosch! The sea swells, boils, and breaks upward. If the boats do not rise with it, they must sink; if they rise, and the chain does not break, the stump must rise with them. At the same moment the heart of cypress is riven; its furthest rootlets quiver; the very earth trembles, and loses courage to hold it; "up comes the stump, or down go the niggers!"[49]

"[U]p comes the stump, or down go the niggers!" . . . this embellished linc suggcsts that divers were expendable, that their lives were worth little more than a stump stuck in the mud. By Olmsted's account, though, they were highly valued, both for their skills and for the revenues they generated. "The success of the operation evidently depends mainly on the discretion and skill of the diver," wrote Olmsted. "Some of them could remain under water, and work there to better advantage than others; but all were admirably skillful." A fishery operator told Olmsted that the previous summer his divers had removed over one thousand stumps in this way.[50]

These divers largely worked free of direct white supervision. When not diving, "and, while the other hands are at work, they may lounge, or go to sleep in the boat." Unlike most slaves, they were permitted to freely consume alcohol, and when "a diver displays unusual hardihood, skill, or perseverance, he is rewarded with whisky; or . . . money." Consequently, these divers earned substantial monetary bonuses from a "quarter to half a-dollar" a day, which sometimes enabled them to purchase their freedom. Though privileged, these divers were not lazy. Pride in workmanship and material rewards drove them to excel. Olmsted was told "'the harder the work you give them to do, the better they like it,'" and even though they frequently suffered from "intermittent fevers" they could not be kept out of the water. He concluded that these bondmen worked arduously in a perilous, yet privileged, profession. "What! slaves eager to work, and working cheerfully, earnestly and skillfully?" he exclaimed. "Being for the time managed as freemen, their ambition stimulated by wages, suddenly they, too, reveal sterling manhood, and honor their Creator."[51]

A close look at enslaved divers expands our understanding of the lives of skilled bondpeople. All of these divers seem to have enjoyed some genuine privilege. Some were granted their freedom, and many accumulated enough material wealth to purchase their liberty. Fishery divers seem to have been highly trusted. They apparently worked away from white supervision and, while slaveholders typically refused to permit bondpeople to carry weapons, these divers were trained in the use of explosives. Differences in time and location significantly impacted how divers were treated. Pearl divers apparently received harsher treatment than other divers. While the reasons for this are unknown, perhaps it was because Spanish colonists were able to import significant numbers of slaves with diving skills, and there were still considerable, though dwindling, numbers of indigenous divers. Importantly, though, pearl divers received privileges denied most Latin American plantation laborers.

While most skilled slaves' positions of privileged exploitation depended upon skill in Western artisanry, divers' abilities were African-based. Divers probably took great pride in their special skill. They knew that they could descend to depths few others could and that they had proficiencies whites did not possess. They braved cold waters, the dangers of underwater pressure, and sharks. Their diving ability not only made them exceptional among slaves, but they, along with Greek sponge divers and Japanese and Middle Eastern pearl divers, were an exception within the human race.[52]

This study demonstrates that bondpeople's swimming activities touched their everyday lives in important ways. In an age when few Westerners could swim, many slaves mastered the skill. Recreational swimming allowed field slaves to relax and cleanse themselves. When bondpeople competed in swimming contests, they exhibited their skills and won material rewards, enhancing their prestige and self-esteem and increased the slave communities' sense of cohesion.

Slaveholders probably had to treat enslaved swimmers and divers differently from most other skilled bondpeople. Slave owners doubtlessly had to concede some autonomy to them and had to temper their claims to absolute authority. Most slaves who possessed land-based proficiencies could be replaced by other competent slaves without considerably interrupting production. Divers, however, could not have been dismissed without causing significant work disruptions and even stoppages. When salvaging goods from sunken ships far out at sea or clearing debris from fisheries, slaveholders did not have the luxury of discharging a diver to exhibit their authority, and severe beatings could render divers unfit for work. Slave owners wanted diving jobs completed quickly and successfully, and they could not easily replace divers. Furthermore, slaveholders probably realized that they were privileged to own slaves possessing such a rare and lucrative ability. Thus, slaves employed in salvage, fishery, and pearl diving had leverage to exact privileges from their owners.

Though the work was grueling, enslaved swimmers and underwater divers welcomed the escape from the monotonous, backbreaking labor their enslaved brothers and sisters performed in the agricultural fields of the Americas. But slavery, no matter the occupation, was always hard work, and the privileges divers enjoyed were restricted by the fetters of bondage. Being a slave, even an enslaved diver, meant subjugation, harsh treatment, and never-ending toil. Still, enslaved swimmers and divers used skills of African origin to make slavery a little more bearable, and sometimes obtained existences of privileged exploitation.

"Intercourse with the Spaniards, Cuimas, California," reflects George Little's view of America's social and commercial interactions with foreign cultures.
(George Little, *Life on the Ocean* (Boston, 1844), G.W. Blunt White Library, Mystic Seaport)

5

Ambassador in the Forecastle: The Reflections of an American Seaman Abroad

Brian J. Rouleau

George Little concluded his memoirs of a life spent at sea with a curious admonition for his fellow mariners. "An American sailor, when abroad," he argued, "should recollect that he is a representative of his countrymen." As such, he continued, it was "in their power to convey to those among whom he mingles a favorable impression of the general conduct, manners, and morals of his countrymen, or to excite their prejudice against the name of an American." Therefore, "if they have a proper love for their country," they ought to be "desirous of gaining a good name among foreigners, civilized or barbarous." Clearly, when George Little looked across the deck at a vessel's crew, he was less inclined to see a penniless, disenfranchised class of men than he was to reflect upon the great power and responsibility of a group of Americans "whose deportment in foreign lands would establish our national character as good or evil." Throughout the several pages that he dedicated to thoughts such as this, the theme he repeatedly returned to was the concept of national reputation and the real stake that seamen possessed in projecting American values abroad. In George Little's eyes, the exports of the new nation were not merely the fruits of its farms and plantations, but instead included the very men hired to transport those goods. American seamen abroad were not to sell only the country's produce. They were to sell the country itself. To do so was to promote the existence, even the legitimacy, of a place previously solidly British and birthed only recently in a fantastic burst, depending upon one's place in the Atlantic, of either patriotism or treason.[1]

As George Little was fully aware, American character would be put on display by the nation's seamen, who themselves became informal ambassadors representing the noble new experiment in liberty that was then taking shape along the eastern seaboard of North America. In the crucible of intercultural contact that often characterized voyages abroad, mariners from the new United States were placed into foreign contexts that could not help but invite reflections upon national identity. Their descriptions of the people and places they encountered present a particularly special opportunity for scholars to survey ideas held about race and nation by a largely lower-class group of men. Intriguing questions emerge from the observations of seamen abroad. What did the world appear as through American eyes? How did mariners describe the different peoples they came to associate with and how did meetings such as these in turn invite reflection upon their own national character and racial identities? The answers are, as usual, harder to come by than the questions. But to turn to the life of one of the forecastle's ambassadors, George Little, born in Boston in 1791, is to begin to understand the ways in which seamen themselves were often fascinated by the very same issues that currently stimulate historical scholarship. The ruminations of one man might provide an interesting place to start for historians interested in the ways that ideas about America began to disseminate around the globe.[2]

An 1807 voyage into what was then Spanish territory along the Pacific coast of the Americas presented Little with his first shipboard experience, as well as his first encounter with peoples outside the United States. The descriptions he offered of such places as Chile, Peru, Mexico, and California, while varying to some extent, share a common obsession with the contrast between what he termed "Yankee ingenuity" and the "proverbial indolence of the Spaniard." In one instance, a seemingly banal complaint about the absence of fresh vegetables aboard ship quickly escalated into sarcastic condemnation. Why should he expect to find produce of any kind, he fumed, when, after all, "labor and industry are required for their cultivation," neither of which his South American hosts exhibited. Another instance found Little pontificating about the orderliness and cleanliness of the American vessel in comparison to the slovenly streets and unkempt inhabitants of Callao. Indeed, those Spaniards granted the honor of boarding the ship, Little noted, marveled at its meticulousness and "appeared to regard the officers and crew as a superior race of beings." Repetitive distinctions drawn between American vigorousness and Spanish slothfulness, between Yankee industriousness and Castilian lethargy, emphasized the energy and dynamism that characterized a new, youthful republic amidst the decay of Old World imperialism.[3]

Yet Little's scattered observations about the relative inferiority of the wider world reached new heights as he described the myriad romantic encounters between the crew and local women. This Casanova of the forecastle, following what must have been several eventful nights ashore, was quick to gloat that "the great contrast of complexion, beauty, and manliness of many of our crew, to those of the Spaniards, caused a number of young Spanish damsels to lose their hearts." But beyond whatever delusions Little and his fellow seamen entertained concerning their sexual conquests, it is interesting to note the ways that he wove together sexuality, race, and national identity. He laid particular emphasis on not only the whiteness of the ship's crew but also their American-ness as a means to explain their appeal to the opposite sex. In ascribing all action and vigor to himself and his fellow Americans, Little underscored the confidence and assurance with which the new nation ought to approach the world with which it traded. As American men, they were desirable and in demand, which was more than could be said about those foreigners Little cast as effeminate Others.[4]

But even as the miscegenation that Little slyly winked at threatened to demolish the barriers he avidly drew between Americans and their perceived inferiors, he was quick to emphasize that his mission was only to objectify these native women, not to countenance any sort of meaningful connection between the two peoples. So it was that "their passions did not become so violent as to induce them to abandon their ship and country and remain among the Spaniards." There were limits to the transgressions of these seamen abroad, and here, loyalty to country was more heavily prized by Little than the fleeting pleasures of the flesh.[5]

Wrapping up his story about his South American adventures, Little somewhat flippantly stated that "this ended [our] intercourse which to them was highly gratifying, and to us was exceedingly profitable." The gratitude that Little infers the Spanish felt serves as a fitting conclusion to a series of descriptions that quelled whatever doubts that he, his shipmates, or his fellow Americans reading at home may have had about the importance and influence of the new nation abroad. Fears of international illegitimacy could be reduced in part by the aggressive performance of national self-importance abroad, and the narration of such exploits at home. The frequent failure of all things Spanish to measure up to rigorous American standards carried with it the implication that these would become the benchmark of civility. An idea such as this, contradicted by the relative weakness and vulnerability of the United States in its early history, led Little to retreat into the shallowest of over-compensation characterized by his frequent boasts about his hosts "never having seen better," "never having heard better," or "never having tasted better" than what those Yankee lads had to offer. Frequently, the author's observations of foreign cultures were not meant to describe exotic customs so much as to laud American ones.[6]

Prone to be judgmental in most instances, it is instructive to note those occasions where George Little seemed relatively pleased with his surroundings. And the place that shone above all others in his travels were the Hawai'ian Islands. In one sense, this is not hard to imagine, given the climate, abundant fruit, and plethora of sexually available women the archipelago boasted. Yet Little, when he did speak of the place, did not mention any of those qualities but in passing. When he did discuss them, it was only to note that the natives probably did not deserve what they had, seeing as how they were "idolaters of the grossest kind," who worshiped "a variety of hideous images." Where the indigenous peoples of Hawai'i did come in for praise was in their defense of values and ideals that Americans increasingly claimed as their own special gifts to the world. According to Little, he had rarely seen more respect paid to the laws of proper governance, "and the maintenance of equal rights of life, liberty, property, &c than among this people." There was never any doubt in Little's mind that he dealt with his racial and spiritual inferiors, as the stress laid upon their "dusky" complexion and heathenism might suggest. But at the same time, Little clearly identified something admirable in the ways that they seemed to mimic some of those sacred virtues laid out to the world in the Declaration of Independence.[7]

Thus when he, and presumably at least some of his shipmates, looked out into the world, they looked for reflections of themselves. When they found what was good about various foreign societies, what they had really found, what they truly cherished, were those values that an incipient American nationalism had raised highest in their own consciousness. Yet to some extent, the power of such national self-searching and self-recognition led Little to lament "how little our countrymen appreciate the blessings of civil and religious liberty, and the superior advantages which they enjoy over the greater part of nations." In something of a rebuke to the readership of his memoir, Little's comments also suggest the ways that, despite the detachment of some mariners from the physical boundaries of the United States, they insinuated themselves into the construction of an American identity rooted in a sense of superiority over other, less fortunate peoples. In contact with a wider world and its confusing array of humanity, sailors may have grounded themselves by laying claim to a nationalist ideology that granted them a sort of dignity that abusive officers, a hierarchical command structure, and an embarrassing dependence on racial inferiors abroad might otherwise have denied.[8]

The American experience abroad, though, often involved more than the search for an abstract ideology. Events themselves were often made intelligible, for both reader and author, by relating them to incidents then unfolding within the nation. This phenomenon came across most obviously during an episode where, on yet another voyage to South America, Little claimed to have been captured and tortured by native peoples dwelling along the Colombian coast. Ambushed while searching for water, the author found himself bound to a stake, and, as he saw it, being prepared as the main course in a "savage, barbarous feast." In some ways, the account of these proceedings, and his miraculous escape, seems so sensationalized as to cast doubt on their ever having happened. But setting aside the question of veracity, Little expected his travails to resonate with an American audience versed in a colonial and national tradition of both demonizing native peoples as peculiarly blood-thirsty foes and celebrating civilization's triumph via the genre of the captivity narrative.[9]

Words like "squaw," "tomahawk," and "war whoop" pervade his rendering of the entire affair, suggesting the transferable nature of the language used to describe native peoples and the ubiquity of Indian cruelty. Thus, he implies, the sailor's struggle abroad mirrored similar racial conflicts at home between the benevolent hand of white civilization and the fiendish plundering of Indian aggressors. By suggesting the transnational nature of the Indian "problem," George Little seemed to portray it as the particular lot of American men everywhere to pacify such a menace. Moreover, the burden and glory of doing so would not be confined to the western frontiers. Rather, the seaman abroad might also insinuate himself into a developing national narrative of Indian-hating expansionism. Nothing could have been more American than the racial slurs George Little used to describe his captors. Nothing could have been more satisfying for his readers than to envision the gruesome deaths suffered by those "savage miscreants" at the hands of vengeful American seamen doing honor to comrades and country across the sea. If racial violence and ethnic cleansing represent at least one element giving form to an American identity at this time, American seamen were in no way absent from this process. Rather their writings and behavior abroad might provide crucial insight and contrast to the "pioneer" experience traditionally dominant in both popular and scholarly accounts.

Throughout his book, George Little called for all men afloat to "prove themselves American seamen." What did this mean, exactly? The expected characteristics of stoicism, bravery, and camaraderie were all a part of his vision of the American seafarer. But there was more to it than the sort of stock elements of character one might expect. Years before Rudyard Kipling ever lifted a pen, Little described his own vision of the "white man's burden" that befell mariners wherever they may travel. The way he saw it, the business of sailing would always "lead sailors among the less informed, uncivilized portions of mankind." This being the case, American seamen would do well to remember "that the examples taught by white men, who mingle with the natives, may have a mighty influence on their conduct." The reason why this was so self-evident to him: the white man was "known to possess a mind of a higher order than the savage, and is by him looked up to as a superior being." American seamen were at all times to "set before the ignorant savage a copy for his imitation." This was their duty, one that transcended the working orders of the ship and its officers, a duty to the white race and the American nation. In the mind of George Little, these elements of color, nation, and orderliness aboard ship were not separate, but rather intertwined and part of a larger calling that was the responsibility of the nation's maritime population to heed.[10]

It is important to remember that in some ways, George Little was more exceptional than representative of American seamen. He was more articulate and at least somewhat more literate than the average mariner. Furthermore, he committed his experiences to paper at the end of his career, shaping them to meet the expectations of the increasingly popular genre of nineteenth-century sea voyage narratives made famous by Dana's *Two Years Before the Mast*. Yet for all this, the issues raised by Little's account provide a fruitful starting point for a more comprehensive study of the way that mariners described the world they came into contact with and the ways that these descriptions help provide insight into issues such as class, race, gender, and nation. A common assertion, advanced most forcefully by Marcus Rediker and Peter Linebaugh, holds that sailors tended to be more accepting of difference, were almost proto-multiculturalists, in the interests of both class solidarity and the success of a voyage unburdened by conflict. In some instances, this was undoubtedly a reality. But in many other cases, to suggest that seamen were less than burdened by the questions of racial and national allegiances may reflect our wishes more than the world in which they lived.[11]

Another way of stating this would be to say that even if this world of heterogenous, transoceanic citizenship ever existed, George Little was a mariner who wrote within a very different context. He was born at a time when the Age of Revolution had fragmented the wider Atlantic world into a set of composite nations. He was raised within the confines of one of these new nations, an American state that predicated citizenship upon whiteness and implicitly taught the inferiority of racial Others. The re-drawn political and territorial boundaries of the late eighteenth century tended to strengthen the sort of rhetoric of racial and ethnic exclusivity that George Little used to organize the world he encountered. For this reason, scholarly accounts that continue to emphasize a relatively static culture of the sea may miss the ways that the nation-building process may have altered the manners by which mariners related to the world with which they came in contact. And while the truly pathbreaking work of Jeffrey Bolster, Julius Scott, and others, has addressed the question of interracial allegiance and conflict aboard ships at sea, we might profit from a more thorough investigation of the way that sailors perceived the peoples they encountered. Race was as much an issue ashore as it was afloat.[12]

The writings of George Little at least, condescending toward and contemptuous of a wide variety of races and ethnicities, suggest how deeply powerful and truly resonant evolving concepts of difference and prejudice at this period were. That he might so forcefully mock the slavish tyranny and ignorant savagery that nine-tenths of the non-white, un-American world existed in, while himself a sailor subject to perhaps the harshest discipline and most rigid hierarchy his or any country had to offer, ought to suggest the power of these ideas to obscure reality itself. Following the War for Independence, many Americans placed faith in a policy of neutrality that would allow the fledgling nation an opportunity to become both the world's pre-eminent carrier and its primary breadbasket. Even Alexis de Tocqueville, in an infrequently cited aside from his masterful *Democracy in America*, remarked that "America will one day become the foremost maritime power of the globe because they are born to rule the seas as the Romans were to conquer the world."[13] Other observers in antebellum America were no less sanguine about the role of American commerce, and more particularly about the nation's white seamen, in world affairs. Congressman Simeon North, speaking in New Haven in 1847, remarked that "our sailors are the men whose enterprise explores every land, and whose commerce whitens every sea." Senator Augustus Dodge, of Iowa, claimed in 1853 that the "Anglo-Saxon race was gradually taking possession of all the ports and coasts of the world." Most grandiloquent of all was the *Southern Literary Messenger*, which boasted that "every ocean will swarm with American Anglo-Saxon ships; every coast and island will be occupied with their establishments; their language, their science, their literature, and their religion will pervade all the kindreds and tribes of Heathendom."[14] Assertions such as these might be dismissed as the ravings of an isolated societal elite, were it not that the writings of George Little suggest the ways that ordinary seamen were prepared to accept their role as bearers of civilization and white supremacy. Accounts that continue to privilege westward territorial expansion as the crucible of American racial ideology do not tell the complete story of an era when the nation's maritime destiny seemed as manifest as its landward one. Historians have much to learn from those decades when multitudes of American seamen plied the oceans in search of trade, ambassadors in the forecastle representing a country and a race they deemed superior. It is hoped that a careful analysis of their reflections abroad can help reveal, both intrinsically and historically, valuable human voices.

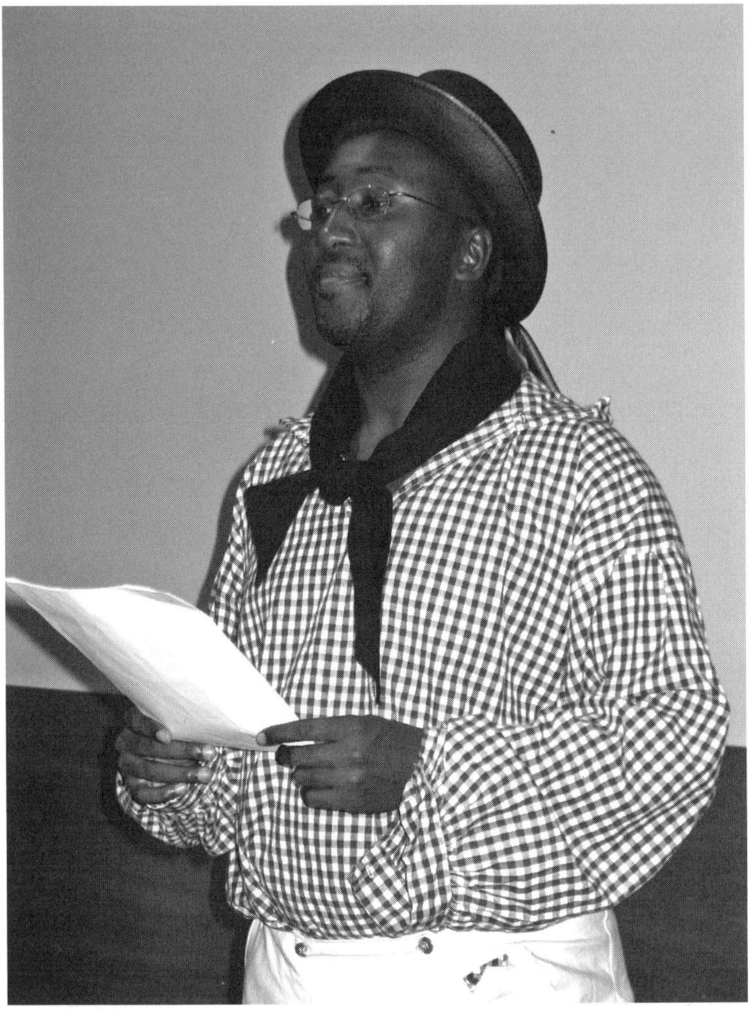

Rashaun Martin portrays USS *Constitution* crewman David Debias in a performance developed at the USS Constitution Museum.
(Courtesy USS Constitution Museum, Charlestown, MA)

6

"I never had any better fighters": Black Sailors in the United Sates Navy during the War of 1812

Lauren McCormack, Anne Grimes Rand, and Kristin L. Gallas

Historical Background

Lauren McCormack

Jesse Williams joined USS *Constitution* in Boston as an ordinary seaman on August 2, 1812. At 40, he was older than most of his shipmates. Besides his advanced age, he fit right in. Born in Pennsylvania, Williams stood 5 feet, 7-1/2 inches tall; he was stoutly built with a round face and black hair. During the battle with HMS *Guerriere*, Williams served as the first sponger for the number-three long gun on the gun deck. Soon after the battle, the navy transferred Williams to the Great Lakes, where he was wounded, captured, and sent to the infamous Dartmoor prison. In 1820, the state of Pennsylvania awarded Williams a silver medal for his service on the Lakes.[1] Jesse Williams's story was similar to that of any one of the thousands of sailors who served in the United States Navy during the War of 1812, with one exception: Jesse Williams was a black man.

The history of black seamen in American naval service goes back at least to the colonial navies of the French and Indian War period.[2] During the Revolutionary War, the Provincial naval forces "used black sailors quite extensively aboard [their] naval vessels, some of whom were native sons and others acquired from captured British ships."[3] Despite this tradition of black naval service, in August 1798, Benjamin Stoddert, the secretary of the new United States Navy, declared that "no Negroes or Mullatoes are to be admitted" into the service.[4] This followed similar regulations issued by the Marine Corps and the U.S. Army in March of that same year.[5] Despite this seemingly official prohibition, it is clear that blacks maintained a consistent presence in the U.S. Navy throughout the Early Republic and especially during the War of 1812.[6]

When war broke out between the United States and Great Britain in June of 1812, the American navy needed to swiftly bring its ships' complements up to full strength. Navy captains, competing with the more lucrative positions offered by privateers and merchant ships, struggled to find skilled seamen willing to sign on.[7] Race often became, therefore, a secondary issue to the need to enlist a crew.

Unfortunately, it is unclear how these naval recruits fared aboard ship. Gerard T. Altoff, a historian who worked for the National Park Service, writes that black seamen faced "varying degrees of racism and were denied unconstrained liberty and equality because of their color."[8] However, Altoff's argument lacks verification by specific, firsthand examples. W. Jeffrey Bolster, the preeminent scholar of the black experience in the merchant service, found evidence that black sailors on board *merchant* ships were integrated with their white counterparts.[9] Naval surgeon Usher Parsons remembered that, immediately after the war in 1816, white and black seaman messed together on USS *Java*. Parsons also recalled that, at that time, one in six or eight sailors was a black man. The same was true, he wrote, on USS *Guerriere* in 1819, where "the proportion of blacks was about the same in her crew [and] there seemed to be an entire absence of prejudice against the blacks as messmates among the crew."[10] He continued, "What I have said applies to the crews of other ships that sailed in [U.S. Navy] squadrons."[11] It should be noted, that Parsons wrote these descriptions in 1862, in the midst of the Civil War. It is possible, therefore, that the nation's current climate influenced his memory of events almost 50 years in the past.[12] All in all, the only certainty is that black naval sailors were paid the same wage as the white sailors.

Of course, hierarchy ruled on naval vessels, and race relations may have been determined to some extent for the sailors by their commanding officer. To the author's knowledge, only one example of forced segregation is documented from the War of 1812, though other, similar examples may also have existed. In the "Internal Rules and Regulations" of USS *Constellation*, written about 1813, both petty officers and "colored" men are ordered to mess "by themselves."[13] Here is an example of a white officer, the *Constellation*'s commander, establishing a policy of separation.

How this segregation affected race relations aboard ship is unknown.[14] However, it is important to note, that this separation only applied to messes, implying that white and black sailors interacted during their other activities aboard ship. Indeed, it would be difficult, if not impossible, for one group to be isolated from another on board a heavily manned frigate.

Still, it is difficult to argue that white sailors, inculcated with racial prejudice on land, could entirely cast off such feelings on board ship. In fact, one key example seems to prove that prejudice, even if subdued while aboard ship, lingered in the minds of white sailors. By 1814, bleak Dartmoor Prison in England was home to approximately 6,000 American prisoners of war. Of these, about 1,000 were black men from privateers and naval vessels, as well as sailors who were serving in the British Royal Navy when war broke out and refused to fight against the United States. Once incarcerated, white prisoners of war—the same ones who supposedly served without complaint beside their fellow black sailors—requested that their black counterparts be housed separately. British officials agreed to the request.[15] As Robin F. A. Fabel writes, "there is no doubt that segregation sprang from the racism of white prisoners."[16] If white sailors agreed, perhaps grudgingly, to work, live, and eat alongside their black colleagues at sea, once freed from the cramped, controlled quarters of the ship, they immediately reverted back to the discriminatory lifestyle they were accustomed to onshore. In fact, the white sailors' request to physically segregate the black prisoners in a separate barracks presents an even stricter separation than most poor, white sailors would have known in America's coastal cities. In most Northern seaports during this period, poor, laboring blacks lived alongside whites of the same class and situation. Why, therefore, did white prisoners of war at Dartmoor demand absolute separation? Perhaps white sailors, now freed from the oversight of their ship's officers, gave in to their personal prejudices; or, possibly, the white prisoners desired to degrade the black sailors in order to claim some measure of superiority even in the midst of their captivity. Whatever the reason, black prisoners in Dartmoor were often the victims of white taunts and violence.[17] The black experience there poses interesting problems for the oft-cited belief that blacks aboard ship were relatively safe from white prejudice.

However, along with these examples of racial animosity at Dartmoor, there are other recorded instances of camaraderie, or at the very least acceptance. White and black prisoners boxed with each other. Occasionally, they also participated in interracial dancing. Though each race produced its own theatrical events, white and black inmates attended each other's productions.[18] As one white prisoner, Benjamin Waterhouse, recorded, "however extraordinary it may appear," whites took fencing, boxing, music, and dancing lesson from black inmates, while other whites chose to live with the black prisoners to avoid white harassment.[19] It is unclear how to reconcile these seemingly conflicting aspects of prison life, segregation on the one hand, and integration on the other. Perhaps more than anything, these incongruities point to the ambiguous and often enigmatic nature of race relations during the Early Republic on land and at sea.

Unfortunately, but not surprisingly, all of the firsthand accounts of black service on board U.S. Navy vessels during the War of 1812 are from a white perspective. Almost all of these accounts speak favorably of black sailors. After his victory over HMS *Guerriere* in August 1812, USS *Constitution*'s Captain Isaac Hull wrote, using the discriminatory language of the day, "I never had any better fighters than those niggers, they stripped to the waist and fought like devils . . . seeming to be utterly insensible to danger and to be possessed with the determination to outfight the white sailors."[20] When Master Commandant Oliver Hazard Perry wrote to Commodore Isaac Chauncey to complain that his crew was "a motley set, blacks, Soldiers, boys,"[21] Chauncey angrily replied, "I have yet to learn that the Colour of the skin, or cut and trimmings of the coat, can effect a man's qualifications or usefulness. I have nearly 50 blacks on board of this Ship, and many of them are amongst my best men."[22] After the Battle of Lake Erie, Perry changed his tune, praising his black sailors to Chauncey, who remembered, "'Perry speaks highly of the bravery and good conduct of the Negroes, who formed a considerable part of his crew.'"[23]

Though the U.S. Navy's 1798 restriction against black sailors does not appear to have been strictly enforced, the navy officially reversed its policy on March 3, 1813, with an act authorizing: "That from and after the termination of the war in which the United States are now engaged with Great Britain it shall not be lawful to employ on board any of the public or private vessels of the United States any person or persons except citizens of the United States or persons of color, natives of the U. States."[24] As written, this policy did not take affect until after the War of 1812 ended. However, the intent behind it indicated a relaxation of official policy. In fact, many historians claim that all of the official ships involved in the War of 1812 contained at least some black sailors.[25]

Since the U.S. Navy did not designate race on muster rolls or other official documents, the average number of black seamen who served aboard naval vessels is debatable. Naval historian Christopher McKee argues that blacks composed an average of 9.7 percent of ships' crews.[26] USS *Independence*, while fitting out in Boston Harbor in 1814, had 34 black crewmembers out of its total complement of about 215 (15.8 percent).[27] In an account of the crew of USS *Hornet* attending a theatrical event in New York City held in their honor, a journalist wrote that the crew "marched together into the pit, and nearly one half of them were Negroes."[28] Ned Myers, who told his personal story to James Fenimore Cooper, recalled that at least eight of USS *Scourge*'s 32 crewmembers—or 25 percent—were black.[29]

Perhaps the most reliable sources for determining the percentages of black sailors aboard naval vessels are the prisoner-of-war records from various prisons and prison ships collected by historians Ira Dye and Christopher McKee. These records provide richly detailed information about naval and merchant sailors during the early nineteenth century.

Of the 666 naval prisoners in Ira Dye's database, 7.36 percent were recorded as black or "mulatto."[30] Christopher McKee, using a slightly smaller sample of 546 naval prisoners, found 51—or 9.34 percent—black and "mulatto" prisoners.[31] Together, these percentages average out to just over 8 percent. Based on these calculations and the ones mentioned earlier, it is probably safe to assume that anywhere from 7 to 15 percent was the *average* percentage of blacks on any given naval vessel.[32]

For USS *Constitution*, which carried approximately 450 men, that 7-15 percent would mean that between 32 and 68 of her sailors were black or mulatto. Unfortunately, discovering just who these men were is extremely difficult. In the course of our research into the lives of *all* of *Constitution*'s War of 1812 crewmembers (approximately 1,300 men), we have found substantial demographic and personal information on more than 450 sailors. Unfortunately, among those 450-plus, we have definitively identified only three black sailors. One is Jesse Williams, whose history was recounted at the beginning of this paper. We have a short pension application for a sailor named James Bennett, who was born in Delaware and killed on the Great Lakes in 1814. The third sailor, David

Debias, was an 8-year-old from Boston who served in the rank of Boy during USS *Constitution*'s last cruise of the war. However, the treasure trove of information from the prisoner-of-war records allows us to draw a composite picture of the "average" black naval sailor during the War of 1812 and compare that composite to the "average" non-black naval sailor.

The black sailors who served in the United States Navy during the War of 1812 were predominately able and ordinary seaman. Able seamen were the most experienced enlisted men and were more adept at sail-handling and the other duties on the ship. Ordinary seamen had some experience aboard ship but were not fully skilled. Unfortunately, the prisoner-of-war records do not differentiate between the two. Approximately 85 percent of the black and "mulatto" naval prisoners were seaman, whereas only 7 percent were designated as servants and slaves and only 7 percent were labeled boys (an indicator of lack of skill rather than age; see Table 1). Most of these black sailors, then, had at least some seafaring experience, and they definitely were not kept in the lowliest shipboard positions because of their race.

Table 2 • **Rank of Black and "Mulatto" Prisoners of War**

Ira Dye's Sample

RANK	NUMBER	PERCENTAGE
Master at Arms	1	2.04
Servants/Slave	3	6.12
Boys	2	4.08
Seamen*	43	87.76
TOTAL	49	

Christopher McKee's Sample

RANK	NUMBER	PERCENTAGE
Servants/Stewards	4	7.84
Boys	5	9.80
Seamen*	42	82.35
TOTAL	51	

* There is no differentiation between Able and Ordinary Seamen in the records.

Table 2 • **Birthplace as Given by Black and "Mulatto" Prisoners of War**

Ira Dye's Sample

PLACE	NUMBER	PERCENTAGE
Pennsylvania	10	20
New York	8	16
Massachusetts	6	12
Virginia	5	10
Louisiana	5	10
Rhode Island	3	6
Delaware	3	6
Maryland	3	6
South Carolina	2	4
New Hampshire	1	2
Holland	1	2
Peru	1	2
Dominica	1	2
Curacao	1	2
TOTAL	49	

Christopher McKee's Sample

PLACE	NUMBER	PERCENTAGE
New York	15	29.4
Pennsylvania	12	23.5
Massachusetts	6	11.8
Maryland	5	9.8
Delaware	3	5.9
Louisiana	3	5.9
Rhode Island	2	3.9
Virginia	2	3.9
South Carolina	1	2.0
Peru	1	2.0
Dominica	1	2.0
TOTAL	51	

Where did these men come from? When taken prisoner, British authorities required the men to give their birth state and city. Though these cannot be entirely trusted, three states made up the majority of entries for black sailors in both McKee and Dye's data: New York, Pennsylvania, and Massachusetts (Table 2).[33] Men from Maryland, Louisiana, Virginia, and Delaware were also a significant, yet smaller, presence. With few exceptions, most notably for Pennsylvania, the percentages are similar to those for non-black or "mulatto" prisoners of war. It must be recalled that during this period, Philadelphia had a very large and important black community, many of whose members were involved in seafaring. The same is true for Massachusetts and New York, both of which were home to maritime-oriented cultures and economies. But in the case of Pennsylvania, the numerical influence of black sailors is clearly shown. Also, more Southern states are represented in the listing of white sailors' birth states (Table 3). It is not surprising that there is a dearth of black sailors from states where plantation slavery and stringent race laws were the norm. It is quite possible that black sailors would never admit to being from the Southern states for fear of being labeled runaways.

Table 3 • **Birth States as Given by Non-Black and Non-"Mulatto" Prisoners of War**

Christopher McKee's Sample

PLACE	NUMBER	PERCENTAGE
Massachusetts	172	33.27
New York	93	17.99
Pennsylvania	40	7.74
Foreigners	39	7.54
Maryland	32	6.19
Virginia	31	6.00
Connecticut	21	4.06
New Jersey	18	3.48
Rhode Island	16	3.09
New Hampshire	14	2.71
Delaware	10	1.93
Louisiana	9	1.74
North Carolina	4	0.77
Vermont	2	0.39
South Carolina	2	0.39
Kentucky	1	0.19
TOTAL	517	

The average age of black and "mulatto" sailors is almost the same as that of white naval sailors: 24.6 years (black/mulatto) vs. 26.5 years (white). This statistic suggests that the factors encouraging young white men to enlist in their mid-twenties may also have influenced their black compatriots. The proximity in age also dispels the possibility that a racist shipboard culture kept black sailors in the lower enlisted positions longer than their white compatriots. During the War of 1812 at least, young black sailors fought alongside their white contemporaries.

Though the prisoner-of-war records allow for a superficial analysis of black sailors, they do not illuminate the black naval experience. Other sources do little to help. The fact that we have no direct evidence of racial prejudice aboard naval vessels is not proof of its absence. It can only be assumed that the racial attitudes of his officers and shipmates determined a black sailor's experiences. It is hopeful to think that, like Perry, other officers and crewmembers changed their pre-existing racist attitudes after witnessing the bravery, hard work, and discipline black sailors exhibited throughout the war. Perhaps the most telling proof of some measure of racial equality on board naval vessels during the War of 1812 is the fact that black naval sailors routinely held the rank of seaman, either ordinary or able. That put them on par, at least on paper, with the majority of their white shipmates. However, the reality of these black sailors' lives largely remains a mystery.

Bringing the Research to Life

Anne Grimes Rand,
Kristin L. Gallas

How best to share the research on USS *Constitution*'s 1812 crew with a broad, general audience? This is the challenge faced by the USS Constitution Museum. Families with children dutifully march along the Freedom Trail-a red stripe on the sidewalk linking Boston's historic sites. The USS Constitution Museum, located at the end of the Trail, welcomes a large intergenerational audience of intrepid travelers who have come to Boston to "do history." Most families arrive exhausted from a busy day walking in the sun and learning about Boston's role in the American Revolution. With no charge for admission, the museum welcomes 250,000-300,000 visitors each year. The not-for-profit museum serves as the memory and educational voice for the frigate that floats across the pier, still an active-duty commissioned warship. U.S. Navy sailors lead visitors on tours of USS *Constitution*, the undefeated wooden warship that earned the nickname "Old Ironsides" during the War of 1812. Those who continue across the pier to the USS Constitution Museum discover an innovative museum providing a hands-on, minds-on environment where visitors seeking an enjoyable, educational experience can have fun and learn as they explore history together.

Research on USS *Constitution*'s 1812 crew is coming to life in an exhibit that invites visitors to sample the daily life of an enlisted sailor in the U.S. Navy.[34] As visitors scrub the deck with a holystone or snooze in a hammock, they learn the stories of sailors who served in 1812 and see life-size photos of both black and white men in period clothing. Exhibit text is written in a conversational, first-person voice and presented by the life-size historic figures that people the exhibit. This thematic story, developed with an advisory panel of scholars supported by the National Endowment for the Humanities, explores topics such as recruiting the crew and joining a seafaring community. Visitors learn how individuals train together to forge a fighting team and then face the ultimate test in battle. Visitors gain an appreciation of both the individual and collective experience of sailors on board USS *Constitution*, recognizing how different the daily lives of 1812 sailors are from the experience of people today.

As visitors enter the exhibit, they hear a conversation among three sailors discussing why they have come to join USS *Constitution*'s crew. There are many reasons, but the primary drive is the need for a job and to earn money. Text in this area points out that seafaring offers free black men the opportunity to earn a living wage through a respectable career with pay equal to that of whites. Many visitors arrive with an assumption that black sailors in this period must be slaves and are surprised to learn of the substantive participation of free blacks in the early navy. A graphic panel based on Ira Dye's research on 6,537 prisoners at Dartmoor Prison brings his research to life in a physical form. The panel asks visitors, "How do you compare to the Average Sailor in 1812?"

- How tall are you?
- How old are you?
- What color are your eyes?
- What color is your hair?
- Are you African American?
- Do you have any tattoos?

The panel stands 5 feet, 6-1/2 inches tall (the average height of sailors) and invites visitors to compare themselves to sailors in 1812. Visitor surveys reveal that 47 out of 80 family groups stopped to read this panel, making it the panel most frequently read in this area of the exhibit. When asked, "What do you recall about the men who signed on as sailors?" 22 percent commented on age, that sailors could be younger than today's sailors, and 19 percent commented about black sailors.

After joining the crew, visitors can try their hand at some of the jobs of sailors in 1812. A daily routine chart lets visitors see the different jobs of crewmembers and how the schedule is staggered to provide 24-hour coverage for a ship at sea. The experience of Jesse Williams is suggested with his likeness on the daily routine chart, showing the responsibilities of an ordinary seaman. Visitors see him again in the "below deck" portion of the exhibit where they can sit on the deck and have lunch with Jesse Williams and his messmates. Visitors can also try furling a sail or resting in a hammock, just as Jesse Williams would have done.

Of the visitors surveyed as they left the exhibit, 58 percent recalled that African Americans served on board USS *Constitution*. When asked, "What does your family recall about African American opportunities?" a remarkable 33 percent of visitors quoted the percentage of free black sailors that they had read in the exhibit introduction. The exhibit employs a broad range of hands-on techniques that encourage families to participate and discuss their experience. This results in families spending three times longer in this exhibit than in a more traditional museum gallery. As visitors engage with exhibits and spend more time in the gallery, they are also absorbing many of the key messages presented. Visitors to the USS Constitution Museum are learning about the important service of free black men at sea through the exhibits and through a museum theater program.

The theater program enables the museum to breathe life into the stories of the sailors and provides visitors with an opportunity to experience a different method of interpretation. Museum staff decided to bring to life the story of David Debias, an 8-year-old free black from Boston. David enlisted on USS *Constitution* in 1814 and took part in her victory over HMS *Cyane* and HMS *Levant*. In 1838, when David was 32 years old, he was captured as a suspected runaway slave in Mississippi. The theater production was a one-man show, with David recounting his story to Judge Thomas Falconer. In 1838 the judge composed a letter for David to the Navy Department asking for documents that declared him free. The goals for the production were to share the experiences of a free black sailor on USS *Constitution* through "his own words"; to connect visitors with the live person of David instead of just a photograph/text; and to utilize primary sources as much as possible then fill in the context with historical research.

Over 1,000 visitors saw a performance of "A Sailor's Life for Me: The Story of David Debias" during its five-week run. Rashaun Martin, a museum staff member and Program Director for History at Boston Latin School, portrayed David, bringing to the role his own experiences as a black man and historian. He breathed life into a man who so bravely recounted his experiences on USS *Constitution* in hope of redeeming his life from bondage. Martin found the experience both challenging and rewarding. Following the performance, Martin stepped out of character, answering questions and explaining to the audience how we know about the life of David Debias and that we do not know if he was ever released from prison.

Formative evaluation with our visitors demonstrated that they could recall several pieces of information about David's life after seeing the performance. Interviews revealed that the performance personalized David's story; that the story of an individual helps visitors learn more about the ship; that the actor "opened up history to us that we didn't know"; that the character was easy to relate to; and that the play was clear and straightforward.

Throughout the development and implementation of the program, staff learned some valuable lessons on bringing life to people of the past. First, it is possible to use just one primary source—in this case a letter written by a third party-and create a dramatic one-man show. Second, there is a gray area where facts end and one must use historical context to fill in the story. Third, it is reasonable to make up dialogue for a theatrical presentation, but be sure to cite it and base it in historical research. And finally, stepping out of character at the conclusion is a good technique for telling visitors what we do and do not know from primary sources.

Bringing David's story to life was a major accomplishment for the USS Constitution Museum. Buoyed by this experience, the museum is creating new theatrical presentations that bring to life other USS *Constitution* crewmembers from the War of 1812. Primary research reveals many fascinating stories, and the USS Constitution Museum seeks to share these stories and engage visitors in learning about the past in compelling new ways.

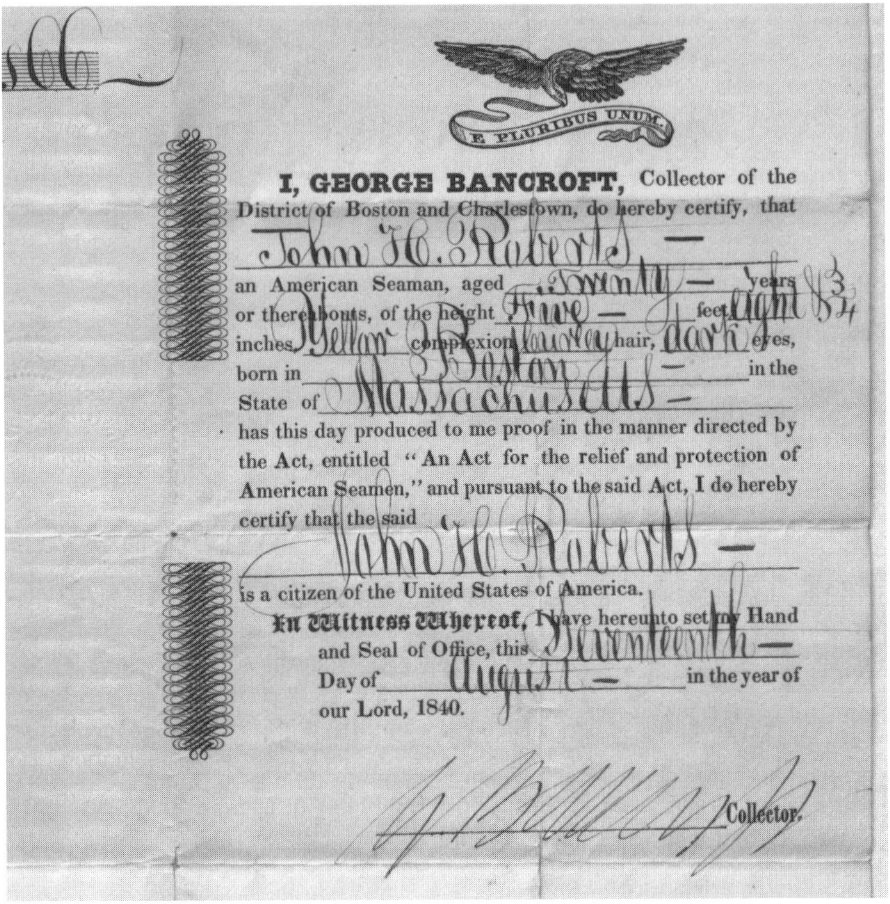

E PLURIBUS UNUM.

I, GEORGE BANCROFT, Collector of the District of Boston and Charlestown, do hereby certify, that John H. Roberts — an American Seaman, aged Twenty — years or thereabouts, of the height Five — feet eight 3/4 inches, Yellow complexion, Curly hair, dark eyes, born in Boston — in the State of Massachusetts — has this day produced to me proof in the manner directed by the Act, entitled "An Act for the relief and protection of American Seamen," and pursuant to the said Act, I do hereby certify that the said John H. Roberts — is a citizen of the United States of America.

In Witness Whereof, I have hereunto set my Hand and Seal of Office, this Seventeenth — Day of August — in the year of our Lord, 1840.

[illegible signature] Collector.

Bearing the federal eagle, this seaman's protection certificate was issued to black seaman John H. Roberts in 1840.

(Coll. 238, box 2, folder 11, G.W. Blunt White Library, Mystic Seaport)

7

Citizens, Sailors, and Slaves

Bryan Sinche

In March 1830, white sailor Edward Smith shipped as a steward aboard the brig *Columbo* and sailed a passage from Boston to Charleston, South Carolina. According to Smith, the day before he left, "a colored man of decent appearance & very genteely [sic] dressed called on board the vessel and asked [Smith] if he would do a favor for him. . . . The man then said that he wished [Smith] to bring a package of pamphlets to Charleston for him and to give them to any negroes he had a mind to, or that he met, that he must do it privately and not let any white person know anything about it."[1] Upon arriving in Charleston, Smith was arrested, tried, fined $1,000, and sentenced to one year in prison for distributing three copies of David Walker's incendiary *Appeal to the Coloured Citizens of the World*. David Walker, who owned a used clothing store in Boston, solicited seamen to distribute his *Appeal* and may have even sewn copies into clothing he sold to sailors heading south.[2] Walker needed to enlist the help of white sailors because free black seamen—thought to be spreading what Jeffrey Bolster names "the contagion of liberty"—were usually put in prison (or, at the very least, required to remain on board ship) in Charleston and other Southern ports.[3] Though Smith claimed he never would have handed out the pamphlet had he known its contents, his willingness to distribute it without letting "any white person know anything about it" betrays his complicity. Whatever Edward Smith's personal investment in the abolition movement, he was willing to trust the black man in Boston who gave him the pamphlets and was willing to risk his own safety by distributing them to blacks in Charleston. Smith's role in circulating Walker's *Appeal* suggests that some white seamen were both friends with their black peers and advocates for enslaved laborers.[4]

In the years following Smith's arrest, black and white writers contemplated the revolutionary possibilities inherent in the maritime world—

a world in which long-standing social, economic, and political hierarchies could be destabilized—and imagined new identities for both sailors and slaves. Though the sea was not an idyllic space for these men, it did serve as a proving ground wherein whites and blacks could show they were fit to carry the title of American citizen. While Herman Melville and Richard Henry Dana Jr. focused on the class divisions and unfair labor practices that restricted the full citizenship of white sailors, Frederick Douglass used the sea (and the conventions of the sea narrative) to make a claim for citizenship for himself and for the fictionalized slave rebel Madison Washington. Douglass's maritime world is one in which landed definitions and identities no longer hold; it is a space in which American laws, symbols, and freedoms are contingent rather than absolute. Douglass's savvy heroes use the fluidity and freedom of the sea in order to assert their own worthiness, and, at the same time, eviscerate the myth of American essentialism.[5]

Parallels between Frederick Douglass—a chattel slave—and white sailors are not so far-fetched as they might seem today, for in narratives and news reports of the antebellum period, white sailors—who were subject to the caprices of all-powerful captains able to flog them for any offense—were often described as "white slaves." The slippage from white sailor to black slave is most famously evident in Richard Henry Dana Jr.'s *Two Years Before the Mast* when Captain Thompson of the *Pilgrim* whips a white sailor and announces to the crew, "You've got a driver over you! Yes, a *slave driver—a nigger driver*! I'll see who'll tell me he isn't a nigger slave!"[6] Thompson's enraged denigration of the men performs the same work as his whip by rendering the sailors "slaves" aboard ship and thereby ensuring his control and the crew's unquestioning servitude. Sailors had little recourse when faced with such treatment, as Dana explains, "If a sailor resist his commander, he resists the law, and piracy or submission are his only alternatives. Bad as it was, it must be borne. It is what a sailor ships for."[7]

In the year before Dana's book was published, naval reformer William McNally bemoaned the unmitigated power of the captain to remake white sailors into cowering slaves, arguing that abuse was not what a "sailor ships for." McNally sailed in the U.S. Navy in the 1820s and 1830s before being court-martialed and dismissed, and his *Evils and Abuses in the Naval and Merchant Service* ranges widely over the abuses of power he located within maritime hierarchies. Insistently linking sailors and slaves, McNally wrote to arouse Northern activists: "Those who exclaim loudest against slavery, had better turn their attention to objects of suffering and benevolence at home, before they look for them abroad, hundreds of whom will stand as much in need of their assistance, and emancipation from the yoke of tyranny of oppression, as the swarthy sons and daughters of Africa." Indeed, in McNally's comparison, sailors were not "as much in need" but more in need of assistance, as "masters of merchant vessels are vested with greater authority than the magistrates or judges, and with the same power as the negro driver, or slaveholder, who has so often been stigmatized with the epithets of tyrants and brutes, by a society whose object is declared to be equal rights and privileges to all."[8] For McNally, the stakes were clear: Sailors needed to be "emancipated" from a system that allowed incursions against their rights as free-born citizens. Arguing that sailors elected to serve only out of ignorance of conditions prevailing aboard ship, McNally claimed that "seamen know that they are born free, and freemen will never submit to the lash of slavery."[9]

The ideas of natural rights invoked by McNally were especially meaningful to nineteenth-century sailors, perhaps because seamen were so often removed from the institutions and protections that guaranteed rights to landed citizens. Within the Declaration of Independence, Thomas Jefferson defines those rights as "life, liberty, and the pursuit of happiness," and Jefferson's conception of natural rights derives from Locke's *Second Treatise on Government*. According to Locke, man in nature is in "a state of perfect freedom to order [his] actions and dispose of [his] possessions and persons as [he sees] fit," though natural law demands that "no one ought to harm another in his life, health, liberty, or possessions."[10] Years after Locke and the Declaration, Francis Asbury Roe argued that the ordering of the naval world mimicked the meritorious ordering of society ensured by the Declaration:

> The American Declaration—the most sublime declaration that ever sounded through the ages—permits men the noble privilege to struggle with their destiny, and attain superiority wheresoever and howsoever they can, without human hindrance, and unfettered by arbitrary law. The right to competition among men, gives the right to its rewards, and the enjoyment of that superiority which claims honor and obeisance from inferiority, wheresoever it may assert its right.

> Naval rank and superiority are based on these broad principles, the same as others. . . . Naval rank is the reward of merit as much as it is in civil or military life, and he who fails to recognize a superior, fails in his conception of human virtue.[11]

Superiority, as Roe conceives it, inheres in superior rank because the Declaration guarantees freedom of movement and competition to any man. Therefore, if a man fails to recognize superiority in an officer, it is because the man himself lacks something; whether the sailor submits to his superior or admits his own inferiority—submission is a given. The sea and its ships, according to Roe, are a proving ground for natural abilities and merit, and those who command at sea are worthy of admiration and respect both on ship and on land.

These ideas did not accord with those of reformers like McNally, who believed that many captains were not, in fact, meritorious. McNally despised the laws that protected the captain's right to abuse and demean common sailors with neither cause nor evidence. Like other antebellum naval reformers, McNally claimed that the situation Roe described in 1865 was the exact opposite of the actual situation aboard American vessels, and that American freemen had both their natural rights (to bodily integrity) and their political rights (to trial by a jury of peers) threatened aboard ship. The abrogation of those political rights was the essence of "white slavery" since seagoing American citizens did not enjoy the same protections as their fellows on land. Arguments like those advanced by McNally helped to turn the tide against corporal punishment on ships, and Congress outlawed flogging on all national vessels in 1850.

In the same year, Congress passed the Fugitive Slave Law, which extended slavery's reach into the formerly free Northern states. At the very moment when sailors were finally enjoying the full protection of citizens, slaves were being further limited in their quest for freedom. It should come as no surprise, then, that abolitionists and advocates of racial equality argued that chattel slavery (as opposed to the "white slavery" of naval reformers) was rooted in the denial of natural rights as enumerated in the Declaration of Independence. For them, slavery proved that the merit-based society promised by the Declaration did not hold sway on land. Though slavery (and the Fugitive Slave Law) may have been legal under the

Constitution, it was inimical to the American ideals first codified in 1776.

The division between Constitution and Declaration, between political and natural rights, points toward the significant differences between "white slaves" and chattel slaves. In light of those differences, it is useful to examine how authors imagined life at sea for whites versus blacks. Whereas in classic texts like Melville's *White-Jacket* and Dana's *Two Years Before the Mast*, the white seamen's revolt is stymied though the use of physical and rhetorical violence that turns sailors into slaves, in the autobiographical and fictional works of Frederick Douglass, black slaves use the sailor identity to turn themselves into men.[12] Whether it is Douglass's deception that enabled his escape, or the slave revolt at sea dramatized in "The Heroic Slave," slaves become sailors in order to demand natural rights and make a claim for political citizenship. The sea narrative was a promising genre for an abolitionist writer like Frederick Douglass because while "sailor" may have been something less than "citizen" for whites, it could mean something far more than "slave" for blacks. The fluid and ungoverned space of the sea provides freedom of movement and communication for black men to plan and execute a rebellion that proved their abilities. Douglass certainly makes this point within his novella, but he also questions whether black slaves *cum* sailors could compete with others at sea and thereby gain the "the right to [competition's] rewards," that is, whether black seamen could become American freemen.

II

From the time Frederick Douglass first began working in a Baltimore shipyard in the 1820s, he understood the emancipatory possibilities of the maritime world. Indeed, describing his years in slavery within the pages of his 1845 *Narrative*, Douglass imagines himself as a sailor who can claim bodily freedom: "O that I were free! O, that I were on one of your gallant decks, and under your protecting wing."[13] He would live that fantasy —in a way—when he escaped from slavery riding on a train while dressed as a sailor in 1838. Years later, when he penned "The Heroic Slave," however, the bodily freedom Douglass had imagined as a young man standing alongside the Chesapeake Bay was not enough, and so Douglass created a maritime hero who could claim the rights of a free-born American sailor. The protagonist of "The Heroic Slave" is based on the real-life Madison Washington, a Virginia slave who escaped to Canada and returned to America to rescue his wife. In Douglass's version of the story, Washington's second escape ends in tragedy as his wife is slain and he is captured. The Virginia slaveholders sell Washington and the re-enslaved hero is loaded aboard the slave ship *Creole*, bound from Richmond to New Orleans. During the voyage south, Washington leads his fellow slaves in a rebellion against the white crew of the *Creole,* and he guides the ship to Nassau where he and his fellow slaves leave the ship and parade triumphantly through the streets of the city. The real-life Washington was also successful in his rebellion, though he gained his freedom following years of litigation in American courts.

Using a true story as the foundation for his novella, Douglass invokes the logic later employed by Francis Asbury Roe and celebrates the natural seamanship (and natural abilities) of rebellious slaves. Imagining the men as ideal seamen, Douglass points out the prevailing dichotomies between Declaration and Constitution, between natural and legal rights, and between black and white. In so doing, Douglass shows that while America could protect its white seamen from the lash of slavery, it was not so ready to acknowledge the black slaves who demonstrated courage and manliness on the high seas. In particular, Douglass reveals the persistent tension between sea freedom and black slavery through his literary imaginings of the American eagle as a symbol of sailor liberty, American citizenship, and legally authorized violence in the antebellum United States.

The American eagle was a popular symbol for American sailors and scrimshanders during the age of sail. It appeared on countless whale-tooth engravings of the period, often spreading its protective wings above Jack Tar himself. Sailors, perhaps anxious to reaffirm their landed citizenship in the fluid spaces of the maritime world, frequently tattooed the American eagle on their arms and shoulders.[14] This symbol recalls the "swift-winged angels" that Douglass describes in his *Narrative*, wherein ships and sailors are protected from the yoke of enslavement. However, when Frederick Douglass first invokes the American eagle in "The Heroic Slave" he does so with quite different intent. Upon escaping to Canada, the protagonist Madison Washington writes to Mr. Listwell, a white man who aided him in his escape from slavery: "'Madison is out of the woods at last; I nestle in the mane of the British lion, protected by the mighty paw from the talons and beak of the American eagle. I AM FREE, and breathe an atmosphere too pure for *slaves*, slave-hunters, or slave-holders.'"[15] Washington's eagle is voracious and malevolent, an agent of the government that legalizes slavery and aids the slave-hunters in their attempts to bring slaves back to the South. Far from a symbol of liberty, the American eagle protects not the weak, but rather those who would see personal liberty violated in favor of inhumane property rights—it defends American laws without regard for the natural rights of human beings.

In his *Life and Times*, first published in 1881, Douglass revealed the means of his escape from slavery (something he concealed in his 1845 and 1855 narratives in order to protect slaves contemplating escape). In so doing, he revives the symbol of the American eagle in a very different context. Intending to use a friend's seaman's protection certificate in order to leave the South unimpeded, Douglass was sanguine concerning his chances for success because, "The instrument [the certificate] had at its head the American eagle, which at once gave it the appearance of an authorized document."[16] His confidence was increased by the fact that "One element in my favor was the kind feeling which prevailed in Baltimore and other seaports at the time, towards 'those who go down to the sea in ships.' 'Free trade and sailors' rights' expressed the sentiment of the country just then. In my clothing I was rigged out in sailor style." Douglass's preparation served him well, as did his belief in the signifying power of both sailor garb and the American eagle, for when Douglass is asked for his free papers, he responded confidently:

> "I never carry my free papers to sea with me." "But you have something to show that you are a free man, have you not?" "Yes, sir," I answered; "I have a paper with the American eagle on it, that will carry me round the world." With this I drew from my deep sailor's pocket my seaman's protection, as before described. The merest glance at the paper satisfied him, and he took my fare and went about his business.[17]

Douglass makes it to the North safely, and there his life as a laborer, speaker, writer, and representative African-American begins. Describing his escape, Douglass affirms the potency of the American eagle as a symbol of liberty, especially for seamen. The paper he shows does not confirm that he is a "free man," that is, a citizen. Instead, it confirms that he is a sailor—and, as William McNally assumes when he writes that "free born men will never submit to the lash of slavery," the train conductor assumes that the sailor before him is, in fact, free. Far from the violent symbol of proslavery aggression imagined by Madison Washington, Frederick Douglass's American eagle—like the protecting wing of the ships on the Chesapeake Bay—shields him from the proslavery forces that would see him captured and returned south.

Though the American eagles Douglass describes serve different ends, there is little difference between them: Both serve to define citizenship rigidly and definitively. Any being outside the citizenry (such as a slave) is in great danger, while the eagle zealously defends any being who can lay claim to its protection. Though the seaman's protection certificate was intended to protect American sailors at sea from impressment on to other ships, the document signifies on land as well, though not as it was intended. Rather than prove his citizenship in order to protect him from foreign governments, the certificate implies his citizenship and thereby protects him from his own government. During his escape, Douglass controls the American eagle; he appropriates and manipulates the icon to keep the marauding, violent eagle at bay.

The uncertain relationship between black slaves and the American eagle persists through the final section of "The Heroic Slave." Unable to produce an authorizing document along the lines of Douglass's sailor protection certificate, the slave rebels do not obtain the political citizenship supposedly concomitant with an expression of American "principles" and so find protection under the imperial paw of the British lion when they disembark in Nassau. Nonetheless, Washington and the other rebels have proved themselves knowledgeable, strong, fair, and dispassionate—they are ideal republican subjects. Tom Grant, the white first mate of the *Creole*, says as much of Washington as the he describes the revolt to sailors in a Richmond coffee house:

> [Washington] was not indifferent to the dreadful hurricane; yet he met it with the equanimity of an old sailor. He was silent but not agitated. The first words he uttered after the storm had slightly subsided, were characteristic of the man.

> "Mr. Mate, you cannot write the bloody laws of slavery on those restless billows. The ocean, if not the land, is free." I confess, gentlemen, I felt myself in the presence of a superior man; one who, had he been a white man, I would have followed willingly and gladly in any honorable enterprise. Our difference of color was the only ground for difference of action. It was not that his principles were wrong in the abstract; for they are the principles of 1776.[18]

The men of the *Creole* have demonstrated national worthiness by standing for "the principles of 1776" while in the fluid space of the maritime world.

Though Washington's earlier capture and enslavement in Virginia demonstrate the power of laws and institutions to circumscribe personal liberty ashore, the geographic and political space of the sea gives Washington the freedom to rise up with his fellow slaves and seize control over his ultimate destiny. At the same time, "The Heroic Slave" is not simply an example of the dichotomy between natural rights and state power reinstantiated in the dichotomy between sea and land. Using the logic of this sea/land division in which the sea was a space wherein natural rights were primary, white seamen who were made rhetorical slaves would have consistently risen up against unjust masters like Captain Thompson in order to assert their inherent dignity and natural rights. How, then, is Madison Washington different from the beleaguered forecastle sailors of antebellum sea narratives? How does he overcome the shipboard slavery that restricted white sailors?

There are two possible answers to these questions. The first is that Washington is simply more "American" than the white sailors who are cowed by their captains and therefore more willing to stand up to tyranny. Though this would certainly align with much current criticism (as well as Douglass's political goals), such an answer is not entirely satisfactory.[19] It does, however, point the way toward another answer, which is that white sailors are bound by American law (codified in the American Constitution) in a way that black slaves are not. Captains like Claret on Melville's *Neversink* and the vicious Captain Thompson on Dana's *Pilgrim* derive power by creating fear and using violence; they imagine their men as slaves in the hopes that the men will imagine themselves the same way. The rebels aboard the *Creole*, though, are neither imagined slaves, nor rhetorical slaves, but slaves *in fact*. Their very marginality is what allows for successful action in "The Heroic Slave" as opposed to the unsuccessful or absent uprisings in the numerous sea narratives of the antebellum era. Black skin liberates the men aboard the *Creole* because it removes from the slaves obligations of citizenship even as it denies them its protections. The extra-legal status of the slaves is the very thing that sets them free, for though the power of the ship's master was to turn a man into a slave, he could not turn a slave into a slave.

In Douglass's story, it is not just one slave who turns himself into a man, but 19 rebels whose combined efforts bring freedom to all. Moreover, the men reveal the signifying power of seamanship (much like Douglass revealing the signifying power of both the American eagle and sailor garb) as they steer through a squall, and, under Washington's direction, lead the ship to Nassau. The rebels, "not one of whom had ever been to sea before," prove themselves to be far more capable than the sailors who quake in fear during the revolt. Seamanship is not learned in Douglass's tale; rather, it is innate and the embodiment of true American principles, principles that the nation itself was unwilling (or unable) to recognize in black men.

Though the historical Madison Washington's personal qualities may have indeed set him apart, he was no natural sailor. According to Senate testimony regarding the *Creole* uprising, Washington and the other slaves aboard the ship did not navigate the vessel and enlisted William Merritt, a white man, to help them steer the ship toward the Bahamas. The rebels agreed to spare Merritt's life in return for his assistance. In a deposition, Merritt said that he was "in charge of the brig, under the direction of Madison Washington," a story corroborated by other men on the ship.[20] However, Douglass—by accident, ignorance, or choice—obscures the historical record and places Madison Washington at the helm of both the rebellion *and* the ship itself, turning him into something more than simply the master of the *Creole*. Washington is, in every sense, the finest sailor aboard. It is likely that Douglass, while aware of the facts of the rebellion, shaped the final section of "The Heroic Slave" for white readers who were familiar with the plots and devices of popular maritime fiction and nonfiction. In so doing, he capitalizes on prevailing sentiments toward sailors in order to make a case for abolition. As it was in 1838, public feeling toward sailors was largely sympathetic, and flogging on national vessels was outlawed in 1850.[21] Little wonder, then, that Douglass turned his heroic slave into a masterful sailor who—like any American seaman—would resist the impositions of the captain's prerogative and maintain his right to bodily integrity. By choosing the sea narrative as a vehicle, Douglass forces readers to confront the differences between the "white slaves" who were protected by American laws and the black chattel who remained subject to American might. More importantly, he demands that readers confront the differences between idealized notions of the American identity and the American laws that precluded the realization of that ideal.

It is no wonder that Edward Smith—the white sailor whose story begins this essay—was thrown in prison for aiding black rebels, for the antebellum maritime world was a fluid and confusing space in which white American sailors could become slaves and black slaves could become American sailors. Frederick Douglass's various imaginings of the maritime world, in which slaves can easily appropriate the trappings of "Americanness," might suggest an America without a political conscience, without laws that affirm the centrality of its founding principles, without a sense of who gets to belong and why. Such a nation is nothing but a grand, unsustainable, fiction wherein belonging can be manipulated for either good or ill—a nation wherein neither seamanship nor the American eagle signify clearly or accurately. Douglass understood (correctly) that such a nation was destined to crumble under the weight of its own contradictions. At the same time, Douglass's works also point the way toward a new, more capacious era for American citizenship. If citizenship could be claimed by displaying seaman's skills, wearing sailor's garb, or invoking national symbols, then perhaps it is flexible enough to include blacks, women, and a host of other peoples—perhaps political citizenship could be a reality for men like Douglass and Madison Washington. Moving readers beyond the restrictive myth of American essentialism, Douglass's maritime world reveals the possibility of an inclusive citizenship based wholly on character and ability. Yet, as "The Heroic Slave" ends, the only place a true American like Washington can live is a British maritime colony, and Frederick Douglass (who, in 1853, was not yet an American) seems to be asking whether American sailors—all of them—could be American citizens as well.

The San Francisco waterfront reaches out past its roofed-over storeships—several of which are visible at center—toward the large fleet of active and abandoned ships in the harbor in this photograph, ca. 1850. Chilean immigrants contributed to the port's early prosperity and growth.
(Mystic Seaport, 1979.90.141)

8

Feeding "La Boca del Puerto": Chileans and the Maritime Origins of San Francisco

Edward D. Melillo

On April 10, 1866, a young journalist named Bret Harte mailed his weekly installment from California to the Boston-based Unitarian paper, the *Christian Register*. In evocative terms, the letter depicted the author's visit to San Francisco's oldest graveyard, the Mission Dolores Cemetery.[1] Harte contrasted "the strife and turmoil of the ocean" with the serene burial ground, tucked behind the mission's well-worn adobe walls: "The Mission hills lovingly embrace the little graveyard, and break the summer gales." He noted, "The foreign flavor is strong."[2]

The granite headstones of three Chileans contributed to the pervasive "foreign flavor" of the cemetery. Louis de Cross, Marie Ruiz, and Carmelita Besa died young, each receiving a Catholic burial from the padres at Mission Dolores in the mid-1850s.[3] Before their untimely deaths, these three South Americans had traversed the tumultuous seas separating their homeland of Chile from the burgeoning city of San Francisco. They were not alone in their voyages to California; more than eight thousand of their countrymen and women eventually flooded through the Golden Gate during the second half of the nineteenth century.[4]

The promise of extraordinary wealth buried in California's mountainsides and submerged in its waterways inspired many of these Chileans to make the journey northwards. Reports of James W. Marshall's discovery of gold on the American River during the last week of January in 1848 sparked an unprecedented global convergence of prospectors on the foothills of the Sierra Nevadas. Chileans were among the first people in the world to catch *la fiebre de oro* (gold fever). Chile's strategic position within a network of Pacific trading ports, and its opportune location along the predominant sea route from the Atlantic to San Francisco, meant that its citizens learned of California's gold strike before most of the world.

Chileans from every stratum of society responded to the news, boarding all manner of seaworthy vessels to seek their fortunes in the icy mountain streams of North America's El Dorado. This was the final voyage for many of the ships in Chile's merchant marine. By December 1849, 92 of Chile's 119 registered ships lay rotting in San Francisco Bay, while their passengers and crews trekked to the mines or tested their entrepreneurial skills in California's emerging frontier towns.[5]

From the Spanish conquest until the end of the Mexican War, Spanish-speaking Californians had referred to the Golden Gate as *La Boca del Puerto de San Francisco*, or "the mouth of the Port of San Francisco." John C. Frémont, who served as the military governor of California in the early months of 1847, renamed the strait the Golden Gate.[6] Despite the shift in appellation, the underlying metaphor of consumption retained its relevance for the Pacific coast harbor and its port city. It was through San Francisco that immigrants from around the world fueled California's ravenous metabolic cycle.

Chile provided more than its share of the ingredients to maintain the spectacular growth-rate of its northern neighbor. From 1848 onwards, San Francisco's waterfront developers incorporated scores of abandoned Chilean ships into the city's expanding network of wooden wharves. Merchants from both hemispheres sold millions of pounds of Chilean flour to the miners who swarmed into the cosmopolitan city. As primitive wooden and canvas structures gave way to modern stone buildings, Chileno brickmakers laid the foundations for the budding metropolis, while their compatriots sold pick axes, panning bowls, and packets of charqui (jerky) to eager prospectors. In the smoky saloons and bordello backrooms of San Francisco, prostitutes from the Chilean port cities of Talcahuano, Coquimbo, and Valparaíso appealed to the sexual appetites of lonely miners. The South American immigrants even built a thriving barrio at the foot of Telegraph Hill, which they proudly called Chilecito (Little Chile). For the thousands of Chileans who disembarked onto California's docks, San Francisco served as the aperture through which a strangely familiar world soon came into focus.

One of the quintessential images of the California gold rush is William Shew's five-plate daguerreotype, "San Francisco from Rincon Point." This panorama offers a striking view of the so-called "forest of masts" protruding skyward from the hundreds of ships that crammed San

Francisco's Yerba Buena Cove throughout 1849 and the early 1850s.[7] "The ships in the harbour looks [*sic*] like a cedar swamp," wrote a Bostonian who sailed through the Golden Gate aboard the *Velasco* in September 1849. "Ships are arriving here every day," continued Thomas Reid. "I went up the mast head and tried to count them but they were so thick I found it impossible."[8] It is no wonder that Reid had trouble calculating the number of vessels anchored in the bay. The San Francisco Harbormaster's records show that 39,888 people arrived aboard 805 ships between April 1849 and January 1850.[9]

Many of these vessels never returned to their homeports. As Hubert Howe Bancroft explained, "In July of 1850, fully 500 abandoned vessels lay rocking in front of the city, some with cargoes undisturbed, for it did not pay to unload with costly labor upon a glutted market."[10] Frequently, the crews and captains of the forsaken ships scurried off to pan for gold in the Sierras. Edward Lucett, a merchant-author who arrived in San Francisco on October 20, 1849, recalled, "Not a vessel in San Francisco possesses its complement of men. Mine all quitted as soon as it suited their convenience, and we were compelled to hire others at 5$ a day."[11] Likewise, a Chilean immigrant wrote home from San Francisco that the captain of his vessel had permitted most of the ship's sailors to head for the mines, "so there were only four men to unload approximately one thousand two hundred tons of cargo."[12]

Expressions of amazement at the ship-choked harbor are typical of mid-century accounts. When his ship reached the bay in 1849, Henry Hiram Ellis of Maine recalled, "the harbor was full of abandoned vessels, perhaps 900 of them. Masters and crews had gone to the mines. In some cases masters were left with their ships on their hands. Hundreds of these abandoned ships, such as the *Mada Kay*, an old slaver, rotted and sank in the bay, and today (1904) many hulls lie under the lower streets of the city, having been moored at the wharves and abandoned."[13]

Some of the forsaken boats fell victim to entrepreneurial scavengers who salvaged leftover cargoes, brass and copper fittings, and rare hardwoods, all of which fetched high prices in the city's teeming markets. In the 1850s, pioneer businessman Charles Hare employed Chinese laborers from a nearby fishing village to disassemble ships moored off of the Market Street Wharf. Hare reclaimed and sold everything from the iron bolts to the cordage of the waterlogged wooden carcasses.[14] Other vessels succumbed to the flames of the eight separate fires that blazed throughout the city between December 1849 and June 1851. Albert Williams, a Presbyterian pastor who lived in San Francisco from 1849 to 1854, recalled, "So frequent and periodical were these fires that they came to be regarded in the light of permanent institutions. Fears of a recurrence of the dread evil, in view of the past, were not long in waiting for fulfillment."[15]

The ships that survived these calamities often ended up as anchor points in an intricate network of wharves, earth fill, foundation piles, and gangplanks. Well over a hundred hulking wooden structures, which had once cruised the oceans of the world, served the rest of their days as makeshift storehouses, hotels, hospitals, prisons, and saloons.[16] A Connecticut pioneer lamented the degradation of his ship into one of these storehouses: "Many buildings have been erected for business purposes, on piles over the waters of the bay, and many hulls of ships that rounded the Horn have been driven as far as possible toward the shores, to serve as storerooms for the rapid increase of merchandise. Among them is the Henry Lee—our old ocean home for over seven months. She failed to realize the poet's vision of '*Ten tons or more of the golden ore–entering Gotham's Bay*.'" British miner William Kelly described the Chilean merchant ship *Niantic*, beached at the foot of Clay Street, as "a fine vessel of 1,000 tons, no longer a buoyant ship but a tenement anchored in the mud, covered with a shingle roof, subdivided into stores and offices."[17]

Lumber was so expensive in San Francisco's early days that the transformation of vessels into impromptu buildings made financial sense. As the captain of the ship *Suliot* found out, spruce boards from Belfast fetched thirty times their purchasing price when sold in California.[18] By 1852, the harbor master concluded that 164 ships served as permanent structures of the city's waterfront.[19] In 1916, Walter J. Thompson, a *San Francisco Chronicle* writer known for spinning romantic tales of "Old California," dubbed these landlocked vessels "the Argonauts' Armada of golden dreams." In flowery prose, Thompson mused over the submerged skeletons of ship hulls, "sepulchered in the clammy ooze beneath the tread of scurrying thousands and uproar of a great city's industry."[20] To this day, archaeologists, construction crews, and landowners have unearthed 42 partially intact ships from beneath the city's surfaces, and many more may lie submerged below decades of accumulated waterfront development.[21]

The sight of so many landlocked ships made a lasting impression on other new arrivals, as well. After disembarking from his own brig onto this city of condemned vessels, Chilean diplomat Benjamín Vicuña Mackenna aptly dubbed San Francisco's waterfront "a Venice built of pine instead of marble."[22] The *Niantic* was just one of many Chilean sailing vessels immobilized within this wooden district. Shipowner Wenceslao Urbistondo found an opportune use for his vessel upon arrival in San Francisco: "taking advantage of the high tide, he beached his ship in San Francisco and transformed it into a comfortable boarding house."[23] Urbistondo toppled his masts and employed them as a ready-made bridge between the stern of his ship and Vallejo Street, thereby connecting his hostel to a thriving commercial stretch of waterfront property.[24] Other ships lodged among the beached fleet served as storehouses for Chilean products. The *John Brewer*, moored near Pacific Wharf, and the *Eleanor* and the *York*, both wedged along the California Street Wharf, became convenient depots for the Chilean flour (*harina*) and wheat (*trigo*) imported by the firms of W. Meyer & Co., Cramer, Rambach & Co., and Isaac Friedlander.[25] It was from waterfront depots such as these that wheat grown half a world away in Chile fed California's hungry population.

Nearly everyone who set foot in California from 1848 to 1853 tasted bread, flapjacks, pies, cakes, or biscuits baked with Chilean flour. During the first five years of the gold rush, Chile's principal agricultural export constituted a ubiquitous ingredient in the meals served at mining camps, restaurants, and home kitchens across the state. This flour was, in the words of Lieutenant Isaac Strain, "of a fine quality, and of a flavour unsurpassed in any part of the world which I have visited."[26] One forty-niner remembered a rest stop along an overland trail into California where he and his companions dined on bread "baked for us by a lady at the ranch, and was very good indeed and made from flour imported from Chile, South America."[27] The first commercial bakers in San Joaquin County, Louis Mersfelder, Charles Potter, and John Inglis, baked their bread exclusively with Chilean flour.[28]

In many cases, milled Chilean wheat was the only available variety of flour. New Yorker Daniel Knower recalled that in Stockton during 1850, "about all the grain and flour came from Valparaiso and Chili, put up very nicely in fifty and one hundred pound sacks, so it was easy to handle."[29] The packaging in which Chilean flour reached California gave the product marked advantages over the small quantities of milled wheat that arrived aboard ships from North America's eastern ports. Bancroft explained that the North American flour came in cumbersome wooden barrels from which the contents had to be unloaded and repacked in bags before supply caravans could carry the wheat into the mining districts.[30]

The journey from Chile to California was comparatively much shorter than the long voyage from the Atlantic seaboard, and the flour from the northeastern United States suffered from double exposure to the humidity and increased temperatures of the equator. Due to the rapidity of the maritime passage northwards to San Francisco, Chilean millers could ship their flour in less-cumbersome burlap sacks of various sizes. Dockworkers unloaded these bags in San Francisco or the inland port cities of Stockton, Marysville, and Sacramento, where they immediately packed the flour sacks onto donkey trains bound for the scores of camps and outposts scattered throughout the Sierra Nevadas.

Chilean *hacendados* responded to California's burgeoning demand for food by expanding the acreage of land under wheat cultivation in Chile. This single-crop regime spread into new areas of the fertile Aconcagua Valley and the regions around Talcahuano and the Maule River. Captain George Coffin, who anchored his ship *Alhambra* at Valparaíso on August 16, 1849, was quick to recognize that "In the staple article of flour California has opened a new and extensive demand, and hundreds of acres are now in wheat where last year was nothing but weeds and thistles."[31]

The development and maintenance of the inter-hemispheric wheat trade depended upon the shipping capacities of a transnational merchant marine. The U.S. customs house officer for San Francisco listed 143 cargo ships of various nationalities that arrived from Valparaíso or Talcahuano between 1849 and 1853.[32] Almost all of the commercial officers aboard these vessels declared Chilean flour as their primary freight. The cargo vessels involved in the wheat trade tended to carry enormous quantities of their valuable commodity, transporting as much as 750,000 pounds of flour per voyage. The brigantine *Castor*, like many of its fellow grain transports, sailed to San Francisco from Talcahuano in 1850 loaded with 3,750 bags of flour, each weighing 200 pounds.[33] Given the success of this oceangoing transportation network and the explosive demand for foodstuffs generated by California's expanding population of miners, it is hardly surprising that Chile's exports of wheat to California grew by nearly 1,000 percent between 1848 and 1850.[34]

In the early years of the gold rush, the system of exchange for a wide range of imported products, including flour, was little more than a waterborne circus. As ships approached San Francisco Bay, tenacious businessmen vied with each other to clamor aboard, survey the contents of cargo holds, and make rapid purchases of valuable goods to sell onshore. Charles Ross, a trader from New Jersey, recounted that in 1849, "merchants would board vessels at the Heads [on either side of the entrance to San Francisco Bay], and offer in some cases a hundred percent advance, without looking at the invoice, for the entire cargo, no matter what it consisted of."[35]

The Golden Gate served as a literal "threshold of exchange" in which the market comprised more of a bounded physical space than an omnipresent organizational principle.[36] The theatrics of nautical commerce at "the Heads" featured the quite visible hands of market players. "We had our boats, and men on the lookout for us, and when a vessel came in, there was quite a rush of boats to board her, and the merchant who got to the vessel first was generally the luckiest fellow," wrote merchant James R. Garniss. "There were no regular prices and we made what we could."[37] Harris Newmark, a merchant of Prussian origin, found that the unanticipated entrance of a cargo ship through the Golden Gate shattered the fortunes of traders who depended upon shortages to drive up prices. Newmark awoke to the chaotic realities of the Californian economy in the 1850s when "red beans then commanded a price of twelve and a half cents per pound, until a sailing vessel from Chile unexpectedly landed a cargo in San Francisco and sent the price dropping to a cent and a quarter; when commission men, among them myself, suffered heavy losses."[38] At other times, however, this unpredictable price variability led to splendid yields for fortunate vendors.

The prices of flour from Chile astounded San Francisco resident William Redmond Ryan. In the winter of 1848-49 he found that in the city, "Chili flour sold lately as high as $45 per sack of 200 lb, on shore: the price is now $26 to $28. Flour has been a splendid speculation lately. In three days, it rose from $8 to $32 per sack of 200 lb, and in a week was up to $45. A vessel came in from Chili when the rage was at its height. She cleared $50,000 gain to the shipper, and made $10,000 commissions to the consignee."[39] Another miner recalled that his party was willing to pay exorbitant prices for Chilean flour "in anticipation of a scarcity."[40] Meanwhile, in the northern mines, where food was in short supply, sacks of Chilean flour fetched $100 apiece during the spring of 1849.[41]

On occasion, a surfeit of flour in San Francisco's storehouses portended disaster for the city's grain traders. A general oversupply of goods, punctuated by shortages resulting from devastating fires, torrential downpours, and unanticipated arrivals of immigrants, ensured the boom and bust cycle of business in San Francisco during 1849 and the 1850s. Wheat offered no exception to this trend.[42] In October 1849, the grain market reached saturation. Thomas Reid lamented the waste of flour that resulted from the market glut: "I saw four or five thousand dollars worth of flour on the beach / it was Chillian [*sic*] flour put up in bags / the bags were rotting off the flour on account of being exposed to the air."[43] So much flour arrived aboard ships from Valparaíso and Talcahuano that sacks of it lay strewn about the city. A French journalist wrote of the bizarre scene, "There was the famous sidewalk in San Francisco on the west side of Montgomery Street composed of 100 pound bags of Chilean flour, a long line of cooking stoves, a damaged piano which bridged a gully, and ending in a double row of boxes of shoes."[44] The adventurers who stepped off boats onto the city's ramshackle walkways for the first time did not find the streets of their El Dorado paved in gold.

By the 1850s, a single commission house, the Chile and California Flour Company, was well on its way towards monopolizing the flour trade with Chile. The U.S. Customs House Records for 1850 are replete with scores of invoices for flour shipped by this prominent importing firm.[45] Although this concentration of purchasing power diminished the chaotic elements of grain buying, it did not stabilize prices for the commodity. J. G. Player-Frowd contended that 100-pound bags of flour, which would have sold for five or six dollars in Chile, went for fifteen to twenty dollars in the mines because merchants withheld quantities of grain in order to stimulate demand.[46] A pioneer merchandiser from New Jersey recalled that the monopoly on grain trading caused prices to rise throughout 1850, driving shipments up. Toward the end of the year, such an enormous surplus of Chilean flour filled the storehouses of San Francisco that the price collapsed, "scarcely paying costs and charges."[47]

The reasons for this crash were quite clear-cut. In 1850, Moorehead,

Whitehead, and Maddington, the representative agents of the Chile and California Flour Company and the owners of the storeship *Niantic*, made a $120,000 contract with the leading mills in Chile and four major San Francisco grain merchants. The company promised to deliver no fewer than 100,000 barrels of flour over the coming months. At the time, California faced a drastic grain shortage and prices stood to hit new highs. The deal seemed like a lucrative proposition to all parties involved, but, in a concerted effort to time their shipments strategically, Moorehead, Whitehead, and Maddington got overzealous with their purchasing orders. When dozens of ships arrived at San Francisco harbor carrying more than 175,000 barrels of flour, the city's grain merchants recognized that the market would soon be glutted. They purchased only 50,000 barrels, paid a modest severance fine, and forfeited their remaining contractual obligations to the Chile and California Flour Company.[48]

Before 1855, the first year when the state's farmers produced a consistent supply of their own wheat, the irregular peaks and slumps in California's grain market had enormous ramifications for the merchants involved. Without the ability to exchange information rapidly on prices, stockpiles, shipping details, and farming conditions, traders had to improvise ways to bridge the vast chasm between demand and supply. Like the miners who squandered the fruits of their labors at monte tables around the state, the shareholders of the Chile and California Flour Company learned the hard way that high-stakes gambling could leave the unfortunate loser saddled with enormous out-of-pocket debts.

Other North Americans—many of them failed miners—started to place their bets on California's agricultural potential. On November 3, 1851, the *New York Daily Times* announced somewhat prematurely that in California "a home agriculture has been introduced, which promises, in another year, to supply the entire population with flour."[49] California still required massive imports of flour, but by the early 1850s, techniques of kiln drying made it possible for the Pacific states to import cheaper wheat from the Atlantic coast.[50] As Henry Clay Evans Jr. pointed out, "on the eastern seaboard of the United States it was found that kiln-dried flour could pass the equator twice without damage. This enabled American farmers in the East to ship their flour to California."[51] Once East Coast exporters began to use swift-sailing clipper ships to transport their agricultural cargo, they mounted a significant challenge to the Chilean dominance of the Pacific Coast flour market.

By 1854, California was still importing the vast majority of its wheat, but the editor of the *California Farmer* suggested that the state's own farmers might soon reach self-sufficiency in grain production.[52] That ambitious goal became reality in 1855. In an ironic reversal of fortunes, California shipped its first cargoes of homegrown wheat to Chile in the winter of 1855-1856.[53] Looking back on the mid-1850s the Reverend Albert Williams reflected, "by degrees, home production has arisen. The fact began to be palpable and make its impression when the soil yielded to the husbandman its teeming product of golden wheat. Chilean and Richmond [Virginia] breadstuffs long since disappeared from our markets."[54] California's farmers were growing wheat on more than 200,000 acres by 1856.[55]

In addition to bringing untilled land under cultivation, the state's residents also continued to create new *terra firma* by filling in the coastal zones of San Francisco Bay. San Francisco was not the first North American metropolis to experience the large-scale "landmaking" of ocean lots along its tidal margin. Many decades before North America's colonies achieved independence from Britain, tenacious developers and savvy commercial interests in New York and Boston extended wharves outwards from their shorelines and then created new property by filling in the spaces between these man-made projections of the landscape.[56]

The process of landmaking in San Francisco occurred in a similar fashion, although the hundreds of abandoned ships in the harbor added a new element to the list of ingredients in the "fill." During his second trip to the bay, Philadelphian Thaddeus S. Kenderdine remarked upon the precipitous transformation of the waterfront district since his previous visit:

> What is now a straight line on the San Francisco front was originally indented with a deep cove, over which, in the most extended portion, are now six squares. This extended from Rincon Point South to Clarke's. In the early years of the city this, called Yerba Buena—Good Herb—Cove, and where [Richard Henry] Dana and his shipmates beached their boats in 1836, was the landing place for vessels drawing eight feet of water, at high tide. Afterwards,

> the streets were extended by wooden wharves to a line from point to point. Between these were several vessels blown ashore in storms or deserted by their crews and these were left and gradually filled around with the gradings from the adjacent hills.[57]

Landmaking on this scale dramatically reoriented the city's relationship to the surrounding waterfront environment.

Ecologists recognize San Francisco Bay as "one of the largest and most extensively modified estuaries in the world."[58] During the mid-1800s the bay's tidelands became areas of profoundly contested usage rights. Cattlemen grazed their herds along the shoreline, salt companies gathered their valuable preservative from bay waters for sale to the salmon canning and silver mining industries, and hunters shot tens of thousands of waterfowl in the bay's tidal estuaries. As environmental historian Matthew Morse Booker points out, all of California's top fisheries centered on San Francisco Bay prior to 1910.[59] Developers battled each of these interests in turn, setting the stage for many of the land-use conflicts that continue to dominate bay shores to this day.

The expansion of shoreline real estate through wharf building was a lucrative venture. San Francisco's wharves served as the gateway for the vast majority of California's maritime commerce, and in 1851, the San Francisco Customs House collected duties totaling over $2 million. Only four other ports in the United States—the well-established harbors in New York, Boston, Philadelphia, and New Orleans—brought in higher tax revenues that year.[60] As of October 1850, four wharves, costing more than $1.5 million, dominated the waterfront and provided the city with nearly two miles of pedestrian boardwalks. The extensions included Long Wharf, 2,000 feet long; Market Street Wharf, 600 feet long; California Street Wharf, 400 feet long by 32 feet wide; and Cunningham's Wharf, 375 feet long, with a 330-bfoot-long by 30-foot-wide T extension at its end.[61] "The wharves and docks are such immense structures that one can hardly find words to describe their extent and importance," remarked Prussian-born Frank Lecouvreur upon seeing the waterfront in the 1850s.[62]

Waterfront development proceeded unabated until the early 1860s. Each expansion further into the bay received notice in the city's papers. On April 8, 1851, *Alta California* reported a new project called "Pacific

Street Wharf—The splendid wharf at the foot of Pacific street, partially constructed at a heavy expense by the city, has fallen into the hands of a number of gentlemen, who have formed themselves into a stock company, with the determination of extending the wharf some eight hundred feet further out. The stock was all taken up previous to the organization or first meeting of the company, and the full amount of capital subscribed. The contract for extending it has been completed and the first series of piles already driven. In forty days the famed Central Wharf will have a competitor equal, if not superior, in every respect."

The unhindered growth of San Francisco's wooden waterfront had serious environmental consequences. Developers extended their search for timber into Oakland's five-square-mile coast redwood (*Sequoia semprevirens*) forest. Lumberjacks cut every one of the trees, some over 300 feet tall, by 1860. Two of the tallest Sequoias that sawyers felled from this stand had once guided captains towards the Golden Gate from 16 miles offshore. By 1872, lumbering activities throughout the state had denuded one-third of California's forests.[63] In many ways the deforestation and marshland development around San Francisco Bay mirrored the patterns of maritime capitalism around the world. From the sixteenth through the nineteenth centuries the ever-expanding mercantile and military demand for ports and sailing ships made demands on laborers and landscapes.[64]

Although San Francisco's "Venice of pine" provided a dense matrix of cargo outlets, storage spaces, dwellings, and commercial establishments for its residents, it proved to be more volatile than durable. The recurrent fires, which ravaged the city in its early years, shook residents' faith in the viability of wood as a sound building material. The fire of May 4, 1851, visited more devastation upon San Francisco than any other conflagration of the nineteenth century. Flames engulfed the commercial district, along with "the most imposing edifice in the city," the four-story customs house.[65] The editors of the *Daily Evening Picayune* wrote of the fire, "The city will feel for years the effects of this visitation." Yet the editors reverted to the city's idyllic geography and the tenacity of its occupants as sources for optimism: "But so great is our confidence in the natural location and advantages of this place, and in the recuperating energies of our fellow citizens, that we do not for a moment hesitate to say that San Francisco will rise again and occupy the position which nature evidently intended her to fill and adorn."[66]

At least one prominent resident of the city saw latent advantages in the disastrous fires of the 1850s: "a real benefit has been the fire; a fine brick building will replace the wretched structures destroyed."[67] The Reverend Albert Williams, founder and pastor of the First Presbyterian Church in the city, concurred, pointing out that the fires actually stimulated commerce by creating an unanticipated demand for building materials and labor.[68] The conflagrations rid the city of outmoded wooden structures and made room for a new array of brick and stone buildings, which required the skills of thousands of construction workers. In the summer of 1853, San Franciscans erected more than 600 brick buildings.[69]

Mexicans and Chileans filled the ranks of the reserve army of laborers who rebuilt the city. While gold might have been San Francisco's cornerstone, bricks comprised its more durable foundation. As William Deverell cogently argues in his account of the Mexicans who made Los Angeles, "The color of brickwork is brown."[70] Latino labor was at the heart of San Francisco's brick-making industry, as well. Chileans brought their brick-making and bricklaying skills with them from the southern hemisphere, putting these abilities to good use in the structural transformation of San Francisco's urban landscape.[71]

"There was a novel method of brick making going on," Forty-niner William M'Collum observed. In the early years of the gold rush, "a large number of Mexicans and Chillians [*sic*], were molding them from clay, 8 by 18 inches, and drying them in the sun. When laid in housewalls they were plastered on the inside with sand and clay, and made a tolerable good substitute for the ordinary burnt brick."[72] Higher-quality kiln-fired bricks, prepared by Chilean and Mexican laborers at brickyards around San Francisco Bay, commanded high prices in the city's construction materials market. At the beginning of 1849, "Garnkirk and Stourbridge" bricks sold at a rate of $45 per 1,000, while at other times, the price of bricks rose as high as a dollar each.[73]

In their homeland, Chilean brick-makers saved their best kiln-fired bricks for the houses of the wealthy. While visiting southern Chile on his way to San Francisco, Samuel C. Upham had noted that high-quality bricks supported upper-class dwellings, helping to stabilize these structures against the tremors of frequent earthquakes. In Talcahuano, "the wealthier classes live in more substantial buildings, the walls being fully three feet in thickness, and in many instances constructed of kiln-burned bricks."[74] The quality and durability of these bricks was so well reputed that Californians imported them for use in their buildings. Jules François Bekeart, a Coloma shopkeeper, used bricks imported from Chile in the cornice of his store.[75]

Likewise, premium brickwork buttressed the elaborate commercial structures of post-1851 San Francisco. At least four Chilean bricklayers worked on William C. Ralston's Palace Hotel at the corner of Market and New Montgomery streets. The eight-floor luxury structure cost $5 million, occupied an entire city block, and required "24,660,596 hard bricks, 28,393 barrels of cement, and 22,160 barrels of lime."[76] Ironically, the walls that working-class Chileans helped to build framed the spatial reconfigurations of an increasingly segregated city. When the hotel opened on October 2, 1875, it divided the wealthy Nob Hill mansions from the working-class neighborhood south of Market Street where many Latinos resided.[77]

Male Chilean brick-makers and masons supplied San Francisco with a literal structural foundation during the mid-nineteenth century. In contrast, the prevailing social theories of the day suggested that women were the only ones capable of providing the moral mortar to stabilize the turbulent social conditions that characterized North America's frontier cities. "Woman, to society, is like a cement to the building of stone," one California immigrant declared.[78]

Prostitution was clearly not the social fortification this commentator sought to promote; the arrival of ships carrying Chilean women to San Francisco's waterfront did less to pacify antagonisms and more to ignite the desires of many of the city's male residents. Initially, San Francisco had been a city of men. Decrying the city's woefully skewed sex ratio, the *Alta California* reported in 1849 that during the month of July, 3,565 men and only 49 women came by sea to San Francisco.[79] This imbalance made the Golden Gate a gendered threshold as well as a maritime doorway to potential riches.

Although some Chilean women found work as dressmakers or maids, they could frequently earn higher wages if they sold their bodies to the lonely men of San Francisco. The most common professional designation for Chilean women in the 1852 and the 1860 censuses is prostitute.[80]

Infamous San Francisco Madam Nell Kimball recalled meeting a retired harlot by the name of "Old Sugar Mary" who had encountered many Chilean and Mexican sex workers in the city during the gold rush years. In Kimball's words, "Old Sugar Mary said she remembered back to the first days of prostitution on any impressive scale; it was in the tents and shacks of the Mexican and South American whores called *Chilenos* [*sic*]. They worked the water front and the long climb up Telegraph Hill. The demand was steady and the work rewarding as the competition was only nigrahs and squaws."[81]

The work might have offered a few financial "rewards," but it generally followed the trends that predominated in the gold mines; a few struck it rich, while most barely kept up with their day-to-day expenses. Patricia Nelson Limerick points out that throughout the American West, prostitution "seldom led past subsistence. A few well-rewarded mistresses of rich men and a few madams skilled in a complicated kind of management may have prospered, but most prostitutes did well to keep revenue a fraction ahead of overhead costs—rent, clothing, food, payoffs to law officers."[82] Beyond these costs, prostitutes, especially women of color, paid a psychological wage to the Anglos of San Francisco.[83]

Anglo men and women tended to refer to these so-called "whores" with the same vulgar economic vocabulary they used when discussing the goods for sale in the city's markets. In his journal entry for Thursday, November 21, 1850, 22-year-old Timothy Coffin Osborn from Martha's Vineyard related crassly, "Had a long and interesting chat with Gurney upon the 'sights' he saw in the little city of Stockton. He informed us of the steady importation of '*Ladies*' from the Atlantic side, and an increased immigration of *females* from Australia and China! Of the latter class he informs us the market is well supplied and 'trade' is light, with market quotations ranging from $50 to $100 *tout la nuit*!"[84]

Sexual encounters with prostitutes embodied the same speculative nature as transactions on the grain market. "I got a crack at a very hansom [*sic*] girl last Sunday," miner Simon Stevens bragged to his Maine cousin in 1853. "It only cos mee a 20."[85] In a letter to "Our loved ones at home" from San Francisco on May 30, 1852, pioneer woman Mary Jane Megquier wrote, "Captain Mann arrived to day [*sic*] with a *cargo* of Chile women."[86] Although "hats were removed and bows executed" when the wealthier madams and their North American or European girls made their way along downtown streets, the men of San Francisco did not always extend the same ostentatious courtesies to the Chilean, Mexican, and Chinese prostitutes.[87]

Her social class, birthplace, and skin color clearly influenced the treatment that a San Francisco prostitute received from white men. Forty-niner Enos Christman complained in August 1851, "The women of other nations, what few there are, are nearly all lewd harlots, who are drunk half the time, or sitting behind the gambling table dealing monte."[88] In a similar derogatory vein, James Buel remarked, "The few women who went to California in 1849, and three or four years after, were generally of the most disreputable class, not merely destitute of decency, but so debased, as to be a caricature on humanity."[89] Another Anglo writer complained, "Excepting saloons and gambling houses there were no other places of amusement, unless one went among the chilean encampment where the lowest of women, owned by men lower than themselves, aided in the robbery, often the murder, of those who came to them; or among the cribs and taverns of the waterfront."[90] The *Daily Alta California* wrote of the women who sold their services in saloons with "walls covered in dingy paper" and "ornamented with Chilian and Mexican flags, and a low bench [which] encircles the room seated on which are some twelve or fifteen women, Mexicans and negresses of different ages from ten to forty. Here may be seen the parent and her offspring practicing the same life of infamy."[91] The *Alta* published a number of stories analogous to this one, in which the editors sought to display the seamy side of San Francisco life, titillating readers while also appealing to their moral indignation and racial biases.

Although the popular press portrayed prostitution as an unfortunate byproduct of San Francisco's explosive growth, the buying and selling of sex was not a phenomenon new to California. Prostitution had become commonplace after the arrival of Spanish soldiers and colonists in the late eighteenth century. As Albert Hurtado notes, "In 1780 Father Serra complained about Nicolas, a neophyte who procured women for the soldiers at San Gabriel. A few years later a Spanish naturalist observed that the Chumash men had 'become pimps, even for their own wives, for any miserable profit.'"[92] The young Boston Brahmin Richard Henry Dana may have been speaking from personal experience when he recounted that during the 1830s, "I have frequently known an Indian to bring his wife, to whom he was lawfully married in the church, down to the beach, and carry her back again, dividing with her the money which she had got from the sailors. If any of the girls were discovered by the alcalde to be open evil livers, they were whipped, and kept at work sweeping the square of the presidio, and carrying mud and bricks for the buildings; yet a few reals would generally buy them off."[93] Official tolerance, and even endorsement, of the practice of prostitution continued unabated throughout the first few decades of statehood.

The availability of a sexual encounter to match one's social status had become a regular feature of San Francisco's urban landscape by the 1850s. In his recollections of the city during its early years, Captain George Coffin quipped, "The most genteel house in San Francisco was a brothel."[94] "One popular French courtesan" about whom Herbert Asbury waxed eloquent in *The Barbary Coast*, "is said to have banked five thousand dollars clear profit during her first year of professional activity in [San Francisco]."[95] Likewise, a few Chinese women managed to ascend San Francisco's social ladder by selling their services to the city's wealthier men. "The first Chinese courtesan who came to San Francisco was Ah Toy," wrote Elisha Oscar Crosby. The former New York lawyer continued, "She arrived I think in 1850 and was a very handsome Chinese girl. She was quite select in her associates, was liberally patronized by the white men and made a great amount of money."[96] The parlors and dance floors of extravagant downtown establishments afforded a socially acceptable meeting place for men to interact with extravagantly dressed female prostitutes.

The opulent veneer of these social settings was only skin deep, however. San Francisco's clubs and bordellos could promptly transform themselves into arenas of bloody confrontation that rivaled any sought-after gold mine as a source of envy and a site of conflict. "Hither I was called one night to attend a Creole girl from New Orleans, who had just been stabbed, at a masked ball in the saloon, by a jealous Chilena," recalled San Francisco physician John W. Palmer. After arriving at the Washington Hall Club "I found the beautiful fury—Camille La Reine, they called her—blaspheming over a gashed shoulder, and devoting the quick-striking vixen of Valparaiso to a hundred fates." The San Francisco underworld balanced its accounts swiftly for, "six weeks after that, the *Pacific News* announced that the notorious Mariquita, the beautiful

Chilian [*sic*] spitfire, had had her throat cut with a bowie-knife, in the hands of the splendid Creole Camille, in a 'difficulty' at one of those mad masked balls at La Señorita saloon."[97] In sensational cases such as this one, the press named the women, but for most Latina prostitutes, life in San Francisco consisted of an anonymous and transient affair.

Obscurity and evanescence were the consuming passions of San Francisco's sex trade. During his passage to California on the French vessel *Staouéli*, Vicente Pérez-Rosales launched into a vivid description of one of the three women onboard, a prostitute named Rosario Améstica. Rosario "had been born as Izquierdo in Quilicura, lived in Talcahuano as Villaseca, in Talca as Toro, and in Valparaíso, till the day before, as Rosa Montalva."[98] Although the harbormaster in Valparaíso questioned her for applying for a passport under an assumed name, the male passengers protested his inquiries. He finally allowed her to remain aboard the ship. Upon arrival in San Francisco, "Rosarito [*sic*], dressed to kill in a magnificent silk gown, cape, and parasol, fawned and fluttered over by everyone who came on board, soon went ashore and, surrounded by a crowd of admirers, disappeared into the low fog or semi-drizzle that obscured everything."[99] The city of men had devoured another object of desire.

In the end, many of the Chileans who followed the Humboldt Current northwards to San Francisco never returned to their homeland in the Southern Hemisphere. Instead, they lived, labored, died, and received burial along the California coast. Mark Twain, who spent the 1860s "Roughing It" in California, mused, "No real estate is permanently valuable but the grave."[100] Yet many California cemeteries did not offer their residents the promise of a reliable, long-term place of rest. At the turn of the century, the San Francisco Board of Supervisors yielded to the demands of land speculators and banned further burials in the city. They also ordered officials at the Laurel Hill and Calvary Cemeteries to remove the interments and deposit the bodies elsewhere. Developers turned the Golden Gate Cemetery into Lincoln Park Golf Course in 1906, and summarily dumped the grave markers at Ocean Beach. Over the following three decades, tombstones from the Masonic Cemetery became landfill for the approach to Golden Gate Bridge, and builders used the remains of the monuments from the Odd Fellows Cemetery to shore up the Aquatic Park seawall at Fisherman's Wharf. As the Chilean Benjamín Vicuña Mackenna deftly noted, "The dead have no friends in San Francisco."[101]

The surviving burial sites have fared no better. Only two cemeteries remain in the city, the San Francisco National Cemetery at the Presidio and the Mission Dolores Cemetery from which Bret Harte wrote his paean to the serene Spanish past. During the summer of 1993, while excavating the ground around the Palace of the Legion of Honor for renovation and expansion of the museum, construction crews found "about 300 corpses from the Gold Rush era—two of them still clutching rosaries, others were wearing dentures and Levis."[102] There were, no doubt, anonymous Chileans among the bodies of this Potter's Field. After a short hiatus from the digging, during which archaeologists scrambled to identify artifacts and skeletal remains, the excavation continued. The episode served as a poignant reminder of the Californian tendency to exhume the past only to bury it again beneath a new veneer.

Many who revisit California after an absence from the Golden State feel that its former landscapes have been irredeemably lost beneath waves of unprecedented expansion. Richard Henry Dana Jr., who first sailed to California from Boston in 1835, returned in 1859 and found his surroundings altered beyond recognition. As Dana wrote, "when I saw all these things, and reflected on what I once was and saw here, and what now surrounded me, I could scarcely keep my hold on reality at all, or the genuineness of anything, and seemed to myself like one who had moved in 'worlds not realized.'"[103]

California's explosive economic growth from the gold rush of the 1840s through the high-tech boom of the 1990s has left the past buried beneath new consumer trends, rapid changes in crop emphasis, and unpredictable demographic shifts. Foreigners were involved in all of these developments. As Carey McWilliams observed, "The single most distinctive fact about the culture of California has been the perpetually high proportion of newly arrived residents among its inhabitants."[104] New arrivals to the state have remade it time and again by contributing elements of their home cultures to the reconstitution California's natural and social systems.

More often than not, these revitalizing influences have come via transoceanic connections between California and the outside world. Beyond the overland trail routes across the American West, the Pacific was the main conduit to the gold fields of California.[105] As historian James P. Delgado points out, "the general impression [of immigration to California] depicts a nation's trend westward by the Oregon Trail. It is important, however, to remember that the California Gold Rush was first and foremost a maritime event."[106]

Chile's maritime influences on San Francisco have become part of a "world not realized," a row of mossy granite headstones and ship hulls entombed in layers of concrete and asphalt. As his vessel departed from California's shores, carrying him back to Chile in the summer of 1852, one-time prospector Ramón Gil Navarro reflected on what he was leaving behind in the Golden State: "With the last rays of sunshine we lost sight of the golden land of California, the country of marvels, the country of the thousand and one nights, the country that was the scene of so much happiness and so much suffering of mine. The last hills of Monterey with their beautiful pine trees disappeared with yesterday's light of day."[107] History is always a process of becoming and disappearing. Though Gil Navarro lost sight of the golden land, the words in his journal testify to the profound Chilean presence that shaped North America's Pacific shores.

Captain William T. Shorey and his family, ca. 1901. Julia Ann Shelton Shorey sits at right, daughter Zenobia sits at left, and Victoria stands. (Mrs. Victoria Francis Collection, San Francisco Maritime Museum (Image P21578), Courtesy Oakland History Room, Oakland Public Library, Oakland, CA)

9

Black Ahab of the Bay: William T. Shorey and the San Francisco Whale Fishery

Timothy G. Lynch

As Jeff Bolster showed in his seminal article, "To Feel Like a Man: Black Seamen in the Northern States, 1800-1860," the American merchant marine was one of the few industries where persons of color could find acceptance in the first half of the nineteenth century.[1] Freed from the constraints of shoreside society, African Americans took comfort in an occupational milieu where they were judged less by the color of their skin and more by their abilities as a sailor or strengths as a longshoreman. Indeed, in some antebellum ports, African Americans made up a sizable percentage of the maritime workforce, and they were substantially over-represented in most maritime occupations. However, as control of hiring practices drifted from salty captains to land-based shipping agents, African Americans began to lose their places of refuge (and relative privilege) in the years after the American Civil War. While white crews were the standard in most areas of the American merchant marine by that later period, opportunities for persons of color remained in the American whale fishery, where polyglot crews that ranged the racial spectrum remained the norm through the end of the century. The lengthy voyages, low pay, hard work, and dangerous conditions associated with whaling all served to make this segment of the industry less attractive for native-born whites, leaving the berths to be filled by foreigners, African Americans, and other marginalized members of society.

From its inception along the East Coast in the early colonial period, the American whale fishery was multiracial and multinational: indigenous persons, Cape Verde Bravas, Portuguese seamen, and blacks made up a cosmopolitan crew that shipped out in pursuit of the leviathans of the deep.[2] Previous treatments of these individuals, and of men such as

William T. Shorey, have mirrored Bolster's approach and have focused on the ways in which persons of color were able to rise through the ranks of a segregated society to make a place for themselves in an inhospitable and segregated America.[3] These treatments, however, border on the myopic: important questions of race, gender, power, and ethnicity go unanswered, or unasked, as a triumphant narrative of success in the face of overwhelming odds is the preferred interpretation. Research suggests, however, that Shorey—rather than serving as a unique model of black ascendancy—should be considered as an example of transcendent themes that were being played out in the American whale fishery as it approached its ultimate decline. Rather than seeing Shorey as reflective of the unique experiences of black seamen, it is, perhaps, better to see him as reflective of the experiences of his times, times that can tell us much about the nature of race and power in maritime America. While Shorey may have been remarkable, his experiences were in many ways typical of what one would expect of the American whale fishery in this era.

William Thomas Shorey was born in Barbados on January 25, 1859, to Rosa Frazier, a "beautiful Creole woman," and Scottish-born sugar planter William Shorey.[4] The eldest of eight children, he was apprenticed to a plumber, but he ran away from this trade and shipped out as a cabin boy aboard a Boston-bound vessel. During the voyage, he was taught some rudimentary navigational skills; this training continued subsequently, when he was introduced to a Captain W. A. Leach of Provincetown, Massachusetts.[5] Leach was a well-known whaling master, and he spent much time teaching his young charge the arts of navigation, seamanship, and, evidently, how to control a crew. In 1876, at the age of 16, Shorey shipped out on his maiden whaling voyage; sailing as a greenhand, he progressed up the ranks and returned as a boatsteerer, a position of some importance and responsibility.[6] The presence of a teenaged West Indian sailor was not uncommon at a time when the composition of an American whaleship crew saw two out of every three individuals born outside of American borders; many of these, moreover, were of liminal age, having recently entered the workforce, but not yet having any dependants. On November 8, 1880, Shorey shipped out of Boston as third mate aboard the whaling bark *Emma F. Herriman* in a globe-girdling, three-year expedition that was typical of the far-ranging whaling voyages of the day. The voyage took Shorey and the

Herriman across the Atlantic, around the Cape of Good Hope, through the Indian Ocean, around Australia, and into the Pacific, calling at Valparaiso, Callao, and other ports. During this voyage, Shorey received a baptism by fire: years later, he recounted a harrowing tale of this early voyage, where he almost lost his life while pursuing a sperm whale. "Evidently enraged" he related, "the whale attacked first one boat, smashing it, then a second one, and then attacked the one I was in. By good fortune we were able to fire a bomb into him which, exploding, killed him and saved us."[7] By the time the 385-ton, 119-foot vessel arrived in San Francisco in 1883, Shorey had risen to the rank of first mate.[8] The seas and the whales were not the only thing that Shorey contested: when the vessel arrived in San Francisco, Shorey was arrested and charged with beating and wounding John A. Peterson, a sailor on the *Herriman*. After forfeiting his bond, Shorey pled guilty to the charges. The charges did not, apparently, worry the shipping company of McGee and Moore; Shorey shipped again aboard the *Herriman* in 1884 and 1885, sailing as second and then as first officer on the short, 10-month voyages, which were typical of West Coast whaling.

Shorey's indiscretions did not ruin his personal life, either. Described as "handsome, charming, ebullient and articulate" he courted one of the doyens of black San Francisco, Julia Ann Shelton, and they married in that city in 1886.[9] During that same year, Shorey was made captain of the *Herriman,* becoming the only black whaling captain in San Francisco's fleet. The newlyweds journeyed together to Mexico and Hawai'i aboard that vessel on their honeymoon; while his bride remained in Honolulu, he sailed off on a highly profitable voyage to the Sea of Japan.[10] In 1889, Shorey took command of the *Alexander*, a 136-ton brig built just three years earlier.[11] Described as a "smallish, but trim and graceful vessel," the *Alexander* made two successful runs to the Arctic in 1889 and 1890; regrettably, the vessel was lost the following year at St. Paul Island in the Bering Sea when it was crushed by a massive ice floe.[12] Denied assistance by the American warship *Yorktown,* and the revenue cutters *Bear, Corwin, and Albatross*, the resourceful Shorey was still able to deliver 28 of his crew back to San Francisco.[13] This was quite an accomplishment, as Shorey was still recovering from a broken leg sustained the previous March.[14]

The crushing ice was not the only issue Shorey had to deal with. When confronted with a "sick" crewman, Shorey offered that he had "good medicine aboard his ship . . . medicine that would fix him up in a jiffy." The captain proceeded to bash his charge over the skull with a revolver, opening a gash that required several stitches. During the attack, Shorey was quoted as saying that he "would teach you who is master aboard this ship." The aggrieved seaman, an Irishman named Slim, signalled the passing revenue cutter *Corwin*. A pair of agents boarded the *Alexander* and were told of the beatings routinely administered by Shorey, whom one sailor described as a "brute." It was all for naught; for the next three months "Slim" had no more than 12 hours rest in any 48-hour period. In the words of one of his shipmates, the experience nearly killed him.[15] Upon returning to San Francisco, "Slim" pressed criminal charges, claiming that Shorey, by forcing him to work constantly on deck for 24 consecutive days with no more than four hours of sleep per night, had inflicted cruel and unusual punishment. Despite having an eyewitness to the assault, Seaman John Rentford was unable to prove his case. Consequently, Shorey was found not guilty.[16]

The owner of the *Alexander* certainly did not lose faith in Shorey, and upon his return to San Francisco he was immediately placed in command of another vessel, the 111-foot bark *Andrew Hicks*. In the decade between 1892 and 1902, the *Hicks* completed eight successful voyages under Shorey's command, but this was not the only ship that Shorey commanded in this period.[17] In December 1895, Shorey headed north on the steam-powered whaling bark *Gay Head*, one of the most illustrious of all San Francisco whalers. This run was to be one of his most successful, netting 500 barrels of oil and 9,000 pounds of whalebone. After this brief interlude, Shorey returned to the *Hicks* in 1896 for six more voyages; on many of these he was accompanied by his wife and their young daughter. In a San Francisco newspaper article, "Love Guided the Wheel," three-year-old Victoria Shorey (whom her mother described as a perfect sailor, "one who knows all the ropes and has perfect command of her father") was credited with guiding the *Hicks* into home port. Shorey later intimated that his success as a sailing master was in some measure due to his happy marriage and family life.[18] This domestic bliss did not spill over to the crew of the *Hicks*: although a 1901 newspaper account of the *Hicks* states that "all hands were friendly throughout the long and tedious cruise," this was not the case; one seaman stabbed and seriously wounded another.[19]

Shorey's final command was the 114-foot whaling bark *John and Winthrop*, built at Bath, Maine, in 1876 by Goss, Sawyer, and Packard. Shorey made five voyages in command of the *John and Winthrop* in the half-decade between 1903 and 1908, and it was on this ship that Shorey may have encountered his biggest challenge. On his final voyage, he brought his ship home safely through two typhoons and an imposing fogbank. After securing four whales, the ship encountered a terrible storm. As a crew-member attested: "All sails were taken down, but the vessel was nonetheless driven along at fifteen knots. The ship was battened down and all hands, as much as possible, remained below decks. Wind and sea increased in fury, smashing the davits, and carrying away everything that was not tied down; for days none on board ate or slept."[20] Despite losing four boats and all their sails during the 42-day passage from the Sea of Okhotsk, the voyage was a marked success, bringing in 200 barrels of oil and 2,500 pounds of bone, including some that was salvaged from the wreck of the *Carrie and Annie*. The men aboard said that nothing but Shorey's "coolness and clever seamanship saved a wreck."[21]

Perhaps chastened by this experience, perhaps wanting to spend more time with his wife and their two surviving children, Shorey retired from the sea in 1908.[22] Living in the same West Oakland residence since 1884, Shorey threw himself into community service and activism.[23] He remained an active member of the Episcopal Church, as well as of numerous charitable and fraternal organizations, including the Home for Aged and Infirm Colored Persons, where he held a seat on the board of directors.[24] But Shorey could never really get the sea out of his veins, and he retained his master's license up through the time of his death. Maintaining his maritime connections, he was appointed a special police officer in January of 1912, working on the docks of the Pacific Coast Steamship Company, in the employ of legendary inspector John K. Bulger. Shorey became a citizen of the United States on November 27, 1912, finally taking a step that the peripatetic existence of a whaling captain had made all but impossible. On April 15, 1919, at the age of 60, William T. Shorey passed away at his home, one of many who succumbed to the influenza pandemic then raging across the world.

There can be no doubt that William Thomas Shorey was an extraordinary man. As an immigrant and a person of color, his ascension through the ranks of American society is exceptional. In an age when racial discrimination and prejudice were widespread, and in which segregation was the law of the land, Shorey's success, which included commanding crews that were largely white, flies in the face of societal norms. On one of Shorey's commands, his crew included citizens of Australia, Austria, British Guiana, Canada, China, Denmark, France, Ireland, Norway, Poland, Scotland, and Sweden.[25] Attesting to the cosmopolitan crew, one observer, using the racist language of the day, commented that the vessel represented "the most heterogeneous ship that made port in many a day. Bright, active Americans are in the forecastle with rugged Northmen, yellow-skinned Chinese, brown Esquimaux, and kinky-haired sailors as black as ever walked the plank of a river packet."[26] But while Shorey may have been an extraordinary man, his experiences were far from extraordinary, and by extrapolating from the particulars of his life, we can gain a better understanding and appreciation of the generalities of what life was like in the American merchant marine towards the close of the nineteenth century. As Yankee whalers ventured further afield in pursuit of their prey, San Francisco became the center of the American whale fishery. This had serious implications for the composition and management of the industry. With longer journeys to more dangerous climes, captains and masters needed to rely on tried and true tactics. The use of crimps and shanghaiers were common in San Francisco at this time, and many of the men who were employed on Shorey ships were acquired in this fashion. According to records kept by notorious San Francisco shipping agent James Laflin, 19 of the 24 seamen aboard the *John and Winthrop* had been introduced to the vessel in this manner. Shorey's name, likewise, can be found in the database constructed from this record, as both receiving advances and accepting shanghaied sailors aboard his vessels.[27]

Other elements of the waning age of sail are also seen in Shorey's life. Abuse of seamen, was, as we know, not unique to the whale fishery. The use of bucko mates, armed with belaying pins, to keep order on these sailing vessels was widespread: in fact, Shorey was once one of them, as evidenced by his behavior onboard the *Herriman*. Moreover, while Shorey was twice bought up on charges of cruelty, this is less than what one might expect to find in the historical record. We need look no further than the *Coast Seaman's Journal*, the periodical of the Coast Seaman's Union, the self-proclaimed "lookout of the labor movement." Between 1887 and

1894, the *Coast Seaman's Journal* published its well-known "Red Record," which listed cases of abuse aboard merchant ships. In that seven-year period there were 64 incidents, 40 of which originated in San Francisco.[28] The occasional presence of women and children aboard Shorey's vessels, a not uncommon practice among Pacific whalers, likewise sheds light on the interesting role of gender in the seafaring world as the nineteenth century drew to a close.

Thus, it is perhaps better to see in William Shorey, not the triumph of a person of color above Jim Crow-era intolerance, but the continued maltreatment of merchant seamen by cruel masters during the waning days of the age of sail. The defining element of William Shorey's existence may not have been his race, but his privileged status as master of an American sailing ship. His crew—and the American courts—routinely deferred to Shorey, not on the basis of his ethnicity, but due to his being in command of a whaleship, where order and discipline mattered far more than race and ethnicity. Thus, in this one instance at least, power and class mattered far more than race and ethnicity at sea.

Perhaps the clearest example of the interplay of race and power in maritime America can be seen in Shorey's last voyage. Limping back into port after surviving two typhoons and nearly stranding in the fog-shrouded Bowsail Channel, the *John and Winthrop* was delayed by customs officials in San Francisco. Among those on board were seven Japanese, who were not allowed to land and who were subsequently deported in compliance with the Gentleman's Agreement of that year.[29] While it is tantalizing to suggest that this injustice was one of the reasons Shorey turned his back on the sea, there is no evidence to suggest that this is the case, and for those who see Shorey's career as a triumph over the segregationist policies of his day, it is clear that many others still toiled under this iniquitous system. Indeed, for every William Shorey, the "Black Ahab of the Pacific," there were countless others whose stories have remained untold.

Despite decades of discrimination, Chinese salmon processors did much of the work in the salmon canneries of Astoria, Oregon, as shown in this photo, ca. 1900.
(Mystic Seaport, 1999.33)

10

"Hands full with the Chinese": Maritime Dimensions of the Chinese-American Experience, 1870-1943

Joshua M. Smith

The story of Chinese labor on the West Coast is typically seen as one of immigration issues, the need for cheap labor, and hardening racial attitudes in communities like San Francisco. It is only relatively recently that popular histories such as the late Iris Chang's *The Chinese in America* have attempted to place the Chinese-American experience within a larger American experience.[1] But there is an important maritime dimension to the Chinese community that remains largely unexplored. These maritime aspects reveal important episodes such as the use of environmental concerns to bolster racist antagonism toward Asian immigrants, the perceived economic threat of Chinese mariners to white sailors, and popular views on white "superiority" and Chinese "docility." The picture thus assembled is a far cry from the "model minority" image of Asian immigrants still perpetuated in this country; yet it is not a part of the narrative Chinese Americans have constructed about themselves, either.[2] The maritime dimension of the Chinese-American experience is thus an opportunity to shed new light on an important immigrant group.

Three vignettes reveal to a large degree the role Chinese immigrants played in maritime matters from the late nineteenth through the early twentieth centuries. The first considers Chinese fishing communities on the West Coast and alleged destruction of fishing grounds. The second is based on the congressional testimony of West Coast labor leaders anxious to eliminate the Chinese competition for seafaring jobs. The third is the 1900 account of a Chinese sailor "mutiny" on the steamship *City of Peking* in 1900 as it crossed the Pacific at the height of the Boxer Rebellion. Uniting these episodes is an important aspect of white racism against the Chinese: the idea that the Chinese community was composed of "perpetual foreigners," an alien presence in

American society that existed solely for the utility of the white community.[3]

The central document to understanding the Chinese-American experience is the Chinese Exclusion Act of 1882, the first American law to single out a specific nationality for discrimination. This law effectively sealed off Chinese immigration by banning Chinese laborers because white Americans assumed the Chinese were "inassimilable," simply too different to ever integrate successfully, an assumption carefully handed down to their children. In the early twentieth century, schoolbooks continued to describe the San Francisco Chinese as exotics, with yellow faces, eyes "set aslant" and alien customs. This schoolbook also found that so many Chinese came across the Pacific that

> our people feared they might do all the work, while some good American citizens would be forced to go idle. They found also that the Chinese who came seldom wished to remain and aid in building up the country, and were not inclined to become citizens. Therefore we came to the conclusion that it was best not to have too many of them; and now all ships arriving from Asia are carefully watched, and the Chinese laboring people upon them are not permitted to land.[4]

The prosaic language aside, this is a remarkable mangling of the facts. Chinese were excluded from citizenship by law; if many chose to return, a significant factor must have been the violence and discrimination they found in America.

The schoolbook excerpt also touches on the maritime dimensions of the Chinese Exclusion Act. The law placed the onus of enforcing the Act on shipmasters, with substantial penalties for ship captains who broke the law. It apparently had the desired effect: out of over 13,000 immigrant mariners who legally entered the country between 1899 and 1902, exactly three were Chinese.[5] The term "legally" is very important here; a close look at American-flagged ships such as the Pacific Mail Company's SS *Mongolia* reveals that many more Chinese mariners found their way into the country illicitly, often with the complicity of other Chinese seafarers who hid them among their number in return for hefty fees. In 1914, an anonymous informant told American customs authorities that the *Mongolia*'s Chinese boatswain harbored 8 stowaways, a fireman 25, the head waiter 20, and that white officers such as the chief engineer received $100 in gold per stowaway to remain silent.[6]

Given the illicit nature of much of this movement, and the transient nature of seafarers, forging a convincing narrative of the Chinese-American maritime experience offers historians some challenges. Furthermore, the immigrants themselves left few written records of their own, a problem compounded in this instance by language. Thus, while we have Frank Besse's account of carrying Chinese passengers to America in 1882 in the ship *William J. Rotch*, there is a definite scarcity of Chinese accounts of such voyages, especially from the viewpoint of Asian seamen working on American vessels.[7] Second, while the historiography of the Chinese-American experience is rich and increasingly growing, the maritime dimension of that experience is largely ignored. In part this may be because like many immigrant groups Chinese Americans tend to emphasize their success as a "model minority"—and seafaring does not play much of a role in a narrative of bourgeois respectability.[8] An example of this occurred in 1975, at the first national conference on the history of the Chinese in America. Only one paper presented was dedicated to anything maritime, and that was by a non-Asian: Charles A. Nash presented his research on "China Gangs" in the Alaska canneries.[9] In fact, fisheries remain almost the only marine element commonly explored in the history of Asian Americans. For example, Ronald Takaki's *Strangers from a Different Shore* neglects any reference to shipping or the merchant marine. Its only concession to seafaring is a small section dealing with the passage of Asian immigrants across the Pacific, and an even smaller section on Filipinos in the Alaskan salmon canneries.[10]

The West Coast Chinese community that fished in coastal waters or worked in shoreside canning plants is a good starting point from which to consider these immigrants' maritime connections. Such is the case because they were a visible, recorded, and remembered presence. Government agencies and other white observers, many with little sympathy for Asian immigrants, reported that well into the 1890s, as much as a third of all California fishermen were Chinese.[11] Perhaps the most notable observer was David S. Jordan, a young scientist who would become a very influential ichthyologist and president of Stanford University.[12] Jordan compiled a report on West Coast Chinese fishermen for George Brown Goode's seven-volume *Fisheries and Fishery Industries of the United States*, a monumental effort that investigated the commercial, environmental, technological, and societal aspects of the nation's fisheries as part of the 1880 U.S. Census.

Jordan's report reflected a number of prejudices held by many Americans against the Chinese. First, he commented on the squalor in which Chinese fishermen lived, but this was a common feature of many fishing communities, which were proverbial for their poverty. More noteworthy were his comments that the "Chinese take risks in stormy weather which no white man in this region would dream of taking."[13] This off-hand remark played on the stereotype that Asians valued human life less highly than whites. No account is taken for the grinding poverty that forced these fishermen to go out in wretched conditions to fish or to recover valuable gear.

More troubling yet is Jordan's labeling of Chinese "avarice." Jordan charged that the Chinese had virtually wiped out the abalone in southern California, and threatened other fisheries with the use of fine-meshed nets imported from China. Jordan concluded that the "Chinese caring nothing for the future fisheries." He never connected the fact that discriminatory laws that denied citizenship and land ownership to most Chinese meant they had no stake in future fisheries. This separated the Chinese fishermen from other ethnic groups on the West Coast. Italian immigrants, for example, while only marginally "white" by the standards of the day, could become citizens, and could and did petition the California legislature as early as 1876 to curb what they perceived as the wasteful practices of the Chinese fishermen. In so doing, Italians bolstered their own claims to membership in a larger white community that partially defined itself by preserving natural resources from exploitation by outsiders.

The white claim to preserving resources, however, falls apart under scrutiny. For example, Jordan never censured the American fish-buyers and others who facilitated Chinese fishermen in their wasteful practices. Arthur McEvoy revealed in his seminal work, *The Fisherman's Problem,* that California's legislative efforts to preserve fish stocks in the late nineteenth century were actually part of a larger state and federal effort to chase the Chinese from the West Coast. While California's legislature used a variety of environmental laws to hound the Chinese fishermen out of the state, the federal government worked to halt the flow of immigrants. In 1880 the California legislature passed a law that prohibited Chinese from fishing in California waters; in 1882 Congress passed the Chinese Exclusion Act. In 1899 the California Fish and Game Commission prohibited shrimp fishing from May to September—exactly when Chinese fishermen wanted to dry their catch of shrimp in the sun. Congress assisted with legislation such as the McCreary Act of 1893, which defined fishermen as laborers, who thus could be excluded from the country under the Chinese Exclusion Act. Further California laws banned exporting shrimp in 1901, and delivered the coup de grace to the Chinese fishermen in a 1911 law that forbade the export of fish to China and the use of Chinese-style nets.[14] The casual violence that accompanied California's enforcement of these environmental laws is apparent in Jack London's autobiographical short story "Yellow and White."[15]

Jordan's report on the salmon packing industry on the Columbia River also reveals the degree of racism Asians faced. About 3,000 seasonal Chinese workers labored in packing plants, supervised by white managers, foremen, and bookkeepers. Jordan claimed, "No other race of people could work at such [low] rates and upon such terms as these, and in the present state of things but for Chinese labor the canneries must needs be closed." American society valued the Chinese only for their cheap labor in the canneries; Jordan noted that it was generally understood that any Chinese caught fishing in the Columbia would be "killed on sight."[16] Jordan's views on the Chinese in the salmon canneries were not unusual. Rudyard Kipling in his travels to a West Coast salmon cannery dehumanized the Chinese workers as "yellow devils" with "yellow, crooked fingers."[17] Cannery owners who sought to maximize profits through automation also dehumanized their workers when they bought an automated fish-butchering device named the "Iron Chink."[18]

Nonetheless, while often reviled by the whites and sometimes in conflict with other groups, the Chinese remained an important part of the West Coast fisheries; as late as 1912, nearly 2,400 Chinese worked in Alaska's salmon canning industry, who garnered over a half million dollars in payroll.[19] The Chinese were often widely despised in these communities, yet they were also vital to their prosperity, for few others were willing to engage in the grueling labor called for in the canneries.[20] The Chinese Exclusion Act of 1882, which was regularly renewed into the twentieth century, thus posed a dilemma for the cannery owners, who's source of labor gradually dried up. While in the 1880s virtually all of the cannery labor was Chinese, by 1912 only 40 percent was Chinese, and other groups such as Filipinos, Japanese, Puerto Ricans, and Mexicans began to replace them, but in insufficient numbers. Thus, by 1912 the cannery owners called for the repeal of the Chinese Exclusion Act.[21]

The sum of these white views of Chinese fishermen is clear. It was held that the Chinese, as perpetual foreigners, had no interest in stewarding fish stocks; as a presumably temporary presence, they would destroy local fish stocks and then move on. The white community, however, as the presumed permanent population of the West Coast, could somehow be trusted to preserve fish stocks. Furthermore, the Chinese were at the bottom of a multi-tiered system that placed whites firmly in control of the means of production; Chinese rose within that framework only as newer Asian and nonwhite groups entered at the bottom of the system.[22]

While cannery owners and operators might argue for more cheap Chinese workers, working-class whites on the West Coast often viewed the Chinese as competitors, and serious racial tensions between whites and Asians developed.[23] San Francisco's white-dominated labor community criticized the Chinese for their "bad moral habits, their low grades of development, their filth, their vices, their race differences from the Caucasians, and their willing status as slaves" and actively called for their removal from the entire Pacific Coast.[24] The idea was prominent enough in California state politics to became a plank in political platforms, as when one party proclaimed that "we find the presence of the Chinese in our midst as an unmixed evil, ruinous alike to the people and the state," and called for the abolition of the Pacific Mail Company's federal subsidy unless it rid itself of its Chinese sailors.[25]

By 1905 Chinese mariners dominated the American transpacific steamship lines in what were known as "mixed crews," featuring white American officers and Chinese unlicensed personnel. For example, the steamer *Tremont* had white American licensed officers in the deck, engine, and stewards departments, but Chinese firemen, sailors, and kitchen and pantry staff.[26] White shipping executives and officers consistently praised their Chinese crews as capable seamen, and preferred them to whites for their "temperance and servility."[27] White labor leaders, however, strongly opposed all Asiatic seamen, but singled out the Chinese as the greatest threat in driving whites from the stokeholds, decks, saloons, and galleys of transpacific shipping. When one man tried to argue for inclusion of Asian seamen at a meeting of the Sailors' Union of the Pacific, howls and laughter drowned him out and the chairman ruled him out of order.[28]

Some Scandinavian seafarers proved especially vocal in criticizing the Chinese, and the most powerful and articulate of these voices was Andrew Furuseth, the nation's foremost advocate for merchant seamen. Furuseth, a Norwegian immigrant and career sailor, was an important labor leader who repeatedly appeared before Congress to advocate changes that improved working conditions for American seafarers. His success in pushing through the Seamen's Act of 1915 earned him the sobriquet "Abraham Lincoln of the Seas." Yet Furuseth, who was thoroughly unforgiving of those of Asian extraction, was a determined and largely effective opponent of Chinese mariners working on American-flagged vessels. As early as 1898, he petitioned President McKinley to remove Chinese seafarers from the U.S. Army's transports. In response, the War Department promptly fired its visible Chinese deck force, but retained the less visible firemen, cooks, and waiters.[29] Furuseth's determination to eliminate the use of Asian seafarers is reflected in a conversation with R.P. Schwerin of the Pacific Mail Company, in which he allegedly said, "Mr. Schwerin, I do not care if there is not an American ship on the Pacific Ocean; I shall do everything I can to stop every American ship, if it has to be sailed with Chinese crews."[30]

Furuseth was particularly critical of the supposed ability of Chinese mariners to react to a crisis. In May 1900, Furuseth testified before a Congressional committee that Asian seamen were practically useless in a storm or other emergency, and that they did not have the "self-control, nor the coolness, nor the courage, nor the strength of the average white man."[31] In 1902, Furuseth's racist proclivities surfaced at the Congressional hearings to renew the Chinese Exclusion Acts, and testified that "I do not think it is safe to put your merchant marine of the Pacific into the keeping of the Chinese, and unless you adopt some law that will give it to the whites, there is where it will go."[32] Notably he failed, and the 1902 renewal of the Chinese Exclusion Act did not forbid Chinese seamen from working on U.S.-flagged vessels, despite the alleged panic among Chinese sailors in the sinking of the SS *City of Rio de Janeiro* in 1901. In 1912, the same year that the *Titanic* sank, Furuseth wrote a newspaper article in which he claimed that in shipboard emergencies, Chinese sailors rescued men first on the basis that a man had present value, then children because they had potential value, and women last, because "a woman is never of any value, what's the use of bothering with saving her, anyhow?"[33] Such claims by a leader in seamen's reform speak volumes about the centrality of race in the Chinese maritime experience.

Much in the same way that California's environmental laws were an attempt to get rid of Chinese fishermen, Furuseth's efforts to reform labor laws to protect mariners were also an attempt to exclude Chinese seafarers from American ships. Furuseth engineered the widely acclaimed "Seaman's Act" of 1915 along with progressive reformer Robert LaFollette in such a way that it virtually barred Asian seamen from American-flagged ships with an English language test. For example, when the Pacific Mail Company's SS *China* put into San Francisco in 1915, 35 of the 154 Chinese in its crew failed the language test, and even then labor organizations complained that many passed the test through the "kindness and indulgence" of the clergymen who administered it.[34]

Shipping company executives and officers responded to Furuseth's attacks with statements about the low cost and efficiency of Chinese crews. In 1905, Pacific Mail representatives claimed that using such a mixed crew versus a presumably all-white American crew saved the company about $65,000 per ship per year; for five ships, for a total of over $300,000 per year—a large sum for the age.[35] Not only were the Chinese paid less, but in one of the curious practices of the day, white Americans received their pay in gold, while the Chinese received their pay in silver dollars—a significant difference because gold dollars were worth more. Chinese sailors could be hired at Hong Kong for $15.00 in Mexican silver a month, or the equivalent of $7.50 in gold, while a white sailor hired in California cost $30.00 gold per month.[36] The captain of the *Tremont* estimated that while he paid a Chinese fireman or sailor $6.00 silver per month, a white sailor received $35.00 and a white fireman $40.00 in gold. Chinese sailors ate differently, too, and compared with a white crew that cost Pacific Mail over $125,000 less a year for their fleet. On board the *Tremont,* it cost $3.00 per month to feed a Chinese sailor, mostly on rice, while it cost up to $20.00 per month to feed a white American seaman. Pacific Mail thus saved a substantial $425,000 per annum by employing Chinese seamen.[37]

The racist assumptions of shipowners and officers were also revealed when they testified to the abilities of Chinese seafarers. While they thought the Chinese were diligent workers, they believed men of European extraction were capable of doing 10-25 percent more work in the engine room, while in the deck force they were fully equivalent in terms of standing watch, and better at cleaning than white sailors because they required less supervision. The representative of Pacific Mail claimed that the Chinese were "more effective than a European sailor—and I know our captains would bear me out in this statement—as being most competent sailors, both fair weather and foul."[38]

Congress ultimately concluded "it can not be wise to surrender to Orientals the forecastles of American ships engaged in trade with the Far East" and urged a subsidy system that would save American ships "for our own race."[39] Apart from the racial issue and the "right of American seamen to protection from ruination," the committee was concerned that in hiring Asians it was training aliens in seamanship operations. The U.S. Navy was having a hard time recruiting experienced sailors and wanted a white merchant marine to provide a pool of skilled mariners in case of war.[40]

Despite the efforts of labor leaders like Furuseth and the suggestions of Congressional committees, Chinese mariners remained on board American vessels into the 1920s, when Furuseth attacked them in Congressional hearings again, citing the tendency of Chinese seafarers to smuggle stowaways onboard ships in Asia, and to smuggle narcotics into West Coast ports.[41] He battled with Dollar Lines over the racial composition of steamship crews, and he complained to the Department of Labor when that company displaced some 500 Americans crewmembers with Chinese. Outraged congressmen investigating the matter pointed out that federal law considered American-flagged ships as U.S. territory, and therefore the Chinese Exclusion Act should be applied, until it was pointed out that the Act was focused within "the limits of the United States," and not all American territory. The Dollar Line also skirted the LaFollette/Seamen's Act that called for the crew to speak the same language as the officers by hiring officers who spoke Chinese—a clever inversion of the law's intent.[42]

Furuseth's Seamen's International Union continued to oppose Asian seamen, asking immigration officials to search for, arrest, and deport Chinese sailors into the 1930s.[43] By then few Chinese seafarers served on U.S. ships, and those that remained found that federal officials banned them from even setting foot in the United States.

The Chinese who remained on American-flagged vessels in the 1930s mostly worked in the steward's department, because white passengers preferred Chinese "boys" as stewards and waiters.[44] The term "boy" is instructive; it indicates the patronizing attitude of whites that either infantilized them as perpetual children or otherwise diminished their manhood by deeming them effeminate and servile. To many white observers, Chinese crewmembers were hardworking and largely effective; they could be brave and uncomplaining. The stereotype of the Chinese was that they were moderate drinkers, but inveterate gamblers, and many whites were critical of the Pacific Mail Company's policy of providing opium dens for the Chinese on its steamers.[45]

An example of the response of white passengers to Chinese crew is found in Wilbur J. Chamberlain's account of his 1900 voyage across the Pacific on the steamer *City of Peking*, which had white officers and Chinese crew. Chamberlain, a reporter for the *New York Sun*, was crossing the Pacific to report on the Boxer Rebellion in 1900, and he recorded his journey in a number of letters to his wife and sister, who published them after his death at an early age.[46]

As an experienced journalist, Chamberlain had a keen eye for details. Like white passengers on other vessels, he praised the Chinese for their hard-working ways and reiterated the commonly held belief that they were willing and obliging servants. Curiosity led him to explore the quarters of Chinese passengers on the ship, including "the joint," as the vessel's opium den was called. But the Chinese did not charm Chamberlain, who ridiculed their eating habits by proclaiming they ate "like hogs."[47]

Whatever good will Chamberlain had for the Chinese evaporated when the crew of the *City of Peking* became restless. The exact cause of the problem is unknown, but the outbreak of the so-called Boxer Rebellion in China seems to have been the root of the problem, and it was exacerbated by several hundred Chinese who boarded the ship in Hawai'i. This behavior manifested itself in "ugly" talk and an assault by a Chinese fireman on a white engineering officer. The officers placed the fireman in irons, shackling both his hands and feet, and confined him on the bridge. The officers largely succeeded in keeping the news about the incident away from the female passengers as they prepared for the coming trouble.

Chamberlain at this point becomes vague, but somehow the officers became aware that the "mutiny" would be attempted at noon on a certain day, starting with the firemen and coal-passers in the engine spaces. In some ways it was the optimum time for an uprising. Both watches would be awake, as would the Chinese passengers, and there naturally would be some confusion as the two watches shifted about. But how did the officers know the exact timing of the "mutiny?" Somebody must have talked to the officers, almost assuredly one of the bi-lingual Chinese who oversaw their countrymen and delivered orders from the officers. Much like slave revolts, someone almost always informed, either for greed or a sense of false consciousness that led them to betray their messmates. Whatever the reason, the white officers were ready. A few minutes before noon, the white officers arranged for the Chinese deck force to go forward to work and ordered the steward's department to complete chores aft. A few extra whites "lounged around" the engine room and stokehold, where the trouble was expected to start.

As the watches changed, some 28 Chinese of the new watch confronted the white engineering officer and announced they would not work until their shackled shipmate was freed. The biggest Chinese fireman on watch made the announcement, and his posture made it clear he and his watch mates were ready to fight. The response of the engineering officer, in the classic style of taking out the biggest man in the crowd, was to strike the Chinese spokesman, who dropped to the deck plates unconscious. According to Chamberlain, the fight quickly went out of the would-be mutineers, but they refused to work, so the officers put all 28 in irons. Seeing the hopelessness of the situation, the Chinese agreed to go back to work. The "mutiny" was over, bar some grumbling on the part of the Chinese.

As Chamberlain put it, the whites on the *City of Peking* did indeed have their "hands full with the Chinese."[48] The incident was a small one, but it highlights the potential for violence that challenges the stereotype of the Chinese as perpetually docile. Like other sailors the world over, these crewmen was ready to defend their rights, but as was commonly the case, they were quickly cowed by harsh authority, quickly proscribed. They frequently lashed out with violence at their white officers, and given the ease with which the white officers snuffed out the intended mutiny, one must assume they were used to this sort of thing. Indeed, they made light of it, and in a heavy-handed prank tricked some male passengers into preparing for a mutiny that was already over.

The above three vignettes shed some light on three larger themes of the Chinese maritime experience. First, it can be said that anti-Asian racism was not solely the province of blue-collar workers. Esteemed native-born college professors and congressmen also viewed Asians as outsiders, along with Italian immigrant fishermen and Scandinavian forecastle hands. Second, it was not necessarily conservatives who sought to exclude the Chinese, but progressives who deeply involved in reform as well. Third, this racism continued well into the twentieth century. Chinese seamen were not welcome into any seafaring union until 1936, when the National Maritime Union opened its doors to seamen of all races.[49] Additionally, the immigration exclusion laws were not dropped until 1943, when China was an embattled ally and there was little chance of immigrants actually arriving.

The story of anti-Chinese racism is becoming better understood and more widely acknowledged. Textbooks increasingly include the story of Chinese persecution in their contents. Too often, however, that story relates only to railroad construction crews or agricultural laborers. There are important maritime dimensions to the Chinese-American experience that remain to be explored, and the more maritime historians uncover the lives of these little-known seafarers, the greater will be the understanding of issues of race and ethnicity in the American story.

These Baltimore oyster shuckers, ca. 1890, may be some of the women who spent their long winters doing similar work in Biloxi.
(Mystic Seaport, 1991.5.3)

11

Sharing the Work: Biloxi Women in the Seafood Industry

Deanne Stephens Nuwer

Biloxi's seafood industry actually had its beginnings in 1867 when George Dunbar, a New Orleanian, experimented with canning shrimp on a floating factory in the Barataria Bay of Louisiana. He towed his processing plant to the shrimping site in order to take advantage of the abundant catches in that area. Once they were canned, he could then transport the shrimp upriver to New Orleans, a ready market for the crustaceans. Dunbar is credited with canning experiments that first used muslin liners in the cans and later parchment protectors so that the shrimp did not turn black as a result of the reaction between their acids and the metal cans. Once these canning methods proved successful, the seafood industry expanded along the entire Gulf of Mexico, creating a commercial enterprise founded on traditional gender roles and supported by conservative immigrant cultures.

When entrepreneurs in Biloxi, Mississippi, decided to create that city's first cannery in 1881 by taking advantage of the rich shrimp and oyster bounty in the Gulf of Mexico, they based their operation on existing cannery technology. However, two other components added to their successful Biloxi enterprise: the New Orleans, Mobile & Chattanooga Railroad that had been built to connect New Orleans and Mobile, Alabama, in 1870, and the invention of artificial ice technology in 1875.[1] With expanded railroad service and refrigeration, Laz Lopez, F. W. Elmer, W. K. M. Dukate, William Gorenflo, and James Maycock started the first cannery in Biloxi with $8,000. The facility opened at the head of Reynoir Street on the Back Bay of Biloxi, canning oysters and shrimp and offering raw shrimp in bulk.

Dukate had traveled to Baltimore, Maryland, to learn more about the seafood industry, and with this new knowledge, the entrepreneurs' endeavor succeeded under the name of Lopez, Elmer & Company.[2] The seafood factory also added to the cultural diversity of the Biloxi area through the use of seasonal workers from the Baltimore region, particularly the Polish and Croatians.

As Lopez, Elmer & Company expanded its operations to include ethnic seasonal workers, it embraced established nineteenth-century gender parameters in the workplace. In the seafood industry, women were mostly relegated to the seafood factory, peeling and packing shrimp, while men harvested the crustaceans from the Mississippi Sound and Gulf of Mexico. These established gender lines included the oystermen who tonged and dredged the bivalves from their myriad coastal beds and the women who shucked the oysters and packed them for shipping.

For Biloxi to develop its profitable seafood industry, entrepreneurs established business practices that facilitated success. In 1890, seafood factory-owners recruited new plant workers and fishermen from Baltimore. Biloxi seafood factory-owners were aware of the Polish workers there because they had studied the successful Baltimore market and had decided that these workers were vital to Maryland's flourishing seafood business. Therefore, they hired them for the expanding Biloxi enterprise. These Polish workers were at first seasonal laborers who worked nine months during the seafood-packing season and then were shipped back to work in Baltimore during the summer off-season in the Gulf. Margaret Filipich Soper, a lifelong Biloxian who worked in the canneries, remembers that the season ended about May.[3] The seafood factories, which numbered 12 by 1902, paid the workers' train passage and provided living quarters or camps of row houses to accommodate them, but wages were generally low. Another Biloxian, Amelia "Sis" Eleuteris, recalled that the Polish workers spoke English and "were good natured people." She also commented that these workers built their own brick communal ovens on the grounds of the camps and baked their own bread since camp living provided few amenities. Locals called the camps "Hotel d'Bohemia." According to Eleuteris, the wages of the Polish workers were "pitiful," yet they continued to work in Biloxi for 28 years as itinerant laborers.[4]

Some Biloxians were fearful of the seasonal workers. Sister Mary Adrienne Curet recalled that when the Polish workers arrived from Baltimore, mule-drawn wagons would haul them and their possessions through the town from the train stop to their camps located near the factories on East Beach of Back Bay. As a young girl then, she was warned by her mother not to go near the workers as the parade of wagons headed to their destinations. "We didn't dare go to the fence [to watch them] because we were scared of them," and "we weren't allowed to go around the camps."[5] Another woman who lived in Biloxi for her entire lifetime recalled that the Polish wore unusual "blousey shirts" and that "they used to like to drink a lot."[6] Certainly, the more exotic culture of the Polish migrant workers attracted attention.

Eventually, some of these seasonal workers chose to stay in Biloxi and work in the seafood industry permanently. By 1904, Biloxi claimed to be the "Seafood Capital of the World." Perhaps this boasting right originated with the Barataria Cannery. It won the Gold Medal Award at the Paris Exposition in 1900 for Best Canned Goods and later earned a Highest Award at the Pan-American Exposition on Sea Products. On the other hand, the claim might rest on the volume of production at the time.[7] Whatever the origin, the seafood industry in Biloxi flourished as a result of its seasonal and permanent workers.

According to Aimee Schmidt, the seafood camps where the workers lived "resembled the paternalistic mill towns that emerged in the Piedmont region of the Southeast [United States]. They were self-contained, self-sufficient communities that worked to the advantage of the owners who provided their employees with basic needs."[8] A 1905 Biloxi city directory listed five "Bohemian Camps" in the city, with most of them on East Beach, or the road that paralleled the Mississippi Sound and where the majority of the factories could be found.[9]

A company-owned store offered rudimentary shopping opportunities for the seafood workers, but it also kept them bound to the factory-owner as credit extensions always left the workers in debt to the company store. Therefore, factory-owners benefited at the expense of the workers. This system of operations continued until after World War I, when two other immigrant groups arrived in Biloxi, one from the Dalmatian Coast of what was then the Austrian-Hungarian Empire and the other from the Cajun region of Louisiana.

Unfortunately, the United States Immigration Service did not distinguish immigrants from the Austrian-Hungarian Empire prior to 1918, so exact numbers for these ethnic groups are unobtainable.[10] However, census officials distinguished between Austrian Italians,

Austrian Slovenians, and Austrian Poles in their reports. For example, in the 1910 Federal Census, Katrina Treoiotich is listed as an Austrian Slovak, as is her husband Mike. Her family was typical of those immigrants who came to Biloxi from the Austrian-Hungarian Empire. She worked as an oyster opener in a cannery, while both of her sons were boatmen on oyster dredgers. Her husband was a laborer. The language spoken in the household was "Slav."[11] Many of the immigrants originally were rural landless peasants, sailors, political refugees, or men who were avoiding conscription in their homeland. Slavonian immigration reached its peak in 1917, while at approximately the same time, seafood factory-owners recruited Louisiana Cajuns from cities such as New Iberia and Lafayette to work in Biloxi's burgeoning seafood industry. Experiencing dire economic times resulting from a failed sugar crop, many Cajuns packed up and relocated to the Mississippi Gulf Coast.[12] When they arrived, they settled in the Point Cadet region of the city, side-by-side with the Slavonians. Mixed into the neighborhood were the Polish. This intercultural interaction created a unique blend even while the ethnicities maintained their individual identities.

Many immigrants to the Mississippi Coast from the collapsed Austrian-Hungarian Empire included Croats, Serbs, and Slavonians. Margaret Filipich Soper's family exemplifies the experience of the people from this region who settled in Biloxi. According to Soper, her parents' marriage was the first between a Slavonian and a French Cajun. Her father, Stephen, was born in Milna Brac, Dalmatia, and arrived in the United States in 1907. After coming to Biloxi, he met and married Clara Leleaux, who was from Cajun Louisiana. Soper does not know the date of their marriage, but she is sure her parents were married in St. Michael's Catholic Church on Point Cadet in Biloxi. Her father eventually owned two fishing boats, the *Nicholas F.* and the *Milna.* Obviously, he was proud of his Croatian heritage as he named one boat after his father and the other after his birthplace. Both of these boats originally were schooners, but later they were converted to gasoline-engine power. Margaret's mother worked in the canneries until her death at age 29; her father continued to shrimp and oyster until 1934, when he died at the age of 39. With the untimely deaths of her parents, Margaret lived with her grandmother Filipich until she married.[13]

Margaret remembered that, in the off-season between oyster and shrimp harvesting times, her family always had watermelons because her father hauled them on his boats from Florida to New Orleans, holding back a few for this children. Her family was an extended one, with relatives living on Pine Street in the heart of the Point Cadet or "Point" area of Biloxi, located in the easternmost portion of the city. Eventually, four Filipich brothers lived in close proximity to one another, with the oldest, Stephen, living with his parents after they arrived in Biloxi. Margaret explained that it was customary for the eldest son to bring his bride home and live with his parents in order to take care of them in the traditional manner.[14]

Because Margaret's mother lived with her Croatian in-laws, she had to learn their language in order to communicate in the house, as she was the only one who spoke Cajun French. As a result, Margaret and her siblings learned Croatian but did not learn her mother's language. However, she did acquire French customs, such as traditional cooking methods.[15] This one Croatian/Cajun culturally blended family ultimately was not unusual in the Biloxi Point region as the seafood industry enticed more immigrants.

By the 1920s, clear gender lines of labor supported the Biloxi seafood industry as the various cultural groups settled into a rhythm of life dependent upon harvesting seasons. By that time, 15 canneries operated in Biloxi, packing in an average annual season 15,000,000 cans of oysters and 130,000 cases or 40,000 barrels of shrimp. Fifty Biloxi schooners plied the Gulf waters with five-man crews in the winter oyster season, while 200 trawl boats with two-man crews caught shrimp in the summer months. The combined annual catch amounted to $3,000,000.[16] Living in single-family dwellings then instead of camps, the immigrant groups clearly maintained divisions of labor. Crews on the boats remained exclusively male, partly because of historical traditional foundations but mostly because of the physical strength involved in working a boat. Factory work was predominately the female domain.

The crew and captain on a shrimp boat operated seines, nets, sails, and dredges that required physical strength. Younger boys who could not contribute to the effort often worked with the women in the factories until they were old enough to secure an apprenticeship as a deckhand on a boat. During a young man's apprenticeship, he learned the art of shrimping and the various tasks in operating the boat and harvesting and storing the catch. More-experienced fishermen mentored the apprentices until they, too, became part of the crew or a captain.

Not all outings on the boats were for harvesting. Soper remembered that her father often would load up his family on the *Nicholas F.* and sail to Deer Island on Sunday. This island is less than one mile from the east end of Biloxi where the family lived. There they would picnic while "scrubbing" the sails. She stated that it was hard work, but with the family working together and picnicking, it was "not so bad." According to her, these sail-cleaning trips were the only times she was ever on a fishing boat, and she has no recollection of any woman ever crewing a boat in Biloxi.[17]

Women were vital to the Biloxi seafood industry even if they did not crew on boats. Once a boat docked at one of the many canneries with its catch of shrimp or haul of oysters, the women went to work. Each seafood plant along Biloxi's Back Bay and Front Beach had its own distinctive factory whistle to alert workers that the boats were in at its wharves, laden with shrimp or oysters. Whenever a factory whistle screamed, regardless of the time, its particular workers or those who needed extra money would show up for work to begin processing the catch. Each factory first allowed its regular pickers or shuckers opportunities to work; then, if the catch was large enough, it offered other workers a place in the picking or shucking rooms.

According to Murella Hebert Powell, who grew up on the Point, trucks often picked up some of the workers to take to the factory while others walked.[18] Children aged 14 could receive a legal work card to labor in the factory, but younger children also worked illegally. Soper recalled that a Mr. Moore, who was probably an inspector for the United States Labor Department, would make rounds through the factories, looking for underage workers. She laughingly explained that all of the laborers knew when he was inspecting, so younger workers who did not have legal work papers would simply hide in the factory or under the picking tables until he passed through their areas. They then resumed their jobs when he left.[19] In many Point families, all members had to work to survive, and that included those younger members.

Working in the factories at a young age often meant that children did not receive an education, especially young girls. Soper is an example of that trend. She attended St. Michael's School through the eighth grade, but then she was told by her grandmother Filipich that she could no longer go to school because of economic hard times. St. Michael's tuition was $.10 per day, and the family needed the money that she could potentially earn in the factory. She indicated that not being able to finish school was one of the biggest disappointments in her life. Her devout Catholic family apparently did not consider sending Margaret to Howard II Elementary School, the public facility also located in her immediate neighborhood.[20] Oftentimes older children living and working on the Point went to the factory before school in the wee morning hours and then returned home still early enough to clean up a bit and go on to school. Their mothers continued to work at the factory while the children readied themselves for school and then walked to St. Michael's, Howard II, or Central High School further downtown.[21] After school, they then went back to work if any was still available. Margaret, however, could not continue her education as her family needed all of her salary when she could work. When asked what she did with her "shrimp nickels," she responded, "Give them to my grandmother Filipich."[22]

After workers carted the shrimp into the factories, rows of women and girls peeled them by hand. Since childcare facilities did not exist, women brought their small children to work with them, often placing the children in seafood boxes for safekeeping while they did their work.[23] Lucretia Buzalich Lee recalled that her mother, Margaret Trebotich, would arise early in the morning when the whistles pierced the air, load her in a buggy along with some food for the day, and walk to the factory, pushing the buggy. As a young child, she remembered a potbellied stove in the factory around which the mothers positioned the babies and young children to keep them warm in the cold factory. Some of the children would be in buggies sleeping, and some would be in makeshift playpens, all bundled for warmth.[24] Since the entire family was involved in the seafood business, no one remained at home to watch the young children while their mothers worked. With their husbands on the boats or unloading at the docks, the women simply brought their children to work with them, regardless of the factory conditions.

The working environment in the factories was "miserable," according to Grace Gaudet Hebert. Hebert recalled that the heat in the summer and the cold in the winter were often overwhelming.[25] Another Biloxi woman, Addie Blanchard Leduc, also verified how hot the factories would be in the summer shrimp season. Leduc also remembered that in the summer months, factories often did not have enough ice to keep the shrimp cool, and maggots hatched in the shrimp and in the peelings on the floor. She recounted that often she would be standing in shrimp peelings up to her knees on some days as the peelers had no where to put them except to drop them on the floor.[26]

Factory owners paid the workers one cent for every pound of shrimp they picked or every pound of oysters they shucked. The picked shrimp and shucked oysters were put into a "cup" that held approximately five pounds when full. Holes in the cup allowed the juices to drip out onto the floor where the workers stood. Once the worker peeled or shucked enough to fill her cup, she turned it into the factory foremen for her nickel. She was paid on the spot. This process was repeated until the catch was completely processed. Margaret Soper recalled that in the factory she and her friends would "race one another to get a bucket filled and make the most money." The acid from the shrimp juice often reacted with the nickel and turned it green. The green "shrimp nickels" were certainly distinct from others. Earlier in the business, factories paid the workers with brass tokens or "shrimp checks" with the company name on one side and the designated amount on the other. Factory workers were suppose to turn in these tokens for currency but often did not. As a result, the merchants in Biloxi and even local banks began to accept these tokens in lieu of currency. Because everyone in the city knew their value, women were able to shop at the company store or local merchants and use tokens as money. Eventually, the federal government forced the plants to stop issuing these tokens as it considered them counterfeit money because they became a major form of currency in Biloxi. At that point, the factories then began paying in "shrimp nickels." Packers, however, were hourly wage-earners and collected their checks on Saturdays. Leduc recalled going to the factory office to pick up her check if she had packed seafood during the week. Sometimes she sent her daughter to pick up the entire neighborhood's checks on Saturday mornings. As most of her neighbors were relatives, this worked out well for everyone.[27]

Seafood factory-owners did not provide workers with the necessary tools to complete their work. Women who worked in the picking and shucking plants told of having to furnish their own cups if they were peeling shrimp, or their own gloves, knives, and cups if they were shucking oysters. Factories did not supply the long, heavy aprons worn by most workers to offer some protection and to help them keep clean, but that was nearly impossible, as the juices from the shrimp and oysters seeped everywhere. Powell recalled that her grandmother made her own seafood apron out of flour sacks.[28] Presumably, most women did the same thing, as money was usually not available to the Point women for items that could be handmade

The smell was often overpowering, as the decomposition of shells and bits of seafood created a strong stench in and around the factories. One worker stated, however, that she "got used to the smell"; it was the smell of money.[29] After the shrimp were peeled, they were blanched in a brine solution, cooled and then hand-packed into cans. Women who worked in the factories learned that if they soaked their hands in an alum solution, their skin would toughen, and they would not be as likely to suffer cuts from handling the shrimp and cans. One woman acknowledged that the solution made the hands "a little rough," but it was a necessity in the factory.[30] Other women wore "finger stalls," which were protective coverings worn only on their fingers.[31] The cans were then sealed, pressure-cooked in a large iron drum to kill any remaining bacteria, and finally packed into boxes to be shipped out by railroad. The women labeled the cans by hand before boxing them for transport.

Work in the factories was not easy. Childcare was unheard of for working mothers. Oftentimes the factories were cold, especially in the winter months of oyster harvesting. Women would resort to wrapping their legs in newspaper over their heavy stockings to keep warm. The shrimps' outer shells often cut the hands of the women as they peeled the crustaceans. The acid from the shrimp also burned the workers' hands, as they usually had multiple skin abrasions because of their work, despite the alum soaking.

Biloxi women who worked in the seafood factories had a difficult life. "Pickin" and "shucking" required stamina and strength since the hours were long and the working conditions were rough. Women were strong on the Point. Powell recalled seeing her grandmother walk home from the factory, carrying a sack of oysters on her back. After she climbed the stairs to their Crawford Street home, she would throw the sack of oysters on the front porch, planning to shuck them later for dinner after she had had her breakfast of coffee and French bread.[32]

Life for women on the Point rhythmically followed the harvesting season. They cared for their families and worked in the factories so that their children would have a better life. Their goal was to help their children move beyond seafood-factory work. One woman who had worked in the factories bragged that her daughter went to work in a bank, with clean fingernails, as if work in the factory was not a worthy employment for the younger generation of women. With little education, however, these Polish, Slavonian, and Cajun French women taught their children the lesson of hard work and lived a life based on frugality and determination. With resolve, they created close-knit neighborhoods that nurtured their children and their culture. As Grace Hebert stated, "It's what you get used to."[33]

Today the seafood industry in Biloxi is recovering from Hurricane Katrina, which flattened the Biloxi Point and many other areas in the city on August 29, 2005. Prior to that storm, the seafood industry underwent many changes. In the 1970s, Vietnamese workers and fishermen became involved in the harvesting, picking, and shucking of shrimp and oysters as the newest immigrants to the Mississippi Coast. Currently, many workers from Mexico, Central America, and South America work in the few remaining seafood enterprises, such as Gollott's on the Back Bay of Biloxi. Still, the majority of those employed in the factories are women. Since its beginnings in 1881, the Biloxi seafood industry has provided opportunities for a multitude of ethnicities that flavor Biloxi's cultural mix. Women have always been vital to its success and continue to sustain the industry.

In the 1920s, Issei and Nisei (perhaps including some future members of the Junior Outing Club) pose in front of Terminal Island's Baptist Mission, one of the institutions like the Junior Outing Club that were part of the community's cultural coalescence. (Los Angeles Maritime Museum Collection)

12

The Junior Outing Club, Nisei Identity, and the Terminal Island Fishing Community

Karen Jenks

> A motion was made; it was carried. Forty-four intended to go on the outing. Everybody going on this outing was requested to gather at the school corner, with her lunch, at 8:00 a.m. sharp. They were also told to speak English as [much as] possible during the outing.
>
> – Teruyo Hamaguchi[1]

During the 1930s, the commercial fishing industry ranked among the largest employers at the ports of Los Angeles and Long Beach. Representative of the multicultural American West, neighborhoods around San Pedro Bay reflected the participation of families of Croatian, Filipino, Italian, Japanese, and Mexican descent. The Japanese-American community on Terminal Island was a vital component: men fished, women worked in canneries, and families operated restaurants and stores that catered to maritime workers at Fish Harbor. Nisei girls, the American-born children of the Issei—the first or immigrant generation of Japanese Americans—grew up in this energetic neighborhood. The commercial fishing industry was an important part of their parents' lives, but would it be the same for Nisei daughters? How did the Terminal Island fishing community prepare girls for the future, and what did girls think about their options?

The Junior Outing Club, a club for girls in middle school at Terminal Island, reflected the community's interest in their futures. Paralleling the work of Valerie Matsumoto, this paper argues that Nisei women teenagers from Terminal Island transformed elements of ethnic Japanese and mainstream Euro-American culture into distinctive Nisei Terminal

Islander identities. The surviving minutes (1936-1942) of the Junior Outing Club provide a close-up view of this incremental process. The club offers insights into generational change and gender behavior in an ethnic fishing community, showing that even girls between about the ages of 13 and 15 were evaluating options and making choices that affected their futures. The club for girls incorporated issues familiar to the regional Japanese-American community in a way that strengthened ties in the fishing community. Their distinct identities as Nisei Terminal Islanders helped them cope with internment and strengthen community ties after World War II.

Primary sources from the fishing community make it possible to look at the club's activities as they unfolded and at the connections that surrounded the club. The Junior Outing Club minutes consist of just over 80 entries written by girls in junior high school. The handwritten entries range from a few sentences to lists and short paragraphs. Since the contents depended on what interested the club secretary and what conversations took place during meetings, the level of detail between entries is uneven. Members (and apparently the club advisor) voted at each meeting to approve them; thus the act of including a topic in the minutes seems significant. This study contextualizes the minutes with oral histories from Terminal Islanders conducted by community members in the mid-1990s. The recollections of the community were generally upbeat, reflecting the value members placed in the community and the friendships they formed there.

HISTORIOGRAPHY

This study builds on earlier studies of the Terminal Islander community and contributes to the historiographies of immigration, gender, and Asian-American studies. Studies of the Japanese-American community on Terminal Island have changed along with approaches to immigration history, from a focus on assimilation to an appreciation of cultural coalescence.[2] The fishing community formed during an era of Asian exclusion. Between 1885 and 1924, about 300,000 Japanese immigrated to the United States.[3] The Gentlemen's Agreement of 1908 stopped the immigration of Japanese laborers. After the Immigration Act of 1924, family members, including wives, could no longer join men already in the United States, although the law also stopped "the most virulent agitation against them in the [American] West."[4] Expanding a 1913 law, the California Alien Land Law of 1920 prevented the immigrant-generation Issei from leasing land or buying it as guardians. Many transferred titles to their children born in the United States, the Nisei, or second-generation Japanese Americans.[5]

Over time, Japanese-American communities in the Los Angeles region grew while coping with increasing restraints on immigration and property ownership. Although San Francisco had a larger and more settled Japanese-American population, by 1930, about 25 percent of Issei in the continental United States lived in Los Angeles.[6] John Modell concluded that there was less "active persecution" of Japanese Americans in Los Angeles than in San Francisco. The "open shop" in Los Angeles "exclude[d] Japanese from some endeavors but not from those which were important to the economy and to the smooth functioning of business in the area."[7] The Japanese-American community on Terminal Island was a significant part of the Los Angeles commercial fishing industry; perhaps this helped to mitigate attempts made at the state level to take commercial fishing licenses from Issei.

Early studies of the fishing community reflected the influence of Emory S. Bogardus and the Chicago School of Sociology. Bogardus believed that the influx of "poorer, ethnic newcomers to the region" was a cause for social concern.[8] In 1921, Edwin Bamford, a student of Bogardus, wrote of immigrants in the Los Angeles commercial fishing industry, "they live in the least desirable communities, often near Americans who, themselves, do not live according to true American standards."[9] In this passage, Bamford applied an ideal standard of American behavior and found some Euro-American communities also lacking. Kanichi Kawasaki, advised by a colleague of Bogardus, wrote in 1931, "During the past ten years much criticism has been heard about the Japanese who live in this so-called free country, the United States of America. Most of these criticisms are not based on scientific research."[10] Kawasaki grappled with assimilation as "giving as well as becoming; it also involves a union of attitudes, which enables people to think and act together."[11] With faith in the American Dream, he expressed his hope that future generations "will participate in all the activities of the United States."[12]

This study of the Junior Outing Club and the Terminal Island fishing community is one among a growing collection of studies of Japanese-American history during the years before World War II. According to David K. Yoo, this earlier period in Japanese-American history has been overshadowed by World War II. Between 1942 and 1945, the U.S. government incarcerated about 120,000 people of Japanese descent, including Terminal Islanders, in ten "War Relocation Centers" across the American West. Yoo writes that studying the prewar years connects the camps to "a racial legacy that dated to the nineteenth century" and shows how Nisei developed a subculture that "helped them to negotiate their times."[13] In 1985, Kanshi Stanley Yamashita's dissertation considered the full sweep of Terminal Islander history. He argued that the fishing community developed "group cohesion, group pride and effectively cop[ed] with outside pressures," while retaining "critical ethnic values."[14] He also considered the meaning of place among Terminal Islanders, who created a "community without physical boundaries" after World War II.[15] A former resident of Terminal Island, Yamashita blended insider information with immigration, anthropology, and ethnic studies. It is the most comprehensive study of the whole community.[16]

Since the late 1980s, historians have been focusing on unequal power across races and classes of women, and have been recovering the contributions of women of color, particularly through newfound and underutilized sources.[17] Valerie Matsumoto's research in Asian-American and women's history seems particularly relevant to this study of the Junior Outing Club. In her analysis of Japanese-American girls' clubs in Los Angeles, Matsumoto examines "the intersection of gender and racial dynamics"—Nisei girls both challenged and reflected gendered practices and racial negotiations of their time. This included taking on a "vivid symbolic role" as community representatives.[18] The activities of the Junior Outing Club also fit well with Shirley Jennifer Lim's study of Asian-American women's public culture between 1930 and 1960. Although the Junior Outing Club was influenced by mainstream popular culture, language, and etiquette conventions, Lim writes, "the adoption of such cultural practices by racial minority women cannot be interpreted merely as assimilation but must be seen as transformative social acts that constituted Asian American culture."[19] The club's activities and friendships took place within Japanese American and more specifically, Terminal Islander culture.

Historians and ethnographers are recovering the significance of women in fishing communities, but less seems to be known about the contributions of girls and how they confronted their futures. As Lisa Norling has asked in a different context, "why was it normal for young women to stay ashore, to marry those men who went to sea, and to take on the risks and burdens?"[20] This study shows some of the ways that Japanese-American girls in the Terminal Island fishing community became aware of available choices in their urban locale and made decisions and connections that affected their futures. Although the club had everything to do with the fishing community, the role of commercial fishing in the daily lives of club participants is oblique in their recorded comments. The club minutes shed some light on girls' American Dreams as they expressed them during club time. In addition, attendance records show that some girls signed up for the club but rarely or never attended. The reasons for their absences—perhaps for family responsibilities or other interests and friendships—are not recoverable from the minutes but would add insights into how girls navigated opportunities and expectations in the ethnic fishing community.

TERMINAL ISLAND

Nisei girls created the framework for their American Dreams out of friendships and shared interests, within the scope of community expectations and available opportunities. These cultural practices had a firm footing in the history of the Terminal Island community. The Japanese-American community grew along with the Los Angeles commercial fishing industry. Plentiful fish attracted Japanese-American fishermen and fishing families to San Pedro Bay. In the early twentieth century, Issei fishermen contributed the pole-fishing method for tuna, increasing the quality and quantity of fish caught.[21] A handful of Issei fishermen in the early 1900s grew into the Terminal Island community of 3,000 or more residents in the 1930s.[22] Many had family ties to fishing communities in Wakayama prefecture in Japan, and many arrived at Terminal Island from fishing and farming communities in California and the Pacific Northwest. The Terminal Island community joined a Pacific World of commercial fishing networks and family connections that stretched across the eastern Pacific, south from

San Pedro to San Diego, Mexico, Panama, and the Galápagos Islands, north to Monterey and Tacoma, and to Japan through family ties to fishing communities in the home islands.[23] These networks evidence the international impact of Japan's commercial fishing industry.

After World War I, canneries built about 350 basic "camp" houses to encourage workers to reside locally and financed the larger boats that were able to reach the increasingly distant fishing grounds.[24] Located at Fish Harbor on Terminal Island, the hub of the Los Angeles commercial fishing industry, the Japanese-American neighborhood was in the middle of the booming urban port. The waters around the island teemed with freighters, passenger liners, fishing boats, lumber schooners, and the U.S. Navy's Pacific Fleet.[25] Access from Fish Harbor to the mainland was by ferry across a 1,000-foot channel; there was also a multiethnic community on the island about a mile away from the Japanese-American community at Fish Harbor.[26] Out of 11,000 people employed in larger industries at San Pedro and Wilmington in 1934, more than 6,000 worked in the commercial fishing industry—on fishing vessels, at fish canneries, and in fresh-fish markets.[27] In 1937, San Pedro packed more cases of fishery products than all the other California ports combined: out of about 6.9 million cases, San Pedro packed about 4 million.[28]

Terminal Islanders created opportunities within racial negotiations, their ethnic fishing culture, the availability of fish, and the framework of the urban port. In the peak years before World War II, more than one-third of San Pedro fishermen were of Japanese descent.[29] In 1937, of the sixteen tuna clippers (the largest and most capitalized fishing vessels) based in San Pedro, Japanese Americans owned four and in 1940 were part of interracial crews on three clippers owned by canneries.[30] For instance, on the *Sea Boy*, a tuna clipper owned by the Franco Italian Packing Company, of a crew of about twelve, there were five Issei. They included the fish boss, Kiyoo Yamashita, an experienced mariner who was a former captain of a tuna clipper. The roster listed the master and the rest of the crew as Euro-American.[31] Issei women were "by far the majority of workers in the canneries."[32] They worked alongside women from ethnic neighborhoods across San Pedro Bay.[33] Emiko Hatashita Matsutsuyu worked as an interpreter during negotiations for Andrea Gómez, organizer of the cannery worker's union.[34] Probably using savings from her job as a cannery worker, Wai Araki owned the *America*, a small fishing boat with a crew of two: her husband, Minezo Araki, and Damaso, a Filipino.[35] Orie Mio and her husband ran two restaurants at Fish Harbor while raising four children. She recalled, "Our Mexican customers would order food in Spanish. . . . I quickly learned Spanish so that I could understand what they wanted."[36] Japanese Americans pursued opportunities in the multicultural fishing industry. However, according to Yamashita's study, multicultural relationships at work did not carry over into social relationships after work.[37]

Terminal Islanders were as self-sufficient as possible. Growing up on the island, Yukio Tatsumi recalled that Terminal Island "was a small 'haven' to us. Everyone knew each other."[38] According to Yamashita in his ethnography, "the extent of discrimination against the Japanese was complete and all encompassing." He wrote, "the probability of finding a job in one's chosen field was remote unless, in some way, it was tied into the Japanese community."[39] Japanese Americans fished, worked in canneries, and in some cases began land-based businesses at Fish Harbor. It was one of the largest, most densely populated Japanese-American neighborhoods in the Los Angeles region, a leading area for Japanese-American settlement in the United States.[40] Even so, Yamashita recalled that "within the Japanese circles, Terminal Islanders were considered subordinate," and they responded with an "island country mentality . . . suspicious of strangers, but very close-knit within the group." He also observed, "regardless of the country in which they exist, fishing communities do not seem to have much status."[41]

Children in the fishing community grew up to be self-reliant. Fishermen were away from home for between a week or two and a month or two at a time, chasing sardines, mackerel, or tuna in the eastern Pacific.[42] The fish catch was cleaned and packed as soon as it arrived. Frank Endo recalled, "My mother, like all of the ladies, had her work clothes ready at all times. . . . Upon hearing the sound of the whistle, my mother would drop whatever she was doing, change clothes and run to work with many others in the neighborhood."[43] Toshiro Izumi recalled his mother going to work at the cannery at night during the sardine season: "She noticed that I had awakened so on her way out the door, she left words that we should prepare our own breakfast and not be late for school. This was an everyday occurrence so I just nodded my head and went to sleep."[44] Orie Mio, an Issei mother of four daughters, recalled, "I can remember washing diapers on the washboard at 1 a.m. after work was done. The restaurant closed at midnight, and during sardine season, I had only about two hours of sleep. . . . Many times, my legs were so swollen that I could barely climb the stairs to our living quarters situated above the restaurant."[45]

The Junior Outing Club was part of an active world of clubs and celebrations in the close-knit community. In particular, Vicki L. Ruiz's concept of cultural coalescence is relevant to this study—through cultural coalescence, "immigrants and their children pick, borrow, retain, and create distinctive cultural forms."[46] The variety of clubs reflected cultural coalescence: Yukio Tatsumi recalled, "Traditional Japanese holidays were celebrated along with American holidays. There were colorful koi-nobori [carp windsocks] on Boy's Day, the doll display on Girl's Day and New Years family visitations."[47] Buddhist or Christian, everyone celebrated Christmas.[48] Girls joined the Junior or Senior Outing Clubs, and piano lessons and Japanese dance lessons were also popular. Some may have joined the YWCA Girls' Reserve.[49] Boys participated in sports, including baseball (San Pedro Skippers) and Kendo (fencing) leagues at championship levels, a Boy Scout drum corps, and the YMCA Friendly Indians. In addition to public school, children went to Japanese language school.[50] Community organizations increased with the growth of families. The initial organizations—a Fishermen's Hall, Baptist Mission, and Japanese Association—were joined by a public elementary school, a language school affiliated with the Baptist Mission, a Buddhist temple with language school, a Shinto Shrine, the Fujin Kai (Women's Association), the Fukei Kai (Parent Teacher Association), and Nisei clubs.[51] The Junior Outing Club for Nisei girls reflected the hopes and dreams associated with this growing community consciousness.

JUNIOR OUTING CLUB

The girls in the Junior Outing Club evaluated options and made choices, thus making the club their own. Children from the fishing community went to kindergarten and elementary school on Terminal Island. When it was time to attend junior high, they took the ferry across the channel to the mainland San Pedro. Attending the school brought new experiences, new pressures, and, for girls, the Junior Outing Club. It met about twice a month during the school year at the elementary school on Terminal Island. The club was popular: with about 55 to 65 girls enrolled in the club each year, almost every junior-high-school-aged girl in the fishing community attended most meetings. The club was a negotiation between the girls, the club's Euro-American advisor, and Issei mothers and clubwomen. Club minutes from September 25, 1936, to January 23, 1942, show how members navigated gendered expectations as Nisei and Terminal Islanders, revealing how cultural coalescence took place on a daily or incremental basis. Whenever possible, girls moved activities more in the direction of their liking. Options and decisions changed over time, reflecting changing interests and constraints as World War II approached.

Japanese-American girls' club culture contributed to the Junior Outing Club and its sister organization, the Senior Outing Club. Valerie Matsumoto's research provides insights into Nisei girls and their incursions into the public sphere in the 1920s and 1930s. Nisei girls' clubs and literary culture fostered peer networks and identities. For instance, Nisei girls in California and the American West considered the etiquette advice of columnist Mary "Deirdre" Oyama and other peer advisors in the Japanese-American press, mediating many cultural influences.[52] Matsumoto also shows how Nisei, especially young women and girls, coped with their roles as community representatives of the ethnic community. Participating in ethnic-cultural performance at public events, second-generation Japanese Americans affirmed ethnic immigrant culture but "were often 'typecast' as exotic and foreign, rather than recognized as home-grown Americans."[53] Through kinship networks and the press, Terminal Island girls were aware of other girls' clubs and had expectations for their own club. January 1937 issues of *Rafu Shimpo*, the leading Los Angeles Japanese-American newspaper, contained news of girls' clubs with activities similar to the Junior Outing Club's programs: winter snow hikes, skating, basketball, and making gifts for the Shonien, or Japanese Children's Home.[54]

The Junior Outing Club reflected the interests of the wider Japanese-American girls' club culture, but in other ways it grew out of the close-knit Terminal Island community. Unlike many other Nisei girls' clubs in the region, the Junior Outing Club was not affiliated with a Christian or Buddhist church or the YWCA.[55] Instead, the club reflected the community's relationship with teachers from the local elementary school. The advisor of the Junior Outing Club was Mrs. Elizabeth Frigon, who, in her early thirties, was a third-grade teacher at the school.[56] Another teacher, Mrs. Mangone, became advisor in about 1940.[57] By that time, there may have been more involvement by Nisei girls in high school as advisors to the Junior Outing Club.

The forerunner of the Junior Outing Club was the "Outing Girls," a teenage club in the early 1930s advised by Mrs. Mildred Obarr Walizer, the first principal of the elementary school.[58] When she retired, the community raised funds to send her to Japan for three months. After her death in 1933, Nisei girls joined the activities at a YWCA clubhouse in San Pedro, but by 1936 the fishing community restarted its own initiative as the Junior and Senior Outing Clubs.[59]

The elementary school in the Japanese-American fishing community reflected larger issues in education. About "99.9 percent" of students at the school were Japanese American.[60] Segregation in education based on language proficiency was "relatively simple to justify" in California and Los Angeles at the time.[61] The San Pedro school district may have justified the separate school based on educational needs and the school's proximity to mothers working at canneries on the island. Parents and teachers worked together to make it an encouraging environment for Nisei.[62] Miss García was the first teacher at the school.[63] Chikao Richard Ryono remembered her as "our quiet, unsung teacher" who was "a trusted counselor and go-between" among teachers and parents. He wrote, "the relationship between the teachers and parents was warm, and they forgave each other's shortcomings. . . . This closeness was the envy of other school communities." Miss García also began a class for Issei learning English: Ryono stated, "I recall how Mom studied and practiced how to write her name."[64]

Mrs. Frigon, the Euro-American teacher advising the club before 1940, drew from her community connections for club programs. Hideyo Ono recorded that the older girls in the club "watched the facial treatment which was demonstrated by Mrs. Boswin, who was [a] friend of Mrs. Frigon."[65] At another meeting, Hideyo Ono wrote that the girls learned about different occupations. The program included Mrs. Frigon discussing the Baltimore Hotel and Girl Scouts, followed by two guest speakers: Dr. Fujikawa on the history of medicine and Mary Campbell,

Mrs. Frigon's sister, on nursing.[66] Mrs. Frigon also found out prices and options for outings. After hearing a comparison of roller skating and ice skating venues—roller skating was less expensive but local and "they will open for our club girls on special" (perhaps meaning the Junior Outing Club would be the only people there)—Fumi Shirokawa wrote, "the Vote was that we would like to go to the ice skating" in Santa Monica.[67] The girls consistently chose outings away from their home locale.

The Junior Outing Club also involved the participation of Issei women in the fishing community. The minutes and later oral histories from Terminal Islanders do not say what Issei women thought about the club and how they viewed their involvement in it. However, the minutes show that Issei women participated in the club in three ways. The girls in the club invited their mothers to attend the club's tea parties and graduation dinners. Club secretaries also recorded the participation of mother sponsors, a formal role that suggests an advisory board for the club. Mother sponsors participated in the club's events, served as chaperones on outings, and stepped in when Mrs. Frigon could not attend. Club secretaries also named the Fujin Kai as part of some club activities on etiquette. According to Yamashita, the Fujin Kai, or Women's Association, "served as a conduit for information of interest to women of the community" and organized traditional activities in the community, such as lessons in flower arrangement and tea ceremony. He also observed that members of the Fujin Kai were primarily wives of business owners.[68]

The minutes show that women from families that ran businesses at Fish Harbor were active as advisors in the Junior Outing Club. For instance, Hideyo Ono recorded that Mrs. Yokozeki, Mrs. Ishii, and Mrs. Iwasaki attended a meeting when Mrs. Frigon could not be there.[69] There are more references to Mrs. Yokozeki in the minutes than to any other Issei.[70] She was fluent in English, active in the Fujin Kai and Fukei Kai (Parent Teacher Association), and her husband was prominent in the Southern California Japanese Fishermen's Association.[71] Mr. Iwasaki ran a barbershop, and Mr. and Mrs. Ishii ran a children's nursery.[72] In addition, Mr. Tsurumatsu Toma, known to everyone as "grandfather" for his civic involvement, arranged for the girls to reserve the fishermen's hall for movie fundraisers.[73] He owned a grocery store and stationery store.[74] Yamashita observed that the "social class structure on Terminal Island was not as sharply delineated as in Japan."[75] In addition, the varied backgrounds of Issei women in the community, many of whom arrived through arranged marriages, prevent a generalization that family occupation determined Issei women's involvement as advisors in the Junior Outing Club.[76] However, according to Yamashita, "the demarcation between the fishermen and the on-shore businessmen also applied to their respective wives. The women who were most active in community affairs and were looked up to were usually the wives of businessmen."[77] Thus, the minutes provide a glimpse into the fishing community's social structure. Issei business networks were evident in the programs of the Junior Outing Club.

The girls made the club their own by making choices in three overlapping areas. According to the club's constitution, "the object of this club is to have good times, go on outings and learn etiquette."[78] The Fujin Kai's interest in the Junior Outing Club reflected community expectations of Nisei. In response, girls both supported and challenged etiquette activities: the last item in the club's three-part statement of purpose, but arguably its top concern, according to its advisors. Etiquette activities involved middle-class, Euro-American, and Japanese conventions. In her study of Asian-American women's public culture, Lim writes that members of ethnic sororities in college used mastery of upper-class skills to "display their social fitness," allowing "women considered to be immigrant non-Americans to transcend that status."[79] In November 1938, Shizuka Ishikawa recorded that the Junior Outing Club would have "an etiquette on tea party" at the next meeting: "The Fujinkai [*sic*] will give us cake and candies and have a real tea party so we will get used to it."[80] Teas were part of Nisei girls' club culture in the 1930s.[81] A few months after the etiquette lesson with the Fujin Kai, the girls invited their mothers and teachers to the club for tea.[82] The minutes do not reveal if the club's tea parties emphasized Japanese or Euro-American etiquette. Mrs. Frigon and later, the girls themselves, held etiquette lessons based on girls' questions. They began as separate "Japanese" and "American" etiquette lessons, but over time they became recorded as "etiquette."[83]

Nisei girls challenged club etiquette through language. According to the club's by-laws, "one must try to speak English during club time."[84] Children in the fishing community spoke a combination of Japanese vernaculars and English, blending words and meanings in original ways that identify a Nisei Terminal Islander anywhere in the world.[85] Educators at the junior high school were concerned. Charlie O. Hamasaki recalled: "When we went to junior high school, we all got taken into this auditorium. You know, what the teacher says, 'Since you're here in San Pedro Junior High School you all have to learn how to talk English.'" He explained: "See that's where my English came out. Out of this Japanese accent, a certain type of Japanese accent, we turn into English."[86] The 1937 club tea party probably involved speaking English: reminders to speak English during club time appeared in the minutes after the tea party. In addition, at a meeting in March 1939, the secretary wrote: "The mother sponsors came over because of Mrs. Frigon's illness. Everyone tried to speak English during club time."[87] The next reminder occurred before a club outing in 1941.[88] Most Issei women had limited English language skills because they accomplished most responsibilities without leaving the island, while most Issei men traveled more widely and, thus, were more fluent in English.[89] Pressure to speak English came from Issei women advising the Junior Outing Club in addition to pressure from the Euro-American majority culture. For the girls, language was an outward sign of being a Nisei Terminal Islander as they navigated mainstream popular culture, increasing their "feeling of belonging" as a generational group in the fishing community.

The club's name—Junior Outing Club—emphasizes the importance of outings, or day trips, the next element in the club's statement of purpose. According to club bylaws, "at least once a year we may have an outing."[90] Girls usually went on two outings each year: girls chose destinations for the winter trip, and club advisors chose the spring trip. The spring trip, always to the grave of Mrs. Walizer, the former principal of the elementary school, reinforced connections with supportive teachers.[91] The impact of the club's annual winter outings went beyond the trip. Selecting the destination and planning the trip gave the girls opportunities to express their opinions and make decisions. The girls voted to go ice-skating in Santa Monica, snow hiking at Mt. Baldy, and to CBS Radio in Los Angeles.[92] They also wanted to go to the Pan-Pacific Auditorium, the museum and zoo, and a broadcast at KNX Radio in Los Angeles.[93] As part of their plans, the girls sewed gifts to deliver to the Shonien or "Children's Garden," the Japanese Children's Home in Los Angeles.[94] The Shonien was the most prominent connection to appear in the minutes between the Junior Outing Club and regional Nisei. From about 1913 until

1942, when the children were moved to Children's Village at Manzanar, as many as 50 Nisei children lived at the Shonien. Founded by Issei, the Shonien became a special project of Nisei across Los Angeles in the 1930s.[95] Through it the girls claimed space in venues different from their fishing community. They strengthened club friendships, positioning new experiences from day trips within Nisei and Terminal Islander culture.

The girls' intermittent debates about a club pin across several years suggest the importance of club identity and public appearance. The quest for a club pin began in February 1937.[96] In an undated entry made between November 1937 and January 1938, Hideyo Ono wrote, "we started discussing about the pins but we couldn't get to any point, so we suggested some places to go on an outing trip, but the discussion was so long that we packed the packages for the orphanage."[97] The club president, vice president, and secretary may have boycotted the Mother's Day program in April 1938 over the lack of a club pin.[98] The minutes hint at disagreement on price and design. Three years later, the pin idea took a new form with widespread support: a club sweater. In October 1941, Masako Terada recorded, "a motion was carried that we have [a] Sloppy Joe v-neck, the color—bright green, emblem—white background with green letters—triangular shape, and the cost about three dollars."[99] In December, the girls planned to wear their club sweater with logo on their winter day trip.

Nisei girls navigated modernity by changing clothes and behavior in response to expectations and interests. In February 1938, Hideyo Ono wrote, "Mrs. Yokozeki ask[ed] us to wear a kimono if you have one and come to [the] auditorium tomorrow night which was [*sic*] Saturday and help [the] Fujin Kai to serve the refreshments. All of us [will] try to participate."[100] The minutes do not record if the event was for Terminal Islanders or visitors. Teruko Miyoshi Okimoto recalled that on Girls' Day in March, visitors came to the island to see "the doll-like girls in their colorful kimonos" perform dances at the elementary school.[101] Orie Mio's daughters studied Kabuki and donated their talents to many events, including the annual Wisteria Festival in the nearby city of Wilmington.[102] In 1926, San Pedro High School invited "Japanese residents of Terminal Island" to attend the "Japanese Program" that included "a Japanese sword dance by the pupils of the East San Pedro School." The program also included "a fanciful Japanese pantomime, Cat Fear, and a well acted

Japanese tragedy, Bushido," with Japanese American and Euro-American players from the high school's Cosmopolitan Club, Drama Association, and Girls' Glee Clubs.[103] Matsumoto writes that Nisei differed in their level of comfort with their participation in ethnic-cultural performances at public events, particularly when requested by Euro-American groups.[104] The Junior Outing Club's diverse activities demonstrate the role of Japanese-American girls as representatives of the ethnic community. The club's programs took place in a wider context of public ethnic-cultural performances by Japanese-American youth.

The third component of the Junior Outing Club's purpose—"have good times"—offers some of the clearest views into the girls' dreams for the future. Good times happened at any time, but the girls also planned good times into club programs through sports, parties, and dancing. The club incorporated sports through "play night." The girls played basketball, volleyball, and softball. Most entries on sports in the minutes were general; for instance, "We played from 8:15 to 9:00."[105] Club secretary Teruyo Hamaguchi was more specific: "It was moved and seconded that we have play night next meeting. The games suggested were basketball and baseball. Baseball won having Yaeko Baba and Julie Fukuzaki as team captains."[106] In his study of sports and the Japanese-American community, Brian Niiya writes that baseball became popular in Japan at about the same time as in the United States, and rather than a sport being "Japanese" or "American," Issei and Nisei transformed sports "into uniquely Japanese-American experiences."[107]

Over time, the girls made dancing a larger part of Junior Outing Club activities. This reflected connections to youth culture. Matsumoto writes, "Nisei clubs provided ample opportunities for flirtation, socializing, and courtship in the context of monitored events—sometimes regulated by peers—that reinforced group ties and standards of behavior."[108] Dancing was sometimes part of play night—some girls danced, some girls played—but mentions of dancing became more frequent in the minutes over time. [109] At the January 1940 planning meeting for the annual graduation party, an event with teachers and mother sponsors, club secretary Aiko Tani revealed some of the negotiations involved: "It was moved and seconded that we have dancing after the dinner and also that boys are not to be invited to this dinner."[110] The group planned the dinner: "Main dish—Roast Beef—peas + carrots, Mashed potatoes, Desert—cookies + ice cream, French Bread, Salad—Fruits (fresh), Drink—Punch, Time—6:30."[111] Kyo Mio recorded a year later: "It was moved and seconded to get a dancing teacher and to learn the correct way of dance. The motion was carried." This meeting ended with a welcome program for new members: "The boys' club was invited too. After dancing we had refreshments."[112] A few months later, club secretary Teruyo Hamaguchi recorded: "Suggestions were made what we should do next meeting. Play night, dancing, and baking were suggested. Dancing won. Several girls were chosen to teach the girls who do not know how to dance."[113] This statement also demonstrates the larger influence girls created in their club over time. During the first few years of the club, programs seemed to be planned several weeks or months in advance and the club's Euro-American advisor was more prominent in the minutes.

As a Nisei Terminal Islander in high school, Mas Tanibata remembered watching girls from the "Outing Club" learning how to dance. He recalled: "We were just too shy to say we'd like to learn how to dance and teach us also. We'd peek from the window and watch them and see what kinds of steps they were doing and go home and try them out ourselves." He attended dances at the Torrance Civic Auditorium with Euro-American friends and recalled, "I used to hang around on the side, watching how to dance and finally I got enough nerve to do it myself." He organized the first group of Nisei to attend the San Pedro High School prom.[114] Kazuye Shibata Kushi recalled that the girl's vice principal encouraged Nisei to attend the prom, and the girls borrowed bridesmaid dresses from friends.[115] Mas Tanibata stated: "Just about every afternoon we'd get in front of Emi Iwasaki's porch and we'd play the records and do the steps . . . from these happenings we all learned how to dance. We went to the prom and really had a good time."[116]

Nisei girls also demonstrated their interest in future choices of careers. In February 1940, Kyo Mio recorded, "it was moved and seconded that [*sic*] to have a student from a higher school and [*sic*] to speak on the subject of what course you should take or the right course to take if you wanted to go to a higher school."[117] The minutes do not show a guest speaker on higher education after the girls' request, although it cannot be ruled out due to a gap in the minutes. Career training for Nisei girls from Terminal Island consisted of learning typing in high school. Other alternatives to cannery work included domestic work.[118] At least three Nisei girls from Terminal Island achieved statewide academic honors at San Pedro High School.[119] Some Japanese-American girls in the Los Angeles region entered UCLA and

Compton Junior College before World War II, but oral histories from Terminal Islanders do not record this option.[120] There was pressure to perfect domestic skills for marriage. Kazuye Shibata Kushi recalled a friend's mother telling her, "you make a perfect nigiri [rice ball], and you get a nice husband."[121]

The club's activities changed as war approached. Girls were more self-sufficient: they ran the programs, most of them unspecified in the minutes, and there were no guest speakers at club meetings in 1941. Bessie Shibata wrote, "we decided that we [will] have [an] etiquette [lesson] next meeting (Nov. 26, 1941)." The club selected a group of girls "to go over [the channel on the ferry] to the library and get some books about etiquette."[122] The girls extended their role as community representatives. In April 1940, the girls sent $20 in response to a fundraising letter from the San Pedro Boys' Club.[123] In March 1941, Teruyo Hamaguchi explained the club's Red Cross project: "While the B10's [younger girls] cut the materials, others played. After the cutting was completed, various things [such] as baby night gowns, diapers, jackets, aprons, and blouses were assigned to the girls to make at home."[124] In October, the girls changed their plans from a play night to making gifts with the Senior Outing Club for the Baptist Church Nursery School in the fishing community.[125] Among their last activities together as a club was to sew dresses for the Shonien. Bessie Shibata recorded on December 5, two days before Pearl Harbor, "the motion was made and second[ed] that we go to the Westwood Iceskating Ring on December 22, 1941 for our outing after we visited [*sic*] the orphanage."[126] The variety of activities in 1940 and 1941, ranging from etiquette to outings, and local to regional community service, positioned the club in the fishing community within a larger youth culture and contemporary events.

CONCLUSION

In the years before World War II, Nisei girls participating in the Junior Outing Club strengthened friendships and developed cultural influences into distinct Nisei Terminal Islander identities. The club's independence reflected the community's close-knit social fabric. Although Terminal Islanders moved fluidly within the multicultural and far-flung networks of the commercial fishing industry, they relied on each other to cope with hostile legislation and discrimination that targeted

Japanese Americans. The arrival of women, the growth of families, and the expansion of the commercial fishing industry fostered community institutions that changed along with the needs and interests of Terminal Islanders. Issei women made significant contributions through the Fujin Kai and other groups in creating a community with a distinct, self-sufficient identity. In particular, the role of the Women's Association in the Junior Outing Club reveals some of the class relationships within the Terminal Island community.

The Junior Outing Club also grew out of the interest among Nisei girls to participate in Japanese-American girls' club culture. During club time girls learned some ways to dance and conduct tea parties, went on outings and listened to programs by guests on music, careers in medicine, and beauty. Their debates included club pins, trip destinations, and sports. They responded to requests to represent the community in kimonos and through social service. As war approached, they increasingly relied on each other and the Senior Outing Club for programs and advice. Their Euro-American advisors and the prominent Issei clubwomen of the Fujin Kai were influential, but ultimately, Nisei girls made their own choices from the available options.

EPILOGUE

Friendships and good times in the Junior Outing Club contributed to the skills Nisei girls needed to be resilient during the turmoil of the next several years. Because of its supposed strategic location, the Japanese-American community at Terminal Island was the first community evicted in its entirety after the Japanese attack on Pearl Harbor on December 7, 1941.[127] The public ignored the fact that the Japanese-American community was there for more than 25 years before the government built the naval base.[128] By the evening of December 7, sentries controlled access to the island and FBI agents began arresting prominent Issei men.[129] Fishing boats returned and canneries fired all their Japanese American employees.[130] The Junior Outing Club continued to plan for the future. At its last meeting, Masako Terada recorded, "it was moved and seconded that we give something to Tsumako Nakachi who is ill. We decided to sent [*sic*] her flowers."[131] The girls selected officers and scheduled a graduation party for the next week.

Within about a month, the community no longer existed on Terminal Island. In early February, the FBI arrested all remaining Issei fishermen.[132] Most families were now single-parent households headed by women. On February 25, the U.S. Navy ordered the remaining Terminal Islanders to leave the island in 48 hours.[133] Art Almeida, then a junior high school student, stated that "teachers let the kids out early so they could say goodbye. Everyone cried."[134] Terminal Islanders sold for low prices or abandoned the possessions they couldn't take with them or put into storage.[135] A member of the community made the courageous decision to save the Junior Outing Club minutes. Terminal Islanders moved in with friends and family or went to multi-family shelters before being incarcerated in "War Relocation Centers."[136] Approximately 800 Terminal Islanders moved to three adjoining blocks at Manzanar, and some former members of the Junior Outing Club appeared in a high school yearbook at camp.[137] Bulldozers destroyed their former homes on Terminal Island.

Scattered across the country after the war, many Terminal Islanders eventually returned to southern California, although only a few families returned to commercial fishing. Chikao Robert Ryono wrote, "Terminal Islanders had no central starting point to start their new lives after the war. That made most of us bitter, but not hopeless."[138] Many participated in reconstructing their Terminal Island community as a community without borders through friendships, gatherings, and a memorial on the island.[139] Terminal Islander culture continues to unfold. The strength of Nisei identity has contributed to its endurance. Ryono stated: "We grew up respecting and helping each other. We were protective of each other. Once a Terminal Islander, always a Terminal Islander."[140]

ACKNOWLEDGMENTS

This essay has benefitted from the suggestions generously offered by Vicki L. Ruiz, David Igler, Jana Bouck Remy, Laura Mitchell, Glenn Gordinier and participants of GREPMA 2006, and Susan Fukushima, Marie Masumoto, and Terminal Islander volunteers at the Hirasaki Resource Center at the Japanese American National Museum.

Notes

1

1. *Virginia Gazette*, December 23, 1773.

2. For a few newspaper examples, refer to *The Boston Weekly Newsletter, The Boston Post Boy, The New York Gazette, The Virginia Gazette, The Newport Mercury, The South Carolina Gazette, The Georgia Gazette, Lloyds Weekly Journal, and The Craftman's Journal;* Darold Wax offers considerable discussion of travelers' view of West African as "violence-ridden" during the eighteenth century, see Darold Wax, "A People of Beastly Living: Europe, Africa, and the Atlantic Slave Trade," *Phylon* 41, no.1 (1980): 17.

3. The growth of studies concerning gender and slavery continue to proliferate as scholars offer nuanced discussions, including the double oppression bondwomen faced, along with the specific instances of resistance black women raged. For further understanding, see Angela Davis, "Reflections on Black Women's Role in the Community of Slaves," *Black Scholar* 3 (December 1971); Deborah Gray White, *Ar'n't I a Woman: Female Slaves in the Plantation South* (New York: W. W. Norton & Company, 1985); Jennifer Morgan, *Laboring Women: Reproduction and Gender in New World Slavery* (Philadelphia: University of Pennsylvania Press, 2004); Stephanie M.H. Camp, *Closer to Freedom: Enslaved Women and Everyday Resistance in the Plantation South* (Chapel Hill: University of North Carolina Press, 2004); Marietta Morrissey, *Slave Women in the New World: Gender Stratification in the Caribbean* (Lawrence: University Press of Kansas, 1989); Barbara Bush, *Slave Women in the Caribbean Society, 1650-1838* (Bloomington: Indiana University Press, 1990); David Barry Gaspar and Darlene Clark Hine, eds., *More Than Chattel: Black Women and Slavery in the Americas* (Bloomington: Indiana University Press, 1996); Hilary Beckles, *Centering Woman: Gender Discourses in Caribbean Slave Society* (Oxford: James Currey Publishers, 1999); Sterling Stuckey, *Slave Culture: Nationalist Theory and the Foundations of Black America* (New York: Oxford University Press, 1987); Betty Wood, "Some Aspects of Female Resistance to Chattel Slavery in Low Country Georgia, 1763-1815," *Historical Journal* 30, no. 3 (1987); Herbert Aptheker, *American Negro Slave Revolts* (New York: International Publishers, 1943); and Alice and Raymond Bauer, "Day to Day Resistance to Slavery," *The Journal of Negro History* 27, no. 4 (October 1942): 388-419.

4. Several monumental works have been published giving attention to the resistance bondpeople utilized towards freedom aboard slave vessels and within the plantation system. See the works of Lorenzo Greene, "Mutiny on the Slave Ships," *Phylon* 5 (1944): 346-54; Vincent Harding, *There is a River: The Black Struggle for Freedom in America* (New York: Harcourt Brace Jovanovich, 1981);

David Richardson, "Shipboard Revolts, African Authority, and the Atlantic Slave Trade," *William and Mary Quarterly* 58 (2001): 69-92; Michael Gomez, *Exchanging Our Country Marks: The Transformation of African Identities in the Colonial and Antebellum South* (Chapel Hill: University of North Carolina Press, 1998); Antonio Bly, "Crossing the Lake of Fire: Slave Resistance During the Middle Passage, 1720-1842," *Journal of Negro History* 83 (Summer 1998): 178-86; Aptheker, *Negro Slave Revolts in the United States, 1526-1860,* Bauer, "Day to Day Resistance to Slavery," and A.H. Gordon, "The Struggle of the Negro Slaves for Physical Freedom," *Journal of Negro History* 13, no. 1 (January 1928): 22-35. Franny Nudelman, in the introduction of her recent work, *John Brown's Body: Slavery, Violence, & the Culture of War,* situates her discussion amidst what she refers to as "the wealth of recent scholarship that can be loosely grouped under the rubric 'Violence Studies,'" see *John Brown's Body* (Chapel Hill: University of North Carolina Press, 2004), 2. Echoing these sentiments, this study locates the environment of violence common between enslaved Africans and their captors aboard slave ships in this same growing field of historical inquiry.

5. Marcus Rediker in his seminal 1987 work is credited with offering detailed discussion regarding the arguably lower class of workers—seamen and ship captains—that operated as employees of merchants traveling across the Atlantic, see *Between the Devil and Deep Blue Sea: Merchant Seamen, Pirates and the Anglo-American Maritime World, 1700-1750* (Cambridge: Cambridge University Press, 1987).

6. Tuohy Papers, 380 TUO 4/4, Liverpool Record Office, Liverpool, England.

7. Slavery Manuscript Collection, Box #1, New-York Historical Society, New York City.

8. DeWolfe Family Papers, MSS 382, Rhode Island Historical Society, Providence, Rhode Island.

9. Emma Christopher offers the first book-length study interrogating the lives of sailors employed aboard slaveships and the often dangerous dynamics they confronted within their employment, see *Slave Ship Sailors and their Captive Cargoes, 1730-1807* (Cambridge: Cambridge University Press, 2006).

10. T 70/2—Abstracts of Letters From September 30, 1707, to July 22, 1713, National Archives, Kew Gardens, England.

11. Harvey Wish offers considerable discussion regarding the unending threat of violence slave traders faced from those enslaved while engaged in trade across coastal regions of West Africa, see "American Slave Insurrections Before 1861," *Journal of Negro History* 22 (July 1937): 300.

12. Winston McGowan, "African Resistance to the Atlantic Slave Trade in West Africa," *Slavery and Abolition* 11 (May 1990): 19.

13. Testimony of Capt. John Ashley Hall, *House of Commons Sessional Paper of the Eighteenth Century,* Vol. 72 (Wilmington, DE: Scholarly Resources, 1975), 226; Winston McGowan posits that kidnapping and raiding persisted as long as the slave trade, see McGowan, "African Resistance to the Atlantic Slave Trade in

West Africa," 10; the author recognizes some people were often sold and born into slavery and thereafter exchanged by seamen without the threat of violence, yet this beyond the scope of this paper's focus on the discourse of violence; for an expanded discussion of the background of enslavement among West Africans, see Richard Sheridan, "Resistance and Rebellion of African Captives in the Transatlantic Slave Trade before Becoming Seasoned Labourers in the British Caribbean, 1690-1807," in Verene A. Shepherd, ed., *Working Slavery, Pricing Freedom: Perspectives from the Caribbean, Africa, and the African Diaspora* (Kingston, Jamaica: Ian Randle Publishers, 2002), 183.

14. Testimony of James Towne, *House of Commons Sessional Paper of the Eighteenth Century,* Vol. 82 (Wilmington, DE: Scholarly Resources, 1975), 16.

15. Testimony of John Bowman, Ibid., 114.

16. Testimony of John Douglas, Ibid., 122.

17. Testimony of William Littleton, Ibid., 292-93.

18. Wilma King speaks of female slaves being consistently faced with sexual exploitation due to their enslaved status, see "'Mad' Enough to Kill: Enslaved Women, Murder, and the Southern Courts," *Journal of African American History* 92 (Winter 2007): 39.

19. Testimony of James Towne, *House of Commons Sessional Papers of the Eighteenth Century,* Vol. 82, 22.

20. For further discussion of the operation of double oppression among enslaved black women, see White, *Ar'n't I a Woman?*

21. Johannes Postma, *The Dutch in the Atlantic Slave Trade, 1600-1815* (Cambridge: Cambridge University Press, 1990), 243.

22. Jay Coughtry, *The Notorious Triangle: Rhode Island and the African Slave Trade, 1700-1800* (Philadelphia: Temple University Press, 1981), 11.

23. Abbe Raynal, *Slave Trade: A Full Account of This Species of Commerce; With Arguments Against it, Spirited and Philosophical.* (Southwark: T. Cox, 1792), 35.

24. Nell Irvin Painter, *Soul Murder and Slavery,* Charles Edmondson Historical Lecture Series, 15 (Waco, TX: Baylor University Press), 9.

25. Evelyn Brooks Higginbotham, "African-American Women's History and the Metalanguage of Race," in Darlene Clark Hine, Wilma King, and Linda Reeds, eds., *'We Specialize in the Wholly Impossible': A Reader in Black Women's History* (New York: Carlson Publication, Inc., 1995), 11.

26. John Newton, *Thoughts Upon the African Slave Trade* (London: J. Buckland, and J. Johnson, 1788), 105.

27. Darlene Clark Hine, "Lifting the Veil, Shattering the Silences: Black Women's History in Slavery and Freedom," in Darlene Clarke Hine, ed., *The State of the Afro-American Past, Present, and Future* (Baton Rouge: Louisiana State University Press, 1986), 224.

28. John Newton, Journal, 1750-1754, Log/M/46, National Maritime Museum, Greenwich, England.

29. Wendy Anne Warren, in her recent article, offers the point that getting pregnant could somehow keep enslaved black women plausibly free from repeated attacks of rape, see Warren, "Rape of a Slave in Early New England Slavery," *Journal of American History* 93 (March 2007): 1047; the present study departs from this particular view, arguing that as human chattel, bondpeople were never free from the lash of violence—sexual or nonsexual—regardless of gender, age, ethnicity, or even if they were carrying unborn children.

30. Painter, *Soul Murder and Slavery,* 10.

31. Robert Stein, *The French Slave Trade In the Eighteenth Century: An Old Regime Business* (Madison: University of Wisconsin Press, 1979), 101.

32. Wilma King makes the assertion that, regardless of race or age, women were often subjected to sexual abuses mitigated by both black and white men, see "'Mad' Enough to Kill," 158.

33. This point builds upon the assertion Wendy Anne Warren poses in relation to the rape of enslaved women. She suggests that, "maybe rape meant little to a woman fully immersed in one of the most violent enterprises the world has ever known," and that as "a proven survivor" these varied victims perhaps "took the rape in stride," see "Rape of a Slave in Early New England," 1047; although the argument could be made that repeated sexual attacks may have induced feelings of numbness, the author of this study argues it is difficult to presume these women became accustomed to these violent attacks; for discussion of the long-term affects regarding sexual exploitation, see Nell Painter, *Soul Murder and Slavery*; Darlene Clark Hine offers details concerning gender relations based on sex common between black women and men during bondage, see, "Lifting the Veil, Shattering the Silences," 226.

34. Jennifer Morgan, "Some Could Suckle over Their Shoulder": Male Travelers, Female Bodies, and the Gendering of Racial Ideology, 1500-1700," *William and Mary Quarterly* 54, no. 1 (January 1997): 170.

35. Alexander Falconbridge, *An Account of the Slave Trade on the Coast of Africa* (London: AMS, 1788) 23-24.

36. Hazel Carby analyzes this phenomenon through the context of master-slave relationship within the American plantation system, see, *Reconstructing Womanhood: The Emergence of the Afro-American Woman Novelist* (Oxford: Oxford University Press, 1987), 27; the author of this study takes a much broader view to understand this dynamic, suggesting that with possible different sexual partners some black women may have endured within the slave trade, seamen were at liberty to flee or even return to Africa to embark upon new forced relationships without the threat of political, economic, or social liability. This process was permitted largely due to the differing status of seamen and female captives within slave societies.

37. Darlene Clark Hine employs the concept of "sexual hostage" in her discussion of black women and migration often owing to their experiences of sexual exploitation, see "Rape and The Inner Lives of Black Women in the Middle West," *Signs* 14 (Summer 1989): 915.

38. Quobna Ottobah Cugoano, *Thoughts And Sentiments On The Evil of Slavery* (1787; reprint, New York: Penguin Books, 1999), 15.

39. King originates this concept of "rite" and its relation to the sexual exploitation of black females; for further discussion, see "'Mad' Enough to Kill," 40.

40. Elaine Scarry, *The Body in Pain: The Making and Unmaking of the World* (New York: Oxford University Press, 1985), 73.

41. Newton, *Thoughts Upon the African Slave Trade*, 105.

42. Raynal, *Slave Trade: A Full Account of This Species of Commerce; With Arguments Against it, Spirited and Philosophical,* 35.

43. Ken Marshall discusses the presumption of women as the weaker sex, which he argues is predicated on "the chauvinistic belief that the physically weaker females represented little if any real threat to the armed crew's safety," see "Powerful, Righteous: The Transatlantic Survival and Cultural Resistance of an Enslaved African Family in Eighteenth-Century New Jersey," *Journal of American Ethnic History* 23 (Winter 2004): 32.

44. Testimony of Thomas Trotter, *House of Commons Sessional Papers of the Eighteenth Century,* Vol. 73 (Wilmington, DE: Scholarly Resources, 1975), 86.

45. Testimony of Henry Ellison, Ibid., 375.

46. Daniel Mannix and Malcolm Cowley, *Black Cargoes: A History of the Atlantic Slave Trade, 1518-1865* (New York: Viking Press, 1962), 113.

47. Falconbridge, *An Account of the Slave Trade on the Coast of Africa*, 23.

48. Paula Giddings pushes this particular argument concerning bondwomen and the emotional ties shared with their children; for further discussion, see *When and Where I Enter: The Impact of Black Women on Race and Sex in America (*New York: W. Morrow, 1996), 45.

49. Moses Brown Papers, MSS 313, Rhode Island Historical Society, Providence, Rhode Island.

50. Sloop *Dolphin*, Logs, 1795-97, MSS 828, Rhode Island Historical Society, Providence, Rhode Island.

51. John Newton, Journal.

52. Darlene Clark Hine and Kate Wittenstein conceived the concept of "gynecological resistance." For an expanded discussion, see "Female Slave Resistance: The Economics of Sex," in Filomina Chioma Steady, ed., *The Black Woman Cross-Culturally* (Cambridge MA: Schenkman, 1981), 289-300.

53. Several scholars have considered the recognition among slave owners of bondwomen's knowledge of how to terminate unwanted pregnancies, see White, *Ar'n't I a Woman?*, 84-88; Jennifer Morgan, *Laboring Women: Reproduction and Gender in New World Slavery* (Philadelphia: University of Pennsylvania Press, 2004), 114; and Barbara Bush, "Women, Childbirth, and Resistance in British Caribbean Slave Societies," in David Barry Gaspar and Darlene Clark Hine, eds., *More than Chattel: Black Women and Slavery in the Americas*

(Bloomington: Indiana University Press, 1996), 204-05. Ken Marshall also offers further discussion of the roles as spiritual mediums some African women played within West African societies, see "Powerful and Righteous," 34. These knowledge systems could have presumably bestowed some of these women with information concerning reproductive capabilities that they carried aboard slave-ships and into enslaved communities.

54. Certificate of Slaves Taken on Board Ships, HL/PO/JO/10/7/982A, Parliamentary Archives, House of Lords Record Office, London, England.

55. Peleg Clarke Papers, MS 75, Newport Historical Society, Newport, Rhode Island.

56. Newton, *Thoughts Upon the African Slave Trade*, 105.

57. David Barry Gaspar, *Bondmen and Rebels: A Study of Master-Slave Relations in Antigua* (Durham, NC: Duke University Press, 1993), 171.

58. John Atkins, *A Voyage to Guinea, Brasil, and the West-Indies* (London: Ward and Chandler, 1735), 72.

59. Wish, "American Insurrections Before 1861," 300.

60. Atkins, *A Voyage to Guinea, Brasil, and the West-Indies*, 72-73.

61. Scarry, *The Body in Pain,* 61.

62. *The Weekly Journal: or the British Gazetter*, July 5, 1729.

63. Sir Phillip Gibbes, *Instructions For the Treatment of Negroes* (London: Printed for Shepperson and Reynolds', 1797), 71.

64. Louis P. Maher, *Rites of Execution: Capital Punishment and the Transformation of American Culture, 1776-1865* (Oxford: Oxford University Press, 1991), 26.

65. Testimony of Richard Miles, *House of Commons Sessional Papers of the Eighteenth Century,* Vol. 68 (Wilmington, DE: Scholarly Resources, 1975), 86.

66. Greene, "Mutiny on the Slave Ships," 348.

67. Richardson, "Shipboard Revolts, African Authority, and the Atlantic Slave Trade," 71.

68. Raynal, *Slave Trade: A Full Account of This Species of Commerce,* 23

69. W. Jeffrey Bolster is credited for turning scholars' attention back to the viable role free black sailors played in both the maritime industry and Northern black communities, see *Black Jacks: African American Seamen in the Age of Sail* (Cambridge, MA: Harvard University Press, 1997).

70. Darold D. Wax, "Negro Resistance to the Early American Trade," *Journal of Negro History* 51, no.1 (January 1966): 2.

71. Richardson, "Shipboard Revolts, African Authority, and the Atlantic Slave Trade," 76.

72. Hebert Klein, "African Women in the Atlantic Slave Trade," in Claire Robertson and Martin A. Klein, eds., *Women and Slavery in Africa* (Portsmouth, NH: Heinemann, 1997), 29.

73. Greene, "Mutiny on the Slave Ships," 354.

74. Kali Gross, *Colored Amazons: Crime, Violence, and Black Women in the City of Brotherly Love, 1880-1910* (Durham, NC: Duke University Press, 2006), 8.

2

1. RG003, New London County Court Records, Native American Box 1, Folder 10, RG003, Connecticut State Library and Archives, Hartford, CT.

2. Ibid., Box 1, Folder 8, Box 1, Folder 10.

3. Marcus Rediker, *Between the Devil and the Deep Blue Sea: Merchant Seamen, Pirates, and the Anglo-American Maritime World, 1700-1750* (Cambridge: Cambridge University Press, 1993); Daniel Vickers, *Young Men and the Sea: Yankee Seafarers in the Age of Sail* (New Haven: Yale University Press, 2005); *Daniel Vickers, Farmers and Fishermen: Two Centuries of Work in Essex County, Massachusetts, 1630-1850* (Chapel Hill: University of North Carolina Press, 1994); W. Jeffrey Bolster, *Black Jacks: African American Seamen in the Age of Sail* (Cambridge: Harvard University Press, 1997). Efforts to understand Indian presence in the whaling industry can be found in the following works: Russel L. Barsh, "'Colored' Seamen in the New England Whaling Industry: An Afro-Indian Consortium," in James F. Brooks, ed., *Confounding the Color Line: The Indian-Black Experience in North America* (Lincoln: University of Nebraska Press, 2002), 76-107; Daniel Vickers, "The First Whalemen of Nantucket," in *After King Philip's War: Presence and Persistence in Indian New England* (Hanover, NH: University Press of New England, 1997); Mark A. Nicholas, "Mashpee Wampanoags of Cape Cod, the Whalefishery, and Seafaring's Impact on Community Development," *American Indian Quarterly* 26, no. 2 (2002):165-97.

4. See Gary B. Nash, *Forging Freedom: The Formation of Philadelphia's Black Community, 1720-1840* (Cambridge, MA: Harvard University Press, 1988).

5. Daniel R. Mandell, *Behind the Frontier: Indians in Eighteenth-Century Eastern Massachusetts* (Lincoln: University of Nebraska Press, 1996) 81-82; Jason R. Mancini, "'We Judge it therefore very Necessary to make Some alterations amongst ourselves': Indians, Land, and Community in Southern New England and Eastern Long Island, 1713-1790," n.d., on file at Mashantucket Pequot Museum and Research Center.

6. RG001 Crimes and Misdemeanors, RG001 Indian Papers Series I & II, RG002 New London County Superior Court Records, RG003 New London County Court Records, Connecticut State Library and Archives.

7. Ibid., RG003, New London County Court Records Native American Box 1, Folder 34.

8. Ibid., Folder 35.

9. Ibid.

10. Marcus Rediker, *Between the Devil and the Deep Blue Sea,*105.

11. Bolster, *Black Jacks,* 69, notes a significant increase in black mariners in the period between 1740 and 1820.

12. Rediker, *Between the Devil and the Deep Blue Sea,* 101.

13. Maureen A. Taylor, *Runaways, Deserters, and Notorious Villains: From the Rhode Island Newspapers, Volume 1, The Providence Gazette, 1762-1800* (Camden, ME: Picton Press, 1995); the author is currently collecting similar data from the *New London Gazette and Norwich Packet.*

14. Several examples appear in these advertisements, including a mulatto man named Francisco who was wearing a "blue jacket, Sailors Trowsers," in July 1769; a mulatto fellow named Harry who "had on when he went away, a striped woolen Shirt, a short blue Sailor Jacket," in December 1771; and an Indian named Daniel Jeffrey who had on a "dark Pea Jacket" in May 1777, see Taylor, *Runaways, Deserters, and Notorious Villains,* 12, 20, 63; mariners were widely viewed as having a distinct way of dressing and even walking that made them readily identifiable to the broader public, see Rediker, *Between the Devil and the Deep Blue Sea,* 11, and Bolster, *Black Jacks,* 91-92.

15. Jesse Lemisch, *Jack Tar vs. John Bull: The Role of New York's Seamen in Precipitating the Revolution* (New York: Garland Publishing, 1997), 6-7.

16. See also Bolster, *Black Jacks,* 216.

17. *New London Summary*, March 12, 1760.

18. Elmo P. Hohman, *The American Whaleman: A Study of Life and Labor in the Whaling Industry* (New York: Longmans, Green and Co., 1928), 55.

19. Rediker, *Between the Devil and the Deep Blue Sea,* 114-15.

20. Laura Murray, *To Do Good to My Indian Brethren: The Writings of Joseph Johnson, 1751-1776* (Amherst: University of Massachusetts Press, 1998), 191-92.

21. Ibid., 92-98.

22. Jason R Mancini, and David J. Naumec, *Connecticut's African and Native American Revolutionary War Enlistments: 1775-1783* (Mashantucket, CT: Mashantucket Pequot Museum and Research Center, 2005).

23. Frigate *Confederacy* Papers, 1776-1786, Collection 222, Folders 18-19, Historical Society of Pennsylvania, Philadelphia. In contrast to tribal records that emphasize groups or lists of men and women, maritime records focus on individuals. This has hampered population-level scholarship, but through record linkage of multiple sources, individual and community activities and behaviors can be reconstructed.

24. Mancini and Naumec, *Connecticut's African and Native American Revolutionary War Enlistments.*

25. For comparison, see Daniel Vickers, "The First Whalemen of Nantucket," *William and Mary Quarterly*, 3rd Ser., 40, no. 4 (1983): 560-83; Nichols,

"Mashpee Wampanoags of Cape Cod, the Whalefishery, and Seafaring's Impact on Community Development,"165-97.

26. An additional two reservation communities, Shinnecock of Southampton, Long Island, New York, and Wangunk along the Connecticut River in Middletown, Connecticut, are about 36 linear miles from New London.

27. RG001, Indian Papers, Series II, Vol. II:33, May 10, 1804, Connecticut State Library and Archives.

28. Mancini, "we Judge it therefore very Necessary to make Some alterations amongst ourselves."

29. Sketches of Indian lives can be seen in the following works: Ruth Wallis Herndon, *Unwelcome Americans: Living on the Margin in Early New England* (Philadelphia: University of Pennsylvania Press, 2001); Donna Keith Baron, J. Edward Hood, and Holly V. Izard, "They Were Here All Along: The Native American Presence in Lower-Central New England in the Eighteenth and Nineteenth Centuries," *William and Mary Quarterly*, 3rd Series, 53, no. 3 (1996): 561-86; Thomas L. Doughton, "Unseen Neighbors: Native Americans of Central Massachusetts, A People Who Had "Vanished," in Colin G. Calloway, ed., *After King Philip's War: Presence and Persistence in New England* (Hanover, NH: University Press of New England, 1997), 207-30.

30. Ruth P. Dixon, "Genealogical Fallout from the War of 1812," *Prologue* 24, no. 1 (1992).

31. Salem, Massachusetts, Crew Lists Index: 1799-1879, G. W. Blunt White Library, Mystic Seaport; Marblehead, Massachusetts, Crew Lists Index: 1799-1879 (Partial), G. W. Blunt White Library. Mystic Seaport; New Bedford Customs Records from New Bedford Free Public Library, and New London Customs records on file at the Mashantucket Pequot Museum and Research Center; Providence customs records from Rhode Island Historical Society, *Register of Seamen's Protection Certificates from the Providence, Rhode Island Custom District, 1796-1870* (Baltimore: Clearfield Co., 1995).

32. Bolster, *Black Jacks*, 234, "Note on the Tables"; Bolster also omitted sailors labeled "Indian" because their number "was very small." I am not suggesting that these other complexion terms are equated with "Indian," only that many Indians were labeled in other ways.

33. Records of the Collector of Customs for the Customs District of New London, Connecticut, 1789-1938 (M1162, RG26), National Archives and Records Administration, Northeast Region (Boston).

34. The surname Cheats appears as a contracted form of Quocheats, and Cinnamon as a contracted from of Cassacinamon, names that appear commonly in the Connecticut Indian Papers and other colonial records; in some instances these race labels were explicitly defined: for example, on April 10, 1765, Jacob Cushman placed a notice in the *Providence Gazette* for his runaway servant, Ezekiel Fuller, "being a mulatto, or half English and half Indian Fellow," Taylor, *Runaways, Deserters, and Notorious Villains,* 7; according to court documents, by 1823, in New England and in the maritime industry, "it was customary" to call

Indians "colored men" or "men of color," see United States Congress, 27th, 3rd Session: 1842-1843, House Report No. 80, Free Colored Seamen: Majority and Minority Reports, State of South Carolina vs. Daley,19. Misrepresentations of individual identity are also evident in Federal Census records where many people of Indian ancestry were labeled as "other free persons, except Indians not taxed" or "free colored persons." This occurs frequently in the Stonington, North Stonington, Groton, and Ledyard, Connecticut, censuses between 1790 and 1840.

35. Records of the Collector of Customs for the District of New London, Connecticut, 1789-1938 (M1162, RG26); SPC#140 does not exist in the New London Customs Records; the SPC records only identify mariners' birthplaces; surrendered crew lists include both birthplace and current residence.

36. Records of the Collector of Customs for the District of New London, Connecticut, 1789-1938 (M1162, RG26).

37. Bolster, *Black Jacks,* 93-101. While the principal concern in the scope of this paper is to identify and demonstrate that these relationships existed, future research may be able to explore whether these fraternities developed in their respective communities, at sea, or in port.

38. Records of the Collector of Customs for the District of New London, Connecticut, 1789-1938 (M1162, RG26).

39. Vickers, *Young Men and the Sea*, 63, 78; Paul A. Gilje, *Liberty on the Waterfront: American Maritime Culture in the Age of Revolution* (Philadelphia: University of Pennsylvania Press, 2004), 15, 20.

40. Gilje, *Liberty on the Waterfront*, 15.

41. Records of the Collector of Customs for the District of New London, Connecticut, 1789-1938 (M1162, RG26); Peter Potter's ancestry is somewhat difficult to ascertain, but it appears that he later married a woman associated with the Mashantucket Pequot community and has descendants among individuals later enumerated as tribal members.

42. Ibid.

43. Individuals with the surname Caujock (and all of its variant spellings) appear only at Mashantucket until it disappears from tribal rolls and petitions in 1774. It appears again with Jonathan Caujock, who was born ca. 1780 on Long Island, suggesting that some type of movement occurred from Mashantucket to Long Island.

44. Ship *Acasta*, September 25,1835, Log 367, G.W. Blunt White Library, Mystic Seaport; Crew Lists Surrendered, Customs Records of New London; Alexander Starbuck, *History of the American Whale Fishery* (1876; reprint, Secaucus, NJ: Castle Books, 1989).

45. Rediker, *Between the Devil and the Deep Blue Sea,* 113.

46. Lisa Norling, *Captain Ahab Had a Wife: New England Women and the Whalefishery, 1720-1870* (Chapel Hill: University of North Carolina Press, 2000), 199.

47. Connecticut Historical Society, Papers of William Samuel Johnson, Micro Pos. #74129, Reel V, Vol. III, Connecticut Historical Society, Hartford, CT; Erastus Williams to William L. Williams, December 13, 1833; Overseers Papers. RG3 Accession 2001-034, Indians, 1716-1855, Mashantucket Pequot 1758-1855, Box 2, Connecticut State Library and Archives.

48. See Vickers, *Young Men and the Sea*, 99.

49. Papers of Eleazer Wheelock, Microfilm Reel 1 742162.1, Dartmouth College Archives, Hanover, NH.

50. See Ann Marie Plane, *Colonial Intimacies: Indian Marriage in Early New England* (Ithaca: Cornell University Press, 2000), 67-128; Laurie E. Pasteryak, "Tradition and Deviance: The Presence of Southern New England Native Traditions in Nineteenth Century Eastern Connecticut," presented at the June Baker Higgins Gender Studies Conference, Central Connecticut State University, April 7, 2006.

51. Female-centered households can be seen in Plane, *Colonial Intimacies*, 112-15.

52. Edward A. Kendall, *Travels through the Northern Parts of the United States in the Years 1807 and 1808*, 3 vols. (New York: I. Riley Publishing, 1809)1: 301.

53. John M. Earle, *Report to the Governor and Council Concerning the Indians of the Commonwealth, Under the Act of April 6, 1859* (Boston: William White, 1861), 34.

54. First appearing on a crew list for the bark *Ceres* in August 1842, Manuel Bastio (though a resident of New London) was unable to provide a protection certificate, verifying his "citizenship." In 1848, he married Tamar Brushell, a resident of the Pequot Reservation at Lantern Hill in [now North] Stonington.

55. Rediker, *Between the Devil and the Deep Blue Sea*, 146-49; Bolster, *Black Jacks,* 160-61; Vickers, *Young Men and the Sea*, 147.

56. Bolster, *Black Jacks*, 163-65.

57. Stonington Land Records 13:480, 13:494; North Stonington Land Records 1:338, 2:50.

58. Lyme Land Records 6:265, 11:100, 11:253, 13:121.

59. Danske Dandridge, *American Prisoners of the Revolution* (Baltimore: Genealogical Publishing Company, 1967), 458.

60. Gideon Tocus [Tokus], "Blackman," and Titus Sinement [Cinnamon], "Blackman," appear together on the sloop *Active* in October 1806 with Joseph Peters, "Blackman," and George Arnold, "Blackman." These men are all identified as residents of Stonington in the 1820 Federal Census.

61. RG002 General Assembly, Box 2 File 37, Document 1a-b, Rejected Bills of Native Americans, May 1856, Connecticut State Library and Archives.

62. Connecticut Historical Society, Papers of William Samuel Johnson, Micro Pos. #74129, Reel V; Vol. III, Letter from Erastus Williams to William L. Williams, December 13,1833; Connecticut State Library and Archives RG002 General

Assembly Papers, Box 68, Document 47a-f, May 1855, Original Bills.

63. Ann Marie Plane and Gregory Button, "The Massachusetts Indian Enfranchisement Act: Ethnic Contest in Historical Context, 1849-1869," *Ethnohistory* 40, no. 4 (1993): 587-618.

64. Rediker, *Between the Devil and the Deep Blue Sea;* Bolster, *Black Jacks*; Gilje, *Liberty on the Waterfront*; Lemisch, *Jack Tar vs. John Bull*; Vickers, *Young Men and the Sea*; Vickers, *Farmers and Fishermen*; Peter Linebaugh and Marcus Rediker, *The Many Headed Hydra: Sailors, Slaves, Commoners, and the Hidden History of the Revolutionary Atlantic* (Boston: Beacon Press, 2000); Norling, *Captain Ahab Had a Wife*.

65. See Daniel Vickers, "Beyond Jack Tar," *William and Mary Quarterly*, 3rd series, 50, no. 2 (1993): 418-24.

3

1. Lorenzo Greene, *The Negro in New England, 1620-1775* (New York: Columbia University Press, 1942), 116; *New-England Weekly Journal,* April 24, 1724; *American Weekly Mercury,* April 25, 1723.

2. John Wood Sweet, *Bodies Politic: Negotiating Race in Early America, 1730-1830* (Baltimore: Johns Hopkins University Press, 2003), 377.

3. My identification of maritime fugitives has largely been based upon a review of more than 4,000 New York, Pennsylvania, and Rhode Island fugitive slave advertisements. These advertisements alone cannot fully describe the world that maritime fugitives encountered and became part of when they fled slavery. To recreate that world my research has included the review of muster rolls, log books, High Court of Admiralty and Vice-Admiralty records, newspaper dispatches, ship captains' journals, account books, military pension records, and secondary sources. This research resulted in the creation of the Colored Mariner Database ("*CMD*"), which now contains more than 8,700 colored mariners from throughout the Atlantic world. *CMD*'s colored mariners include maritime fugitives, any crew member on a ship that had a classical (e.g., Scippio), African (e.g., Quash) or place (e.g., Bristol) name, and those lacking a surname, which typically was an indication during the eighteenth century that an individual was or had been a slave. Due to most eighteenth-century records not providing racial identification, and many dark-skinned mariners having been given Christian surnames, the *CMD* undercounts the number of eighteenth-century colored mariners, although the extent of that undercounting cannot be stated with certainty.

4. Journal of William Richardson, 1780-1819, titled "The Wandering Sailor," 3 vols., JOD/156, National Maritime Museum, Greenwich, United Kingdom; escape via the sea in Northern British North American colonies was largely a tool of resistance used by men, Charles R. Foy, "Ports of Slavery, Ports of Freedom: How Slaves Used Northern Seaports' Maritime Industry to Escape and Create Trans-Atlantic Identities, 1713-1783," Ph.D. Diss., Rutgers

University, 2008, ch. 3; this was due to women having less freedom of movement than male slaves, the masculine ethos of the maritime industry, and women's child-rearing responsibilities, see Lisa Norling, *Captain Ahab Had A Wife: New England Women and the Whalefishery, 1720-1870* (Chapel Hill: University of North Carolina Press, 2000); Suzanne Stark, *Female Tars: Woman Aboard Ship in the Age of Sail* (Annapolis: Naval Institute Press, 1996); Margaret S. Creighton and Lisa Norling, eds., *Iron Men, Wooden Women: Gender and Seafaring in the Atlantic World, 1700-1920* (Chapel Hill: University of North Carolina Press, 1996); Deborah Gray White, *Ar'n't I a Woman: Female Slaves in the Plantation South* (New York: W.W. Norton, 1985); however, there were some women, such as the unnamed Negro woman from Boston, who when they fled, were believed to have sought berths on vessels, see *New-England Courant,* May 11, 1724.

5. David Cecelski, *Waterman's Song: Slavery and Freedom in Maritime North Carolina* (Chapel Hill: University of North Carolina Press, 2001), xvi; Gerald W. Mullin, *Flight and Rebellion: Slave Resistance in Eighteenth-Century Virginia* (New York: Oxford University Press, 1972); Peter H. Wood, *Black Majority: Negroes in Colonial South Carolina from 1670 through the Stono Rebellion* (New York: Random House, 1974), 123-24, 200-05; Tom Costa, "What We Can Learn from a Digital Databases of Runaway Slave Advertisements," *International Social Science Review* 76, nos. 1-2 (2001): 36-43; Philip D. Morgan, *Slave Counterpoint: Black Culture in the Eighteenth-Century Chesapeake & Lowcountry* (Chapel Hill: University of North Carolina Press, 1998), 340-41.

6. Paul Gilroy, *The Black Atlantic: Modernity and Double Consciousness* (Cambridge: Cambridge University Press, 1993), 12; W. Jeffrey Bolster, *Black Jacks: African American Seamen in the Age of Sail* (Cambridge, MA: Harvard University Press, 1997), 3, 11.

7. Foy, "Ports of Slavery, Ports of Freedom," ch. 3.

8. Among the Atlantic seamen whose age was compared to Northern maritime fugitives were Salem mariners (mid-20s), British transatlantic seamen (27.6), Scarborough (25.6) and Plymouth (30.6) crews, New York mariners (26.8), and a sampling of Americans on British naval ships in North America (27.7); Daniel Vickers, *Young Men and the Sea: Yankee Seafarers in the Age of Sail* (New Haven: Yale University Press, 2005), 119, appendix B; Marcus Rediker, *Between the Devil and the Deep Blue Sea: Merchant Seamen, Pirates, and the Anglo-American Maritime World, 1700-1750* (Cambridge: Cambridge University Press, 1987), 156; The National Archives, Kew, United Kingdom, (hereafter TNA), CUST 66/227; TNA CUST 91/111; TNA CUST 91/112; *New York Colonial Muster Rolls, 1664-1775,* 2 vols., *Third Annual Report of the State Historian of the State of New York,* appendix "M" (Baltimore: Genealogical Publishing Inc., 2000); and Foy, "Ports of Slavery, Ports of Freedom," ch. 3.

9. Vivienne L. Kruger, "Born to Run: The Slave Family in Early New York, 1626-1827," Ph.D. diss., Columbia University, 1985, ch. 4; Billy G. Smith and Richard Wojtowicz, *Blacks Who Stole Themselves: Advertisements for*

Runaways in the Pennsylvania Gazette (Philadelphia: Pennsylvania University Press, 1989), 8-9; *New-York Gazette & Weekly Mercury,* October 15, 1770.

10. David Waldstreicher, "Reading the Runaways: Self-Fashioning, Print Culture and Confidence in Slavery in the Eighteenth-Century Mid-Atlantic," *William and Mary Quarterly* 56, no. 2 (April 1999): 243-72; Charles R. Foy, "How Conflicts between Whites Shaped Slave Resistance in Colonial New York City," M.A. thesis, Rutgers University, Newark, NJ, 2002, Table 1-5.

11. Foy, "Ports of Slavery, Ports of Freedom," Tables 3-3, 4-3, and 5-3; *New-York Gazette and Weekly Mercury,* April 24, 1769; John Kolmos, "On the Biological Standard of Living Eighteenth-Century Americans: Taller, Richer, Healthier," University of Munich, http://epub.ub.uni-muechen.de/archive /00000053/01/h-usa.pdf (accessed July 6, 2006), Table 2; *Pennsylvania Chronicle and Universal Advertiser,* February 24, 1772; *New-York Mercury,* December 27, 1762; approximately 50 percent of all of Rhode Island's fugitives for whom their height was indicated were tall maritime fugitives, and some tall fugitives not described as maritime fugitives were owned by ship captains, making it likely that tall maritime fugitives exceeded 50 percent of all fugitives, see for example *Providence Gazette and Country Journal,* July 15, 1780.

12. *New-York Mercury,* October 16, 1765; *Providence Gazette,* August 16, 1777; *New-Jersey Gazette* (Trenton), April 17, 1782; *Pennsylvania Gazette,* May 9, 1751; *New-York Mercury,* March 15, 1756; Bryan Edwards, *Observations on the Disposition, Character, Manners and Habits of Life, of the Maroon Negroes of the Island of Jamaica* (London: J. Stockdale, 1796), reprinted as appendix to vol. 1, *History of the West Indies* (London, 1789), 527. I want to thank Kathleen Wilson for this reference; flight overseas offered the only realistic prospect of a permanent escape from smaller West Indian islands, N.A.T. Hall, "Maritime Maroons: Grand Marronage from the Danish West Indies," *William and Mary Quarterly* 42, no. 4 (October 1985): 481-82; in their review of 662 New York and New Jersey fugitive slave advertisements, Graham Hodges and Allen Brown noted only ten in which the runaway fled to the "backcountry," Graham Russell Hodges and Allen Brown, *Pretends to be Free: Runaway Slave Advertisements from Colonial and Revolutionary New York and New Jersey* (New York and London: Garland Publishing, Inc., 1994), 345.

13. Smith & Wojtowicz. *Blacks Who Stole Themselves,* 12; John A. Sainsbury, "Indian Labor in Early Rhode Island," *New England Quarterly* 48, no. 3 (September 1975): 391-92; *Pennsylvania Gazette,* November 3, 1763; *New-York Mercury,* October 16, 1765; *Newport Mercury,* September 28, 1772.

14. Michael Jarvis, "Maritime Masters and Seafaring Slaves in Bermuda, 1680-1783," *William and Mary Quarterly* 59, no. 3 (July 2002): 612; David Barry Gaspar, *Bondsmen and Rebels: A Study of Master-Slave Relations in Antigua* (Baltimore: Johns Hopkins University Press, 1985), 110-13, 286-87 n51; *New-York Evening Post,* June 19, 1749.

15. Kevin Dawson, "Enslaved Watermen in the Atlantic World," Ph.D. diss., University of South Carolina, 2005, 132, 144, 149, 196, 199; Lt. Gov. Hope to Council of Trade and Plantations, March 20, 1724, TNA CO 37/11, ff. 113-17.

16. Benjamin Douglas to the King, Recognizance Pursuant to the Condition of the Pardon of the Negroe Man Named Falmouth, Misc., Mss. B. Douglas, November 28, 1770, New-York Historical Society (hereafter N-YHS); *Rex v Falmouth,* New York County Supreme Court, July 31, August 3, 1770, Parchment Rolls, G-334, K-314; *Royal Gazette,* November 20, 1779.

17. South Carolinian slaves with maritime experience were exported to Northern ports, TNA CO 5/1222, 54, 224, 255; Morgan, *Slave Counterpoint*, 236-44, 310-11.

18. Jacobus Van Cortlandt to Mr. Jenkins, New York, April 15, 1698, in letter book of Jacobus Van Cortlandt, 1698-1700; Jacob Judd, "Frederick Philipse and the Madagascar Trade," *New-York Historical Quarterly* 55, no. 4 (October 1971): 364; Elias Neau to David Humphreys, June 23, 1721, in SPG Letter Books; Daniel DeFoe, *A General History of the Pyrates,* ed. Manuel Schonhorn (London, 1724; reprint, New York: Dover Publications, Inc., 1999), 247; David Eltis, Stephen D. Behrendt, David Richardson, Herbert S. Klein, and eds. *Trans-Atlantic Slave Trade Database*, vol. CD-ROM (Cambridge: Cambridge University Press, 1999), Voyages #25012 and #25014; *New-York Mercury,* August 7, 1758, October 11, 1762; Virginia Bever Platt, "The East India Company and the Madagascar Slave Trade," *William and Mary Quarterly* 26, no. 3 (October 1969): 548-77; Elizabeth Donnan, *Documents Illustrative of the Slave Trade to America* (Washington, D.C.: Carnegie Institute of Washington, 1930-35), 3:122; *American Weekly Mercury,* August 1, 1723, October 15, 1724.

19. Philip D. Morgan, "Black Experiences in Britain's Maritime World," in David Cannadine, ed., *Empire, the Sea and the Global History: Britain's Maritime World, 1760-1840* (New York: Palgrave McMillian, 2007), 105-33; George E. Brooks, *Eurafricans in Western Africa: Commerce, Social Status, Gender and Religious Observance from the Sixteenth to the Eighteenth Century* (Athens: Ohio University Press, 2003), 7, 52, 141, 177, 207, 297; James F. Searing, *West African Slavery and Atlantic Commerce: The Senegal River Valley, 1700-1860* (Cambridge: Cambridge University Press, 1993), 93, 117, 122; Edna Greene Medford, ed., New York City African Burial Ground History Final Report, http://www.africanburialground.com/History/ABG.pdf (accessed February 22, 2005), 93 (it is estimated that 77 percent of African imports to New York were from Senegambia); West African fishing practices were observed among slaves in other North American colonies, Wood, *Black Majority,* 200-02; Gold Coast West Africans were expert canoe men who regularly brought slaves to European ships, used their boats to fish in the Atlantic, and transported large cargos of goods to European vessels, Roger Quarm, "An Album of Drawings by Gabriel Bray RN, HMS *Pallas,* 1774-1775," *The Mariner's Mirror* 81, no. 1 (February 1995): 32-44; canoe skills assisted North American slaves to escape their masters and obtain berths, *Newport Mercury,* June 24, 1734; *New-York Gazette,* August 13, 1767.

20. Philip Curtin, *Economic Changes in Pre-Colonial Africa: Senegambia in the Era of the Slave Trade* (Madison: University of Wisconsin Press, 1975), 95-100; Bolster, *Black Jacks,* 50-1, 58; Platt, "The East India Company and the Madagascar Slave Trade," 548-77; *Pennsylvania Gazette,* May 20, 1742; *New-York Mercury,* December 27, 1762; few Senegambian children were

imported to the Northern British North American colonies, David Eltis and Stanley L. Engerman, "Fluctuations in Sex and Age Ratios in the Transatlantic Slave Trade, 1663-1864," *Economic History Review* 46 (1993): 308-23; G. Ugo Nwokeji, "African Conceptions of Gender and the Slave Trade," *William and Mary Quarterly* 58, no. 1 (January 2001): 47-68.

21. Foy, "Ports of Slavery, Ports of Freedom," ch. 1.

22. Irving H. Bartlett, *From Slave to Citizen: The Story of the Negro in Rhode Island* (Providence: Urban League of Greater Providence, 1954), 14; Edward H. Knoblach, "Mobilizing Provincials for War: The Social Composition of New York Forces in 1760," *New York History* 78 (1987): 147-72; *New-York Gazette & Weekly Post-Boy,* August 29, 1768; enslaved Muslims transported to the Americas tended to have come from urban settings in Africa and were experienced in dealing with peoples of varied cultural backgrounds, Paul Lovejoy, "The Urban Background of Enslaved Muslims in the Americas," *Slavery and Abolition* 26, no. 3 (December 2005): 349-76; Michael Gomez, *Black Crescent: The Experience and Legacy of African Muslims in the Americas* (Cambridge: Cambridge University Press, 2005), 371.

23. *New-York Mercury,* April 13, 1767; *New-York Gazette & Weekly Post-Boy,* June 16, 1768, November 24, 1777; *New-York Journal or General Advertiser,* March 19, 1772; *Pennsylvania Gazette,* September 8, 1774; Frank J. Klingberg, *Anglican Humanitarianism in Colonial New York* (Richmond: The Church History Society, 1940), 127.

24. Charles Nicolls Account Book, 1758-1760, N-YHS; Joanne Pope Melish, *Disowning Slavery: Gradual Emancipation and Race in New England, 1780-1860* (Ithaca, NY and London: Cornell University Press, 1998), 47; *New-York Gazette & Weekly Mercury*, November 24, 1777; James Lydon, *Pirates, Privateers and Profits* (Upper Saddle River, NJ: Gregg Press, 1970), 44-48, 193-94, 242; *Pennsylvania Gazette*, May 5, 1743, August 29, 1754; *Pennsylvania Chronicle and Universal Advertiser*, May 9, 1768; *New-York Gazette or Weekly Post-Boy,* July 24, 1758. See *American Weekly Mercury*, June 18, 1730; Ann Elizabeth Schuyler Account Book, 1737-1769 (BV Sec. Schuyler, N-YHS, 111 [May 1, 1737] and 185 [April 12, 1740]); James Pitcher Ledger, 1766-1782, N-YHS, for examples of slaves being hired out. See Thomas Witter Ledger Account Book, New York City, 1747-1768, N-YHS, January and July 1747 and May 1750; William D. Faulkner, Brewer, Ledger Book D, 1773-1790, N-YHS; and Inventory and Administration of the Estate of Adolph Philipse, New York Public Library, for examples of slaves hired out as sailors; hiring out slaves was also a common practice in Philadelphia and Newport, Gary B. Nash, *Forging Freedom* (Cambridge MA: Harvard University Press, 1988), 11,15-16, 286n27; examples of hiring out include *Newport Mercury*, February 6, 1764, January 9, February 3, 1775, September 28, November 8, 1776, January 2, 1778; *Pennsylvania Gazette*, July 4, 1768; *Pennsylvania Chronicle & Universal Advertiser*, June 3, 1771, November 7, 1772; *Pennsylvania Packet or General Advertiser*, April 27, 1772; and *Pennsylvania Evening Post*, March 1, 1777, July 11, 1778.

25. Charles Nicoll Day Book, 1780-1781, N-YHS; *New-York Mercury,* April 17, 1758; *American Weekly Mercury,* February 7, 1721, October 12, 1732, April 8, 1736; *Newport Mercury,* February 9, 1762, October 20, 1766, June 27, 1768, September 15, 1774; TNA CO 5/1222, 136; Graham Hodges, *Root & Branch: African Americans in New York & East Jersey, 1613-1863* (Chapel Hill: University of North Carolina Press, 1999), 110; Lydon, *Pirates, Privateers and Profits*, 193-94, 242; slaves "fit for sea service" were regularly sold in Northern ports, *Pennsylvania Gazette,* December 3, 1741, May 26, 1748, October 9, 1755; *New-York Gazette, Revived in the Weekly Post-Boy,* March 6, 1749; *New-York Gazette,* March 14, 1758; *New-York Mercury,* December 13, 1756; *Providence Gazette & Country Journal,* October 7, 1769; *Pennsylvania Packet or General Advertiser,* November 4, 1780.

26. *Connecticut Gazette,* February 17, 1775; *Newport Mercury,* August 15, 1774; Richard Shannon Moss, *Slavery on Long Island: A Study of Local Institutional and Early African-American Communal Life* (New York & London, 1993), 109.

27. Carl E. Swanson, "American Privateering and Imperial Warfare, 1739-1748," *William and Mary Quarterly* 42 (July 1985): 368; *Pennsylvania Gazette,* October 31, 1745; Lydon, "The Role of New York in Privateering Down to 1763," 14-15, 244; McDougall Papers, N-YHS, Reel 1, "List of Men Belonging to the Privateer Tyger."

28. N. A. T. Hall, "Maritime Maroons: Grand Maroonage from the Danish West Indies," *William and Mary Quarterly* 42, no. 4 (October 1985): 490; Lawrence A. Clayton, "Life at Sea in Colonial Spanish America: The New World Experience," in Paul Adam, ed., *Seamen in Society* (Bucharest: Secretarie General de la Commission Internationale d'Historie Maritime, 1980), III, 22, quoting a letter from Lima's Merchant Guild to the Real Tribunal del Consulado, 1753-1754; examples of ship-jumping include *New York Weekly Post-Boy,* April 19, 1756; *New York Mercury,* April 19, 1756; Edward Trelawny to Lords of Admiralty, December 21, 1743, TNA ADM 1/3917; Thomas Franklin to John Cleveland, Esq., April 28, 1757, TNA ADM 1/306; Jane B. Landers, "Garcia Real De Santa Teresa De Mose: A Free Black Town in Spanish Colonial Florida," in Stanley N. Katz, John M. Murrin, and Douglas Greenburg, eds., *Colonial America: Essays in Politics and Social Development* (New York: McGraw-Hill Higher Education, 2001), 609.

29. Landers, "Gracia Real de Santa Teresa de Mose," 595-619.

30. In 1758 a French privateer captured in the West Indies had 34 sailors "of the woolly race" out of a crew of 80. This crew was not unusual as Spanish and French privateers operating in the West Indies could not "get their Privateers mann'd" without black mariners, Letter from the Board of Trade to the Crown, February 10, 1758, TNA CO 318/3, 365.

31. *New-York Gazette,* January 30, 1732; and Daniel E. Meaders, "South Carolina Fugitives as Viewed Through Local Colonial Newspapers with Emphasis on Runaway Notices, 1732-1801," *Journal of Negro History* 60 (1975): 304.

32. Julius Scott, "Crisscrossing Empires: Ships, Sailors, and Resistance in the Lesser Antilles in the Eighteenth Century," in Robert Paquette and Stanley L.

Engerman, eds., *The Lesser Antilles in the Eighteenth Century* (Gainsville: University of Florida Press, 1998), 135.

33. N.A.M. Rodgers, *The Wooden World: An Anatomy of the Georgian Navy* (Annapolis: Naval Institute Press, 1988), 160; F. Holbourne, December 17, 22, 29, 1758, TNA ADM 1/927; *TASD*; see George Van Cleve, "Somerset's Case and its Antecedents in Imperial Perspective," *Law and History Review* 24, no. 3 (Fall 2006): 601-02; Foote, *Black and White Manhattan,* 198; see *Virginia Gazette* (Purdie & Dixon), Williamsburg, September 30, 1773; and Gretchin Gerzina, *Black London, Life Before Emancipation* (New Brunswick, NJ: Rutgers University Press, 1995), 130, for examples of slaves who believed that if they reached England the *Somerset* decision would ensure their freedom. Although Admiralty regulations prohibited slaves enlisting as seamen (they could be employed as servants and stewards), naval officers were known to use slave mariners in their private ventures. During the Seven Years War Admiral Douglas, Commander of the West Indies fleet, manned his private sloops in the Leeward Islands partly with slaves, some free mulattoes, and Negroes captured as prisoners of war and condemned to slavery, *Wooden World*, 159-60; N.A.M. Rodgers, "The Douglas Papers, 1760-1762" in *The Naval Miscellany,* vol. 5, 264, 275.

34. *Somerset v Stewart,* 20 How. St. Tr. (1772) in Helen Tunnicliff Catterall, ed., *Judicial Cases Concerning American Slavery and the Negro* (Washington, D.C.: Carnegie Institute, 1926), 1:15.

35. TNA CO 5/148, folio 70-71 (May 17, 1776), folio 75 (May 19, 1776), folio 86d (May 2, 1776) and folio 92-93 (May 21, 1776).

36. Prior to 1747 Scarborough "crews were not paying the [required seamen's sixpence] dues," resulting in "distress amongst the seamen of the Town." The 1750s saw renewed enforcement of the duty and construction of additional hospital beds, Records of Scarborough Trinity House, North Yorkshire Record Office, ZOX 10/1; out of the more than 3,000 Scarborough crew members in the period between 1748 and 1759, only seven were colored mariners, Scarborough Crew Lists, 1748-1759, TNA CUST 91/111-112.

37. *Pennsylvania Gazette,* March 3, 1743; Zabin, "Places of Exchange," 102; Richard Bond, "Spanish Negroes and Their Fight for Freedom," *New York Archives* 3 (Summer 2003): 13-15; *Boston Gazette,* October 5, 1741; *Boston News-Letter,* October 1, 1741; HMS *Garlands,* Muster Rolls, 1764, TNA ADM 36/7390. For some slave mariners freedom resulted not through active resistance, but rather the capture of their master's ship. In 1781, after the New London privateer *Mercury* was captured by a British warship, the ship's slave cook Romeo found himself "Set at Liberty being a Slave." Romeo's experience was not an isolated event, as a number of British naval officers interpreted Dunmore's Declaration to require them to free other captured slave mariners, Louis F. Middlebrook, Undated biographical sketch of Elisha Lathrop, VFM 405, G. W. Blunt White Library, Mystic Seaport; and HMS *Monk,* Muster Roll, 1781, TNA ADM 36/1999. The risk of mariners of color being sold was not limited to periods of war. For example, in 1725 Peter Van Trump, a free black mariner from St. Thomas, signed on for a voyage to Europe only to find the ship

captain steered the ship into North Carolina where he sold Van Trump, Bolster, *Black Jacks,* 31.

38. Letter from Ben, dated 1774 [1784?], Rhode Island Historical Society (hereafter RIHS), Mss 9003, vol. 16, 99; Ben to "Dear Master," June 16, 1774 [1784?], Mss 9003, vol. 16, 97, RIHS. Captain Battle made slaving voyages to the Gold Coast in the *Happy Return* and *Hawke* in 1776 and 1777, *TASD* # 25017 and 27302. I want to thank Philip D. Morgan for providing the documents from the Rhode Island Historical Society regarding Ben Freebody.

39. Deposition of George Irish, July 1, 1786, Mss 9003, vol. 16, 102, RIHS; the brutality of public whipping in Grenada is described in some detail in the Deposition of James Duncan, July 1, 1786, Mss 9003, vol. 16, 103, RIHS.

40. Bryan Rommel-Ruiz mistakenly believed that Ben Freebody "sailed to live in Nova Scotia as a freedman," Rommel-Ruiz, "Atlantic Revolutions: Slavery and Freedom in Newport, Rhode Island, and Halifax, Nova Scotia, in the Era of the American Revolution," Ph.D. Diss., University of Michigan, 1999, 2. Although a "Ben Freebody" owned by a Samuel Freebody is listed in the *Black Loyalist Directory* as boarding the sloop *Cato* to sail to Nova Scotia in 1783, subsequent proceedings in Rhode Island concerning Samuel Freebody's claim against Captain Brattle for compensation for the ship captain having kidnapped Ben make clear that Samuel Freebody's Ben Freebody detained by Captain Brattle did not go to Nova Scotia, but returned to Rhode Island, Graham Hodges, ed., *The Black Loyalist Directory: African Americans in Exile After the American Revolution* (New York, 1996), 162; Deposition of George Irish, July 1, 1786, Mss 9003, vol. 16, 102, RIHS; August 10, 1790, Note from Samuel Freebody, Mss 9003, vol. 16, 103, RIHS.

41. Ben's belief that Samuel Freebody's "goodness" would result in his freedom and being paid sailor's wages was obviously misplaced, Freebody to Dear Master," June 16, 1774 [1784], Mss 9003, vol. 16, 97, RIHS; Captain Brattle unsuccessfully tried to settle the matter for $200, but the ultimate outcome of the dispute is unknown, George Irish, Deposition, July 1, 1786, Mss 9003, vol. 16, 102, RIHS.

42. Venture Smith, "A Narrative of the Life and Adventures of Venture, a Native of Africa," (New London, 1798), in *Five Black Lives* (Middletown, CT: Wesleyan University Press, 1971), 8-24; Desrochers, "Not Fade Away," *Journal of American History* 84, no. 1 (June 1997): 42, 50-51.

43. Paul C. van Royen, "The National Maritime Labour Market," in *"Those Emblems of Hell"? European Sailors and the Maritime Labour Market, 1570-1870* (St. John's, Newfoundland: International Maritime Economic History Association, 1997), 6, quoting Marcus Rediker and N.A.M. Rodgers.

44. Salem, Massachusetts, was a port that underwent such a significant change. From the 1750s into the mid-nineteenth century, Salem had a vibrant black community in which one-quarter of the black men worked as mariners. By the end of the Civil War only 18 black mariners from Salem were listed on the port's crew lists, and by 1880, only three black mariners, all over 50 years old, remained on the port's vessels, Gary Wills, *"Negro President": Jefferson and the*

Slave Power (Boston and New York: Houghton Mifflin, 2003), 19; Brian S. Kirby, "The Loss and Recovery of the Schooner *Amity:* An Episode in Salem Maritime History," *New England Quarterly* 62 (1989): 553-60.

4

1. Nicholas Orme, *Early British Swimming, 55 BC–AD 1719: With the First Swimming Treatise in English, 1595* (Exeter: University of Exeter, 1983); Richard Mandell, *Sport: A Cultural History* (New York: Columbia University Press, 1984), 179-80; Olaudah Equiano, *The Interesting Narrative of the Life of Olaudah Equiano, or Gustavus Vassa, the African, Written by Himself* (1789; New York, 1995), 258, n167; J. Frost, *The art of Swimming: A Series of Practical Instructions on an Original and Progressive plan. To which is added, Dr. Franklin's Treatise* (New York: P.W. Gallaudet, 1818), frontpiece; "Swimming," *Sailor's Magazine*, 11 (January 1839): 152; Theodorus Bailey Myers Mason, *The Preservation of Life at Sea: A Paper Read Before the American Geographical Society, February 27th, 1879* (New York, 1879), 2-3; Thomas Tegg, *The Art of Swimming* (London: Thomas Tegg, ca. 1805-1824), 5-6; Richard McAllister Smith, *The Confederate First Reader: Containing Selections in Prose and Poetry, as Reading Exercises for the Younger Children in the Schools and Families of the Confederate States* (Richmond: G. L. Bidgood, 1864), 20-21; William Percey, *The Compleat Swimmer: Or, The art of Swimming: Demonstrating the Rules and Practice Thereof, in an Exact, Plain and Easie Method. Necessary to be Known and Practised by all who Studie or Desire their own Preservation* (London: printed by J.C. for Henry Fletcher, 1658), v; Benjamin Franklin, *The Art of Swimming Rendered Easy* (Glasgow: Printed for the booksellers, 1840?), 3-4; 8-9; Archibald Sinclair and William Henry, *Swimming* (London: Longmans, Greens & Co., 1893), 27; 186-280; Everard Digby, *A short introduction for to learne to swimme. Gathered out of Master Digbies Booke of the Art of Swimming. And translated into English for the better instruction of those who understand not the Latine tongue. By Christofer Middleton* (1587; London: Printed by Iames Roberts for Edward White, and are to be sold at the little North doore of Paules Church, at the signe of the Gun, 1595), 3-4; Richard Nelligan, *The Art of Swimming: A Practical, Working Manual. Graphically Illustrated from Original Drawings and Photographs, with a Clear and Concise Description of All Strokes* (Boston: American Gymnasia Company, 1906); Melchisédec Thévenot, *Art de nager. The art of Swimming. Illustrated by Proper Figures. With Advice for Bathing. By Monsìeur Thevenot. Done out of French. To which is Prefixed a Prefatory Discourse Concerning Artificial Swimming, or Keeping ones self Above Water by Several small Portable Engines, in case of Danger* (London: printed for Dan Brown at the Swan without Temple-Bar; D. Midwinter and T. Leigh at the Rose and Crown, and Robert Knaplock at the Angel, in St. Pauls Church-Yard, 1699), i-viii, 1, 4-5.
2. For scholars' discussion of how maritime occupations could ameliorate the conditions of bondage and create degrees of racial parity, see James Farr, "A

Slow Boat to Nowhere: The Multi-Racial Crews of the American Whaling Industry," *Journal of Negro History* 68, no. 2 (Spring 1983): 159-70; W. Jeffrey Bolster, *Black Jacks: African America Seamen in the Age of Sail* (Cambridge, MA: Harvard University Press, 1997); David Cecelski, *Waterman's Song: Slavery and Freedom in Maritime North Carolina* (Chapel Hill: The University of North Carolina Press, 2001); Michael Craton and Gail Saunders, *Islanders in the Stream: A History of the Bahamian People from Aboriginal Times to the end of Slavery* (Athens: University of Georgia Press, 1999); Gail D. Saunders, *Slavery in the Bahamas, 1648-1838* (Nassau, Bahamas: Nassau Guardian, 1985); Virginia Bernhard, *Slaves and Slaveholders in Bermuda*; (Columbia: University of Missouri Press, 1999); Jane Landers, *Black Society in Spanish Florida* (Chicago: University of Illinois Press, 1999); Bayly E. Marks, "Skilled Blacks in Antebellum St. Mary's County, Maryland," *The Journal of Southern History* 53, no. 4 (November 1987): 537-64.

3. Digby, *A short introduction for to learne to swimme*; Percey, *The Compleat swimmer: Or, The art of Swimming*; Thévenot, *Art de nager. The art of Swimming*; Tegg, *The art of Swimming*; Frost, *The art of Swimming: A Series of Practical Instructions*; Orme, *Early British Swimming*; "Swimming," *Sailor's Magazine*, 152; Mandell, *Sport: A Cultural History*, 112-13, 179-80; Sinclair and Henry, *Swimming*; Nelligan, *The Art of Swimming: A Practical, Working Manual*, frontpiece; 12-14.

4. Frost, *The art of Swimming: A Series of Practical Instructions*, 9; Orme, *Early British Swimming*, 164; Benjamin Franklin, *The Art of Swimming Rendered Easy*, 14; Digby, *A short introduction for to learne to swimme;* Mason, *The Preservation of Life at Sea*; Nelligan, *The Art of Swimming: A Practical, Working Manual*, 12-17. Manuscript illustrations suggest that the breaststroke (in various versions) was the most common European swim stroke and that dogpaddle and back- and sidestrokes were widely used, yet they do not depict the freestyle. However, illustrations, as Nicholas Orme warned, are imperfect documentations. Artists may not have understood or clearly observed the swim strokes of their day. Additionally, they may have employed artistic license or adhered to artistic conventions, Orme, *Early British Swimming*, 38-40.

5. For Native Americans and Asians being strong swimmers and using the freestyle, see Mandell, *Sport: A Cultural History*, 180; Thévenot, *Art de nager. The art of Swimming*, vii-viii; Nelligan, *Swimming*, 27; Sinclair and Henry, *Swimming*, 97-105; William Strachey, *The Historie of Travell into Virginia Britania* (1612; London: The Hakluyt Society, 1953), 66; Clements Markham, ed., *The Hawkins' Voyages During the Reigns of Henry VIII, Queen Elizabeth, and James I* (1847; New York: Burt Franklin, 1970), 157-58, 314; George Catlin, *Letters and Notes on the Manners, Customs, and Conditions of the North American Indians: Written During Eight Years' Travel (1832-1839) Amongst the Wildest Tribes of Indian in North America*, 2 vols. (1844; New York: Henry G. Bohn, 1973), I: 96-97; Pierre Antoine Tabeau, *Tabeau's Narrative of Loisel's Expedition to the Upper Missouri,* ed. Annie Heloise Abel (Norman: University of Oklahoma Press, 1939), 74; John Bradbury, *Travels in the Interior of America* (Liverpool: Printed for the author, by Smith and Galway, and published by Sherwood, Neely, and Jones, 1817), 160-61; George Frederick Kunz and Charles

Hugh Stevenson, *The Book of the Pearl: Its History, Art, Science and Industry* (1908; New York: Century Co., 2001); Charles Warren Stoddard, *Cruising the South Seas: Stories by Charles Warren Stoddard* (1904; San Francisco: Gay Sunshine Press, 1987), 93-95, 117-18; Hiram Bingham, *A Residence of Twenty-one Years in the Sandwich Islands* (Hartford: H. Huntington, 1847), 382-83; Walter Colton, *Deck and Port: Or Incidents of a Cruise in the United States Frigate Congress to California. With Sketches of Rio Janeiro, Valparaiso, Lima, Honolulu, and San Francisco* (New York: A.S. Barnes & Co., 1850) 352-53; Mark Twain, *Roughing It* (1872; New York: Penguin Putnam, Inc., 1962); Ben Finney and James D. Houston, *Surfing: A History of the Ancient Hawaiian Sport* (Rohnert Park: Pomegranate Books, 1996).

6. For "ordinary" methods of swimming, see Benjamin Franklin, *The Art of Swimming Rendered Easy*, 15; Richard Ligon, *A True and Exact History of the Island of Barbadoes* (1673; Portland, 1998), 53; P.E.H. Hair, Adam Jones, and Robin Law, eds., *Barbot on Guinea: The Writings of Jean Barbot on West Africa, 1678-1712*, 2 vols., (London: Hakluyt Society, 1992), 2: 545 n50; R.S. Rattray, *Ashanti* (Oxford: Clarendon Press, 1923), 63; Catlin, *Letters and Notes on the Manners, Customs, and Conditions of the North American Indians*, 1: 97.

7. Pieter de Marees, *Description and Historical Account of the Gold Kingdom of Guinea*, trans. Albert Van Dantzig and Adam Jones (1602; New York: Oxford University Press, 1987), 26, 32, esp. 186-87; Pieter Van den Broecke, *Pieter Van den Broecke's Journal of Voyages to Cape Verde, Guinea and Angola, 1605-1612*, trans. J.D. La Fleur (1634; London: Hakluyt Society, 2000), 37; Hair, Jones, and Law, eds., *Barbot on Guinea*, 2: 532; Rattray, *Ashanti*, 63; Horatio Bridge, *Journal of an African Cruiser: Comprising Sketches of the Canaries, the Cape Verds, Liberia, Madeira, Sierra Leone, and Other Places of Interest on the West Coast of Africa* (New York: George P. Putnam & Co., 1853), 174.

8. George Catlin, *Letters and Notes on the Manners, Customs, and Conditions of the North American Indian*, 1: 96-97.

9. For swimming, see de Marees, *Description and Historical Account of the Gold Kingdom of Guinea*, 26; Hair, Jones, and Law, eds., *Barbot on Guinea*, 2: 532, 501 n16, 640; Adam Jones, ed., *German Sources for West African History, 1599-1669* (Weisbaden: Franz Steiner Verlag GMBH, 1983), 103, Bosman, *A New and Accurate Description of the Coast of Guinea*, 121-22; William Smith, *A New Voyage to Guinea: Describing the Customs, Manners, Soil, Climate, Habits, Buildings, Education, Manual Arts, Agriculture, Trade, Employment, Languages, Ranks of Distinction, Habitations, Diversions, Marriages, and Whatever else is Memorable among the Inhabitants. Likewise an Account of their Animals, Minerals, &c. with a great Variety of Entertaining Incidents, Worthy of Observation, that Happen'd During the Author's Travels in that Large Country* (1774; London: Frank Cass & Co., 1967), 210. For nursing practices, see Patrick Manning, *Slavery and African Life: Occidental, Oriental, and African Slave Trades* (Cambridge: Cambridge, University Press, 1990), 55; Peter Kolchin, *American Slavery, 1619-1877* (New York: Wang and Hill, 1993), 44; Richard Steckel, "Women, Work, and Health Under Plantation Slavery in the United States," in David Barry Gaspar and Darlene Clark Hines, eds., *More than*

Chattel: Black Women and Slavery in the Americas (Bloomington: University of Indiana Press, 1996), 57; Barbara Bush, "Hard Labor: Women, Childbirth, and Resistance in British Caribbean Slave Societies," in Ibid., 202-03; de Marees, *Description and Historical Account of the Gold Kingdom of Guinea*, 26; Hair, Jones, and Law, eds., *Barbot on Guinea*, 2: 532, 501, 640.

10. Hair, Jones, and Law, eds., *Barbot on Guinea*, 2: 532.

11. Ibid., 2: 497 n3, 501, 510 n20, 529-32, 544 n545, 545 n46, 545 n550, 573 n8, 640; de Marees, *Description and Historical Account of the Gold Kingdom of Guinea*, 26, 32, 186-87; Jones, *German Sources for West African History*, 12, 103, 109, 219; Crow, *Memoirs of the Late Captain Hugh Crow, of Liverpool*, 34, 39-40.

12. Mungo Park, *Travels in the Interior Districts of Africa: Performed under the Direct Patronage of the African Association, in the Years 1795, 1796, and 1797* (1799; New York: Arno Press & the New York Times, 1971), 71-72, 210-11; Mungo Park, *Travels of Mungo Park containing Book One, The First Journey: Travels in the Interior districts of Africa. and Book Two, The Second Journey: The Journal of a Mission to the Interior of Africa in the Year 1805* (London: J.M. Dent & Sons, 1954), 53-54, 161.

13. Finney and Houston, *Surfing: A History of the Ancient Hawaiian Sport*, 88; Jean Fouch, "Surf–riding sur la Côte d'Afrique," *Note Africaines. Bulletin d' Information et de Correspondence de l'Institut Français d'Afrique Noire* (April 1949): 50-53; C. Béart, Jeux et "Jouets de l'Ouest Africain," *Mémoires de l'Institut Français d'Afrique Noire* 42 (Dakar, Senegal: 1959), 329-31; Ben Finney, "Surfboarding in West Africa," in *Wiener Völkerkundliche Mitteilungen* 5 (1962): 41-42; Jones, *German Sources for West African History*, 109; Hair, Jones, and Law, eds., *Barbot on Guinea*, 2: 532; James Edward Alexander, *Narrative of a Voyage of Observation among the Colonies of Western Africa, in the Flag-Ship Thalia; and of a Campaign in Kaffir-Land, on the Staff of the Commander-in-Chief, in 1835* (London: Henry Colburn, 1837), 192; Thomas J. Hutchinson, *Ten Years' Wanderings Among the Ethiopians. With Sketches of the Manners and Customs of the Civilized and Uncivilized Tribes, from Senegal to Gaboon* (1861; reprint, London; Frank Cass, 1967), 227-28.

14. De Marees, *Description and Historical Account of the Gold Kingdom of Guinea*, 186.

15. Mandell, *Sport: A Cultural History*, 180.

16. Stedman, *Narrative of Five Year's Expedition Against the Revolted Negroes of Surinam*, 214; Benjamin A. Botkin, ed., *Slave Narratives, a Folk History of Slavery in the United States from Interviews with Former Slaves. North Carolina Narratives*, vol 11, part 1 (Washington, D.C.: Works Projects Administration 1941), 208; J.G. Clinkscales, *On The Old Plantation: Reminiscences of his Childhood* (Spartanburg, SC: Band & White, 1916), 7-9, 26, 29, 35-36; Stacy Close, *Elderly Slaves of the Plantation South* (New York: Routledge, 1997), 20; Frederick Douglass, *My Bondage and My Freedom* (New York: Miller, Orton & Mulligan, 1855), 36; 65; Charles L. Perdue, Jr., Thomas E. Barden, and Robert K. Phillips, eds., *Weevils in the Wheat: Interviews with Virginia Ex–Slaves*

(Charlottesville: University of Virginia Press, 1976), 325; Kate E. Pickard, *The Kidnapped and the Ransomed: Being the Personal Recollections of Peter Still and his Wife "Vina" after Forty Years of Slavery* (Syracuse: William T. Hamilton, 1856), 229-30.

17. John Blassingame, *The Slave Community: Plantation Life in the Antebellum South* (New York: Oxford University Press, 1972), 105-09; Eugene D. Genovese, *Roll Jordan Roll: The World the Slaves Made* (New York: Random House, 1972), 569; David Wiggins, "Good Times on the Old Plantation: Popular Recreations of the Black Slave in the Antebellum South, 1810–1860," *Journal of Sport History* 4, no. 3 (1977): 273-74; Mandell, *Sport: A Cultural History*, 180; Betty Wood, *Women's Work, Men's Work: The Informal Slave Economies of Lowcountry* (Athens: University of Georgia Press, 1995), 135; Kenneth S. Greenberg, *Honor and Slavery: Lies, Duels, Noses, Masks, Dressing as a Woman, Gifts, Strangers, Humanitarianism, Death, Slave Rebellions, the Proslavery Argument, Baseball, Hunting, and Gaming in the Old South* (Princeton, NJ: Princeton University Press, 1996), 34-35; Equiano, *The Interesting Narrative of the Life of Olaudah Equiano*, 70; Henry Bibb, *Narrative and Life Adventures of Henry Bibb, an American Slaves* (1850; New York: Negro University Press, 1869), 23; Stedman, *Narrative of Five Year's Expedition Against the Revolted Negroes of Surinam,* 214.

18. Stedman, *Narrative of Five Year's Expedition Against the Revolted Negroes of Surinam*, 214.

19. Wiggins, "Good Times on the Old Plantation," 273; Genovese, *Roll, Jordan, Roll*, 569; Clinkscales, *On The Old Plantation*, 7-9, 26-29, 35-36. Mandel defined "formal" sporting events as those announced in advance with invited spectators, which is what these slaveholders did, Mandell, *Sport: A Cultural History*, xiii, 180.

20. Ligon, *A True and Exact History of the Island of Barbadoes*, 52-53.

21. Blassingame, *The Slave Community*, 105; Wiggins, "Good Times on the Old Plantation."

22. Stedman, *Narrative of Five Year's Expedition Against the Revolted Negroes of Surinam*, 7; Douglass, *My Bondage and My Freedom*, 33-37, 40, 42, 60, 65, 70; Perdue, et. al., *Weevils in the Wheat*, 325; Wilma King, *Stolen Childhood: Slave Youth in Nineteenth-Century America* (Bloomington: University of Indiana Press, 1995), 67-80; Wilma King "'Suffer with them till Death': Slave Women and Their Children in Nineteenth–Century America," in David Barry Gaspar and Darlene Clark Hines, eds., *More than Chattel: Black Women and Slavery in the Americas* (Bloomington: University of Indiana Press, 1996), 147-68; Deborah Gray White, *Ar'n't I a Woman? Female Slaves in the Plantation South* (New York: W. W. Norton, 1985); Elizabeth Fox-Genovese, *Within the Plantation Household: Black and White Women of the Old South* (Chapel Hill: University of North Carolina Press, 1988), 146-91; Lawrence Levine, *Black Culture and Black Consciousness: Afro-American Folk Thought from Slavery to Freedom* (Oxford: Oxford University Press, 1977), passim, especially 90-133; Genovese, *Roll Jordan Roll*, 503-19; Blassingame, *The Slave Community*,

186-88, Kolchin, *American Slavery*, 142; Betty Wood, *Women's Work, Men's Work*, 31-34, 40-43; Schwartz, *Born in Bondage;* Herbert S. Klein, *African Slavery in Latin America and the Caribbean* (Oxford: Oxford University Press, 1986), 169-78; Gail Saunders, *Slavery in the Bahamas,* 258-61; Hilary Beckles, *Natural Rebels: A Social History of Enslaved Black Women in Barbados* (New Brunswick, NJ: Rutgers University Press, 1989), 115-31.

23. Ligon, *A True and Exact History of the Island of Barbadoes*, 52; Robert Walsh, *Notice of Brazil in 1828 and 1829,* 2 vols. (Boston, 1831), 1: 281; Francis Fedric, *Slave Life in Virginia and Kentucky* (London, 1863), 1-2; Stedman, *Narrative of Five Year's Expedition Against the Revolted Negroes of Surinam*, 7-8, 57, 86, 154, 157-58, 164, 192, 214.

24. Schwartz, *Born in Bondage*, 101, 130.

25. Neville Hall, "Maritime Maroons," 387-400; Jorge Chinea, "Quest for Freedom," 51-87; Douglas Hall, ed., *In Miserable Slavery: Thomas Thistlewood in Jamaica, 1750–86* (Hong Kong: Macmilliam Publishers, 1989), 54-55; Jackson, *The Experience of a Slave in South Carolina*, 23-24; James Pennington, *A Narrative of Events of the Life of J. H. Banks, an Escaped Slave, from the Cotton State, Alabama* (Liverpool: J. W. C. Pennington, M. Rourke, Printer, 1861), 37-41; Clinkscales, *On The Old Plantation*, 16-19; Solomon Bayley, *A Narrative of Some Remarkable Incidents in the Life of Solomon Bayley Formerly a Slave in the State of Delaware* (London: Harvey and Darton, 1825), 5-7; James Lindsay Smith, *Autobiography of James L. Smith, Including, Also, Reminiscences of Slave Life* (Norwich, CT: Press of the Bulletin Company, 1881), 16-20; David Turnbull, *Travels in the West; Cuba, with Notices of Porto Rico* (London: Printed for Longman, Orne, Brown, Green, and Longmans, 1840), 365; Allen Parker, *Recollections of Slavery Times* (Worcester, MA: Chas. W. Burbank & Co., 1895), 29, 47-48; Isaac Johnson, *Slavery Days in Old Kentucky. A True Story of a Father Who Sold His Wife and Four Children* (Ogdensburg, NY: Republican & Journal, 1901), 29-30.

26. Pinckard, *Notes*, 2: 149, 321; Clinkscales, *On The Old Plantation*, 26.

27. Robert Haynes, *The Barbadian Diary of General Robert Haynes, 1787-1836* (Hampshire: Azania Press, 1934), 26; H. G. Adams, ed., *God's Image in Ebony: Being a Series of Biographical Sketches, Facts, Anecdotes, etc., Demonstrative of the Mental Powers and Intellectual Capacities of the Negro Race* (London: Partridge and Oakey, 1854), 159-60; Zamba, *The Life and Adventures of Zamba, an African Negro King; and His Experience of Slavery in South Carolina* (London: Smith, Elder and Co., 1847), 1, 168-70; Frederic W. N. Bayley, *Four Year's Residence in the West Indies, During the Years 1826,7,8, and 9* (London: William Kidd, 1833), 486.

28. De Marees, *Description and Historical Account of the Gold Kingdom of Guinea*, 186-87; Crow, *Memoirs of the Late Captain Hugh Crow, of Liverpool*, 44; Equiano, *The Interesting Narrative of the Life of Olaudah Equiano*, 54; Ligon, *A True and Exact History of the Island of Barbadoes*, 53; Stedman, *Narrative of Five Year's Expedition Against the Revolted Negroes of Surinam*, 214.

29. Craton, *Invisible Man*, 142; Betty Wood, *Women's Work, Men's Work*; Morgan,

Laboring Women, 144-65; Beckles, *Natural Rebels*; Kolchin, *American Slavery*, 105.

30. Sinclair and Henry, *Swimming*, 110-11; Bernhard, *Slaves and Slaveholders in Bermuda*, 6-7; Howard Larson, *A History of Self-Contained Diving and Underwater Swimming: Prepared for the Office of Naval Research under the auspices of the Committee on Undersea Warfare* (Washington, DC: National Academy of Sciences, National Research Council, 1959), 7-26; R. W. H. Hardy, *Travels in the Interior of Mexico: In 1825, 1826, 1827, and 1828* (London: H. Colburn and R. Bentley, 1829), 231-60, especially 250; Stedman, *Narrative of Five Year's Expedition Against the Revolted Negroes of Surinam*, 154.

31. Dusinberre, *Them Dark Days*, 179-210, especially 190; Kolchin, *American Slavery*, 51-54; 105-09; Genovese, *Roll, Jordan, Roll*, 294-98, 392-98; Klein, *African Slavery in Latin America and the Caribbean*, 31-32; Bayly Marks, "Skilled Blacks in Antebellum St. Mary's County, Maryland," *Journal of Southern History* 53 (November 1987): 537-64; Littlefield, *Rice and Slaves*, 93-95, 106; Carney, *Black Rice*, 94-97; Richard Sheridan, *Sugar and Slavery: An Economic History of the British West Indies, 1623–1775* (Baltimore: Johns Hopkins University Press, 1973), 107-18, 339-40; Charles B. Dew, *Bond of Iron: Master and Slave at Buffalo Forge* (New York: W. W. Norton, 1994).

32. Dusinberre, *Them Dark Days*, 192, 196-201; Kolchin, *American Slavery*, 109.

33. Price, "Caribbean Fishing and Fishermen"; Farr, "A Slow Boat to Nowhere: The Multi–Racial Crews of the American Whaling Industry"; Bolster, *Black Jacks*; Cecelski, *Waterman's Song*; Linebaugh and Rediker, *Many-Headed Hydra*.

34. Dusinberre, *Them Dark Days*, 178-210; Kolchin, *American Slavery*, 53.

35. Jose de Acosta, *Natural and Moral History of the Indies: Descriptions of Notable Things about the Sky, Elements, Metal, Plants, and Animals, and Rituals and Ceremonies, Laws and Government of the Indians. Including Information on the Religion and Beliefs of the Indians of Mexico* (1590; Buenos Aires: Fundo de Cultura Ecómica, 1962), ch. 15; Sanford Alexander Mosk, "Spanish Pearl Fishing Operations on the Pearl Coast in the Sixteenth Century," *Hispanic American Historical Review* 18 (August 1938): 392-402; R.A. Donkin, *Beyond Price: Pearls and Pearl-Fishing, Origins to the Age of Discoveries* (Philadelphia: American Philosophical Society, 1998), 321-22; Francis Augustus MacNutt, ed., *Bartholomew de Las Casas: His Life, His Apostolate and His Writings* (New York: G.P. Putnam's Sons, 1909), 374-83.

36. De Marees, *Description and Historical Account of the Gold Kingdom of Guinea*, 186.

37. Antonio Vázquez de Espinosa, *Compendium and Description of the West Indies* (ca. 1634: Washington, D.C.: Smithsonian Institution, 1942), 51-52; John Ogilby, *America: Being the Latest and most Accurate Description of the New World; Containing the Original Inhabitants, and the Remarkable Voyages Thither. The Conquest of the vast Empires of Mexico and Peru, and Other Large Provinces and territories, with Several European Plantations in those Parts. Also Their Cities, Fortresses, Towns, Temples, Mountains, and Rivers. Their*

Habits, Customs, Manners, and Religions. Their Plants, beasts, Birds, and Serpents. With an Appendix, containing, besides sever other considerable Additions, a brief Survey of what hath been discov'd of the Unknown South–Land and the Artick Region. Collected from most Authentic Authors, Augmented with later Observations, and Adorn'd with Maps and Sculptures, by John Ogilby Esq; His Majesty's Cosmographer, Geographic Printer, and Master of the Revels in the Kingdom of Ireland (London: Printed by the Author, 1671), 227; Donkin, *Beyond Price: Pearls and Pearl-Fishing*, 323; Markham, ed., *The Hawkins' Voyages*, 313-15; Samuel de Champlain, *Narrative of a Voyage to the West Indies and Mexico in the Years 1599-1602* (London: Hakluyt Society, 1859), 7.

38. De Espinosa, *Compendium*, 51-52; de Champlain, *Narrative*, 7.

39. Acosta, *Natural and Moral History of the Indies*, ch. 15; Ogilby, *America: Being the Latest and most Accurate Description of the New World*, 227; Mosk, "Spanish Pearl Fishing," 295, 399; Donkin, *Beyond Price: Pearls and Pearl-Fishing*, 321-29.

40. J. H. Parry, *The Spanish Seaborne Empire* (Berkeley: University of California Press, 1990), 1; Donkin, *Beyond Price: Pearls and Pearl-Fishing*, 318-24; Mosk, "Spanish Pearl Fishing," 397.

41. Donkin, *Beyond Price: Pearls and Pearl-Fishing*, 324, 327, 328-29; Dunn, *Sugar and Slave*, 10; Van den Broecke, *Pieter Van den Broecke's Journal of Voyages to Cape Verde*, 27, 58.

42. John Viele, *The Florida Keys, Volume 3: The Wreckers* (Sarasota, FL: Pineapple Press, 2001), xii, 3, 5-10.

43. Viele, *The Florida Keys, Volume 3*, 24, 26, 71-72; Daniel McKinnen, *A Tour Through the British West Indies, in the Years 1802 and 1803, Giving a Particular Account of the Bahama Islands* (London: R. Taylor, 1804), 140; Bernhard, *Slaves and Slaveholders in Bermuda*; Craton and Saunders, *Islanders in the Stream: A History of the Bahamian People*.

44. Viele, *The Florida Keys, Volume 3*, 72; Buddington Family Collection, 1706–1986, Coll. 257, G.W. Blunt White Library, Mystic Seaport; Elam, George, and Thomas Eldridge Papers, 1828-1867, Coll. 62, G.W. Blunt White Library, Mystic Seaport; Mason R. Packer Papers, 1835-1872, Coll. 235, G.W. Blunt White Library, Mystic Seaport Museum; Journal, ship *Vesper*, September 15, 1846-June 1849, G.W. Blunt White Library, Mystic Seaport.

45. Charles Ball, *Fifty Years In Chains; or, The Life of an American Slave* (New York: H. Dayton Publisher, 1859), 206-13.

46. Frederick Law Olmsted, *A Journey in the Seaboard Slave States; with Remarks on their Economy* (London: Sampson Low, Son, & Co., 1856), 351-55, especially 351; Cecelski, *Waterman's Song*, 74-75.

47. Olmsted, *A Journey in the Seaboard Slave States*, 353-54; Cecelski, *Waterman's Song*, 88-89; Edmund Ruffin, *Agricultural, Geological, and Descriptive Sketches of Lower North Carolina, and the Similar Adjacent Lands* (Raleigh, NC: Printed at the Institution for the Deaf & Dumb & the Blind, 1861), 183.

48. Olmsted, *A Journey in the Seaboard Slave States*, 353-54.

49. Ibid., 354.

50. Ibid., 354-55.

51. Ibid.

52. Donkin, *Beyond Price: Pearls and Pearl–Fishing*; "The Sponge Fishery," *The Sailors Magazine* 12 (June 1840): 314; Nels Johnson, "Ahmad: A Kuwaiti Pearl Diver," in Edmund Burke III, ed., *Struggle and Survival in the Middle East* (Berkeley: University of California Press, 1993), 91-99; Sinclair, and Henry, *Swimming*, 98-105; Kunx and Stevenson, *The Book of the Pearl*, 85-156; 189-252.

5

1. George Little, *Life on the Ocean; or, Twenty Years at Sea: Being the Personal Adventures of the Author* (Boston: Waite, Pierce, and Co., 1846), 378-79.

2. The traditional avenues to the discussion of Americans and intercultural encounter have been studies of travel literature and the frontier. See, for example, Daniel K. Richter, *Facing East from Indian Country: A Native History of Early America* (Cambridge, MA: Harvard University Press, 2001); Amy S. Greenberg, *Manifest Manhood and the Antebellum American Empire* (New York: Cambridge University Press, 2005); Gregory Nobles, *American Frontiers: Cultural Encounters and Continental Conquest* (New York: Hill and Wang, 1997); Christopher McBride, *The Colonizer Abroad: American Writers on Foreign Soil, 1846-1912* (New York: Routledge, 2004); Bruce Harvey, *American Geographics: U.S. National Narratives and the Representation of the Non-European World, 1830-1865* (Stanford, CA: Stanford University Press, 2001); Amy Kaplan, *The Anarchy of Empire in the Making of U.S. Culture* (Cambridge, MA: Harvard University Press, 2002). A notable exception dealing with seafaring is Robert Allison, *The Crescent Obscured: The United States and the Muslim World, 1776-1815* (New York: Oxford University Press, 1995).

3. Little, *Life on the Ocean*, 64, 111.

4. Ibid., 112. On gender and empire, see Gail Bederman, *Manliness and Civilization: A Cultural History of Gender and Race in the United States* (Chicago: University of Chicago Press, 1995); Kristin L. Hoganson, *Fighting for American Manhood: How Gender Politics Provoked the Spanish-American War* (New Haven: Yale University Press, 2000); Greenberg, *Manifest Manhood*. On gender and maritime history, see Margaret Creighton, *Rites and Passages: The Experience of American Whaling* (New York: Cambridge University Press, 1995); Margaret Creighton and Lisa Norling, eds., *Iron Men, Wooden Women: Gender and Seafaring in the Atlantic World, 1700-1920* (Baltimore: Johns Hopkins University Press, 1996).

5. Little, *Life on the Ocean*, 113.

6. Ibid., 111-14.

7. Ibid., 133. On American seamen in Hawai'i, see Briton Cooper Busch, *Whaling*

Will Never Do For Me: The American Whaleman in the Nineteenth Century (Lexington: University of Kentucky Press, 1994), and Creighton, *Rites and Passages*; see also Paul T. Burlin, *Imperial Maine and Hawai'i: Interpretive Essays in the History of Nineteenth Century American Expansionism* (Lanham, MD: Lexington Books, 2006).

8. Little, *Life on the Ocean*, 261.

9. Ibid., 203-06. On the connections between nationalism and Indian conflict, see Adam Rothman, *Slave Country: American Expansion and the Origins of the Deep South* (Cambridge, MA: Harvard University Press, 2005); Patrick Griffin, *American Leviathan: Empire, Nation, and the Revolutionary Frontier* (New York: Hill and Wang, 2007); Peter Kastor, *The Nation's Crucible: The Louisiana Purchase and the Creation of America* (New Haven: Yale University Press, 2004); Richard White, *The Middle Ground: Indians, Empires, and Republics in the Great Lakes Region, 1650-1815* (New York: Cambridge University Press, 1991); Richter, *Facing East from Indian Country*.

10. Little, *Life on the Ocean*, 358-59, 378-79.

11. Peter Linebaugh and Marcus Rediker, *The Many-Headed Hydra: The Hidden History of the Revolutionary Atlantic* (Boston: Beacon Press, 2000).

12. W. Jeffrey Bolster, *Black Jacks: African-American Seamen in the Age of Sail* (Cambridge, MA: Harvard University Press, 1997); Julius Scott, "Afro-American Sailors and the International Communication Network: The Case of Newport Bowers" in Colin Howell and Richard Twomey, eds., *Jack Tar in History: Essays in the History of Maritime Life and Labour* (Fredericton, New Brunswick: Acadiensis Press, 1991).

13. Alexis de Tocqueville, *Democracy in America,* trans. Henry Reeve (Boston: G. Adlard, 1839), 427.

14. Quoted in Reginald Horsman, *Race and Manifest Destiny: The Origins of American Racial Anglo-Saxonism* (Cambridge, MA: Harvard University Press, 1981), 289-91.

6

1. These medals were awarded to all Pennsylvania natives who served on the Lakes.

2. James Barker Farr, *Black Odyssey: The Seafaring Traditions of Afro-Americans, Culture, Ethnicity, and Nation Series* (New York: Peter Lang, 1989), 109, 110.

3. Ibid.

4. Quoted in Farr, *Black Odyssey*, 114, and Harold D. Langley, "The Negro in the Navy and Merchant Service, 1789-1860," *Journal of Negro History* 52, no. 4 (October 1967): 273-86.

5. Langley, "Negro in the Navy," 275.

6. Langley quotes Commodore Edward Preble in 1803 informing a lieutenant that he was "not to Ship Black Men"; also, in 1807 three of the four seamen impressed by HMS *Leopard* from the USS *Chesapeake* were black; Langley also includes a quote from Dr. Edward Cutbush, a surgeon in the US Navy, who wrote a book for other navy surgeons, recommending that sailors dance during their leisure time, and remarking that "there will be no difficulty in procuring a 'fiddler,' *especially* among the coloured men, in every American frigate, who can play most of the common dancing tunes," Langley, "Negro in the Navy," 276, 277.

7. Gerard T. Altoff, unpublished lecture delivered at USS Constitution Museum, July 2003.

8. Gerard T. Altoff, *Amongst My Best Men: African-Americans and the War of 1812* (Put-in-Bay, OH: Perry Group, 1996), 23.

9. W. Jeffrey Bolster, "'To Feel Like a Man': Black Seamen in the Northern States, 1800-1860," *Journal of American History* 76, no. 4 (March 1990): 1177.

10. Usher Parsons to George Livermore, October 18, 1862, quoted in Joseph T. Wilson, *The Black Phalanx: A History of the Negro Sailors of the United States in the Wars of 1775-1812, 1861-'65* (Hartford, CT: American Publishing Co., 1889), 78.

11. Ibid.

12. Bolster, "'To Feel Like a Man,'" 1179; W. Jeffrey Bolster, *Black Jacks: African American Seamen in the Age of Sail* (Cambridge, MA: Harvard University Press, 1997), 74, 75, 79.

13. "Internal Rules and Regulations to be Observed on board the United States Frigate *Constellation*, Charles Gordon, Esqr. Commander," in Glenn Drayton, untitled Memorandum Book, South Caroliniana Library, University of South Carolina, Columbia.

14. Christopher McKee noted that this ship was berthed in the South at this time. Perhaps if sailors were Southern white men, Gordon felt he was protecting his white crewmembers' racial superiority or notions of propriety by segregating the messes. It may be pertinent to note that the *Constellation*'s commander, Captain Charles Gordon, was a native of Kent County, Maryland, a slave state.

15. Robin F. A. Fabel, "Self-Help in Dartmoor: Black and White Prisoners in the War of 1812," *Journal of the Early Republic* 9, no. 2 (Summer 1989): 170.

16. Ibid., 171.

17. Bolster, *Black Jacks*, 12.

18. Benjamin Waterhouse, *A Journal of a Young Man of Massachusetts* (Boston: Rowe & Hooper, 1816), 174-83.

19. Ibid., 177.

20. Quoted in Altoff, *Amongst My Best Men*, 23.

21. William S. Dudley et al., *The Naval War of 1812: A Documentary History, vol. 2, 1813* (Washington, DC: Naval Historical Center, 1992), 529, 530.

22. Ibid.

23. Quoted in Altoff, *Amongst My Best Men*, 40.

24. United States. Statutes at Large, Act of March 3, 1813, ch. 42, 2 Stat. 809.

25. Wilson, *Black Phalanx*, 79; Altoff, *Amongst My Best Men*, 18, citing Frederick S. Harrod, "Jim Crow in the Navy, 1798-1941," *U.S. Naval Institute Proceedings* 105 (September 1979): 46-53.

26. Altoff, *Amongst My Best Men*, 21; Christopher McKee, unpublished lecture delivered at USS Constitution Museum, July 2003.

27. Edwin C. Bearss, *Historic Resources Study, vol. 1 and 2, Charlestown Navy Yard, 1800-1842* (Washington, DC: U.S. Department of the Interior, National Park Service, 1984), 154.

28. Quoted in Bolster, "'To Feel Like a Man,'" 1179.

30. Prisoners of War Records, Ira Dye Collection, USS Constitution Museum; however, for each ship's captured crew recorded in these records, the percentage of captured black crewmembers ranges from less than 1 percent to 100 percent. All calculations done by the author are based on Ira Dye's list of U.S. Navy sailors in English prisons during the War of 1812. Note, for the calculations of percentages of black prisoners from captured crews, these numbers do not and can not take into account how many crewmembers, white and/or black, comprised each ship's original complement, as well as how many white and black crewmembers were killed in action, escaped, or were not counted. Also, these numbers include any human error on the part of the prison officials who recorded information and who, individually, made the determinations of race. For the 100-percent figure, only one person, a black man, was recorded in the books for the US Brig *Vixen*; therefore the percentage was 100. These calculations must be taken in the context of the prejudices inherent in the available information from which they are based.

31. Christopher McKee, comp. and ed., "United States Enlisted Prisoners of War in England, 1813-1815: Chatham, Dartmoor, Prisonship *Ganges*, Plymouth, Quebec, and Portsmouth," unpublished manuscript.

32. Compare that number to Ira Dye's merchant sailor research, which found that 15 to 20 percent of *merchant* sailors were black, and perhaps we see the effect of the navy's prohibition and/or commanding officers' personal racial politics, Ira Dye Collection.

33. It is possible that some sailors lied about their birth states because they were foreign-born and feared British reprisals, or for other unknown reasons.

34. The Institute for Museum and Library Services, the Massachusetts Foundation for the Humanities, and the National Endowment for the Humanities funded the research and exhibit projects at the USS Constitution Museum, along with many generous foundations and donors.

7

1. Record of Edward Smith's testimony and confession quoted in William H. Pease and Jane H. Pease, "Walker's *Appeal* Comes to Charleston: A Note and Documents," *Journal of Negro History* 59 (1974): 289.

2. See Charles M. Wiltse, "Introduction," in Charles M. Wiltse, ed., *David Walker's Appeal, in Four Articles, Together with a Preamble, to the Coloured Citizens of the World, but in Particular, and very Expressly, to those of the United States of America* (New York: Hill and Wang, 1965), ix.

3. According to Jeffrey Bolster, port imprisonment policies were first imposed in 1822 and remained in place in many Southern ports throughout the antebellum period. Clearly, whites acknowledged the possibility of black resistance or rebellion developing in the watery world apart from landed laws, and, following the distribution of Walker's *Appeal*, Florida, Georgia, and North Carolina passed laws restricting free black access to their states, W. Jeffrey Bolster, *Black Jacks: African American Seamen in the Age of Sail* (Cambridge, MA: Harvard University Press, 1997), 190, 198. Bolster's is the definitive work on African-American maritime culture in the age of sail. Other important works that treat the African-American experience at sea and in port include Peter Linebaugh and Marcus B. Rediker, *The Many-Headed Hydra: Sailors, Slaves, Commoners, and the Hidden History of the Revolutionary Atlantic* (Boston: Beacon Press, 2000), and Maggie Montesinos Sale, *The Slumbering Volcano: American Slave Ship Revolts and the Production of Rebellious Masculinity* (Durham, NC: Duke University Press, 1997).

4. On the distribution and impact of Walker's *Appeal*, see Peter P. Hinks, "Introduction," in Peter P. Hinks, ed., *David Walker's Appeal to the Coloured Citizens of the World* (University Park: Pennsylvania State University Press, 2000), xi-xliv; Peter P. Hinks, *To Awaken My Afflicted Brethren: David Walker and the Problem of Antebellum Slave Resistance* (University Park: Pennsylvania State University Press, 1997).

5. Rogers Smith, writing about America's "civic myths," notes that, "U.S. citizens seem to have wished to hear that their peoplehood was more deeply rooted, and of more intrinsic importance, than liberal republican doctrines have ever indicated." The idea that there is something "essential" and innate in American citizens is what Douglass (and many of his fellow maritime authors) seeks to disprove, see Rogers Smith, *Civic Ideals* (New Haven: Yale University Press, 1997), 38.

6. Richard Henry Dana Jr., *Two Years before the Mast: A Personal Narrative of Life at Sea* (1840; reprint, New York: Penguin, 1981), 92.

7. Ibid., 90.

8. William McNally, *Evils and Abuses in the Naval and Merchant Service, Exposed: With Proposals for their Remedy and Redress* (Boston: Cassady and March, 1839), 129.

9. Ibid., 130.

10. John Locke, *The Second Treatise of Civil Government* (1690; reprint, Indianapolis: Bobbs-Merrill, 1962), 4-5.

11. Francis Asbury Roe, *Naval Duties and Discipline, with Policy and Principles of Naval Organization* (New York: D. Van Nostrand, 1865), 187-88.

12. See Herman Melville, *White-Jacket; Or, the World in a Man-of-War* (1850; reprint, Evanston and Chicago: Northwestern University Press and the Newberry Library, 1970), 499.

13. Frederick Douglass, "Narrative of the Life of Frederick Douglass, an American Slave," in William L. Andrews, ed., *The Oxford Frederick Douglass Reader* (New York: Oxford University Press, 1996), 64.

14. See Ira Dye, "Early American Merchant Seafarers," *The Proceedings of the American Philosophical Society* 120 (1976): 331-60; Ira Dye, "The Tattoos of Early American Seafarers, 1796-1818," *Proceedings of the American Philosophical Society* 133 (1989): 520-54. Dye proves that "patriotic symbols" such as the eagle were the third most popular tattoo design among sailors in the early national period.

15. Frederick Douglass, "The Heroic Slave," in Andrews, *The Oxford Frederick Douglass Reader*, 147.

16. Frederick Douglass, *Life and Times of Frederick Douglass*, in Andrews, *The Oxford Frederick Douglass Reader*, 228.

17. Ibid., 229.

18. Frederick Douglass, "The Heroic Slave," in Andrews, *The Oxford Frederick Douglass Reader*, 162-63.

19. A host of critics have examined "The Heroic Slave" by investigating Douglass's fraught relationship with American ideals and the American nation itself, see William L. Andrews, "The Novelization of Voice in Early African American Narrative," *PMLA* 105 (1990): 23-34; Paul Christian Jones, "Copying what the Master had Written: Frederick Douglass's 'The Heroic Slave' and the Southern Historical Romance," *Southern Quarterly: A Journal of the Arts in the South* 38, no. 4 (2000): 78-92; Helen Lock, "The Paradox of Slave Mutiny in Herman Melville, Charles Johnson, and Frederick Douglass," *College Literature* 30, no. 4 (2003): 54-70; Eric J. Sundquist, *To Wake the Nations: Race in the Making of American Literature* (Cambridge, MA: Harvard University Press, 1993); Ivy G. Wilson, "'I Give the Sign of Democracy': Race, Labor, and the Aesthetics of Nationalism," Ph.D. diss., Yale University; Ivy G. Wilson, "On Native Ground: Transnationalism, Frederick Douglass, and *The Heroic Slave*," *PMLA* 121 (2006): 453-68; Richard Yarborough, "Race, Violence, and Manhood: The Masculine Ideal in Frederick Douglass's 'The Heroic Slave,'" in Eric J.Sundquist, ed., *Frederick Douglass: New Literary and Historical Essays* (Cambridge: Cambridge University Press, 1997), 166-88. Krista Walter makes the strongest argument for a specifically American nationalism underlying the idealization of Madison Washington in "The Heroic Slave," writing that "[Douglass] accepts without criticism a host of nationalistic suppositions underpinning the ideology of American slavery: the primacy of Eurocentric historical

and cultural perspectives, the belief in America's glorious origins, the projection of a kind of manifest destiny based on such origins, and the necessary adherence to patriarchal values," Krista Walter, "Trappings of Nationalism in Frederick Douglass's 'The Heroic Slave,'" *African American Review* 34 no. 2 (2000): 237. There are two problems with Walter's argument (one of which she notes). First, as Walter observes, Douglass's overarching political mission (abolition) forced him to accept certain assumptions in order to challenge others (namely, the humanity, heroism, and natural ability of a black character). Accepting these assumptions causes its own problems, as Andrews, Walter, and Yarborough aver. Second, Walter completely ignores the ending of "The Heroic Slave," in which Madison Washington is parading through the streets of Nassau, safe once more under the paw of the British lion. Thus, though Douglass may have indeed accepted certain nationalistic assumptions, he divorces those assumptions from the United States itself. The only place that American virtues, such as they are, can be celebrated and acknowledged is outside America. This seems to me a potent criticism of American nationalism and a pointed acknowledgment of the distance between the actual and the ideal.

20. See United States, *Senate Documents 51, 27th Congress, 2d Session* (Washington: U.S. Government Printing Office, [1841]); George Hendrick and Willene Hendrick, *The Creole Mutiny: A Tale of Revolt Aboard a Slave Ship* (Chicago: Ivan R. Dee, 2003) contains a thorough look at the historical record of the *Creole* rebellion.

21. On public attitudes toward sailors, see Paul Gilje, *Liberty on the Waterfront: American Maritime Culture in an Age of Revolution* (Philadelphia: University of Pennsylvania Press, 2004), 163-227.

8

1. Mission Dolores, originally known as the Misión San Francisco de Asis, was founded in 1776. It was the sixth mission of the 21 built in California by the Franciscan Missionaries between 1769 and 1823.

2. Bret Harte, "Letter 6: *Christian Register* [Boston], May 19, 1866—written from San Francisco, April 10, 1866," in Gary Scharnhorst, ed., *Bret Harte's California: Letters to the* Springfield Republican *and* Christian Register, *1866-67* (Albuquerque: University of New Mexico Press, 1990), 34.

3. The inscriptions on these three gravestones read: "Louis de Cross, Late of Chili, Died on November 18, 1852, Aged 36 years," "Marie Ruiz of Santiago de Chile, Died in San Francisco, February 16th 1852, Aged 23 years," "Carmelita Besa of Chili, Aged 23 years, Born…1839, Died June 5, 1854."

4. See Edward D. Melillo, "Strangers on Familiar Soil: Chile and the Making of California, 1848-1930," Ph.D. diss., Yale University, 2006, 152.

5. Carlos López Urrutia, *Breve historia naval de Chile* (Buenos Aires: Editorial Francisco de Aguirre, 1976), ch. 3.

6. John C. Frémont, *Geographical Memoir upon Upper California, in Illustration of His Map of Oregon and California* (Washington, D.C.: Wendell and Van Benthuysen, Printers, 1848), 32.

7. Shew's daguerreotype is currently part of the Smithsonian Institution Collections. It is displayed as plate 62 in Beaumont Newhall, *The Daguerreotype in America* (New York: Duell, Sloan & Pearce, 1961).

8. Thomas Reid, "Diary of a Voyage to California in the Bark *Velasco*," October 9, 1849, Bancroft Library, University of California.

9. See James P. Delgado, *To California by Sea: A Maritime History of the California Gold Rush* (Columbia: University of South Carolina Press, 1990), 19.

10. Hubert Howe Bancroft, *History of California*, 7 vols. (San Francisco: The History Co., 1890), 7: 125.

11. Edward Lucett, *Rovings in the Pacific, from 1837 to 1849; with a Glance at California (By a Merchant Long Resident in Tahiti)*, 2 vols. (London: Longman, Brown, Green, and Longmans, 1851), 2: 352.

12. Anonymous, Letter published in *El Mercurio* [Valparaíso] (dated San Francisco, May 15, 1849).

13. Henry Hiram Ellis, *From the Kennebec to California: Reminiscences of a California Pioneer*, ed. Laurence R. Cook (Los Angeles: W.F. Lewis, 1959), 13.

14. Prentice Mulford, *Life by Land and Sea* (New York: F.J. Needham, 1889), 46; Carl Nolte, "Experts Dig Up Nautical Past of Long-Buried 1818 Whaler," *San Francisco Chronicle*, January 28, 2006; Dale Champion, "Gold Rush Fleet's Muddy Ghosts," *San Francisco Chronicle*, July 4, 1988.

15. Albert Williams, *A Pioneer Pastorate and Times, Embodying Contemporary Local Transactions and Events* (San Francisco: Wallace & Hassett, Printers, 1879), 45.

16. Linville J. Hall, *Around the Horn in '49; journal of the Hartford Union Mining and Trading Company* (Wethersfield, CT, Reprinted by L.J. Hall, 1898), 244-45. For a comprehensive treatment of gold rush-era craft moored in San Francisco Harbor, see Albert Harmon, Harlan Soeten, and Karl Kortum, *Notes on the Gold Rush Ships* (San Francisco: San Francisco Maritime Museum, 1963).

17. William Kelly, *A Stroll Through the Diggings of California* (London: Simms and M'Intyre, 1852), 177.

18. Bill Bonyun and Gene Bonyun, *Full Hold and Splendid Passage: America Goes to Sea, 1815-1860* (New York: Alfred A. Knopf, 1969), 160.

19. William H. Pickens, "'A Marvel of Nature; The Harbor of Harbors,' Public Policy and the Development of the San Francisco Bay, 1846-1926," Ph.D. diss., University of California, Davis, 1976, 17.

20. Walter J. Thompson, "The Armada of Golden Dreams," *San Francisco Chronicle*, July 2, 1916.

21. Erin Pursell, "Modern city surrounds what was once forest of ships," *Oakland Tribune*, March 10, 2006; Carl Nolte, "Few clues unearthed about mystery ship

buried after Gold Rush / Dug up at condo project, site of old 'maritime junkyard'" *San Francisco Chronicle*, September 8, 2005; and Kenneth J. Garcia, "Muni Diggers Uncover Bit of S. F.'s Past / Remains may be pieces of Gold Rush-era ship," *San Francisco Chronicle*, December 7, 1994.

22. "Es una Venecia de madera de pino en lugar de mármol," ["It is a Venice of pine in place of marble"] declared Vicuña Mackenna, Benjamín Vicuña Mackenna, "Páginas de mi diario durante tres años de viaje, 1853-1854-1855," in *Obras Completas de Vicuña Mackenna*, 2 vols. (Santiago: Universidad de Chile, 1936), 1: 26.

23. Francisco Antonio Encina, *Historia de Chile: Desde la prehistoria hasta 1891*, 20 vols. (Santiago: Editorial Nascimento, 1949), 13: 506; Roberto Hernández Cornejo, *Los Chilenos en San Francisco*, 2 vols. (Valparaíso: Imp. San Rafael, 1930), 176.

24. Vicente Pérez Rosales, *Times Gone By: Memoirs of a Man of Action*, trans. John H.R. Polt, (Oxford: Oxford University Press, 2003), 269.

25. "Reminiscences: The Last of the Storeships," *Daily Alta California*, May 22, May 29, and June 5, 1882.

26. Isaac G. Strain, *Cordillera and Pampa: Sketches of a Journey in Chili and the Argentine Provinces, in 1849* (New York: Horace H. Moore, 1853), 21.

27. George W. Evans, *Mexican Gold Trail, the Journal of a Forty-niner* (San Marino, CA: Huntington Library Press, 1945), 195.

28. George H. Tinkham, *History of San Joaquin County, California with Biographical Sketches* (Los Angeles: Historic Record Co., 1923), ch. 25.

29. Daniel Knower, *Adventures of a Forty-niner* (Albany, NY: Weed-Parsons Printing Co., 1894), 138.

30. Hubert Howe Bancroft, *The New Pacific* (New York: The Bancroft Co., 1900), 391.

31. Captain George Coffin, *A Pioneer Voyage to California and Round the World, 1849 to 1852* (Chicago: Gorham B. Coffin, 1908), 36.

32. Calculated from "U.S. Customs House, San Francisco—Records. 1849-1897, Key to Arrangement," part 1, Bancroft Library, University of California.

33. "U.S. Customs House, San Francisco—Records. 1849-1897." part 1, box 1, 1849-1850 (A-Gen), Bancroft Library, University of California.

34. Sergio Sepúlveda G. *El Trigo Chileno en el Mercado Mundial, Ensayo de Geografía Histórica* (Santiago: Editorial Universitaria, 1959), 41-46.

35. Charles L. Ross, "Experiences of a Pioneer of 1847 in California," 14, Bancroft Library, University of California.

36. For a superb account of the symbolic and material transformation of *market-places*, spatially and culturally bounded sites where many types of transactions other than commodity exchange might occur, into the *capitalist market*, a realm where the ever-expanding circulation of commodities predominates, see

Jean-Christophe Agnew, "The Threshold of Exchange: Speculations on the Market," *Radical History Review* 21 (Fall 1979): 99-118.

37. James R. Garniss, "The Early Days of San Francisco—Reminiscences for the Bancroft Library, 1877," 10-11, Bancroft Library, University of California.

38. Harris Newmark, *Sixty Years in Southern California, 1853-1913, Containing the Reminiscences of Harris Newmark,* 2d ed., rev. and augm. (New York: The Knickerbocker Press, 1916), 332.

39. William Redmond Ryan, *Personal Adventures in Upper and Lower California, in 1848-9; With the Author's Experience at the Mines*, 2 vols. (London: W. Shoberl, 1850), 1: 407.

40. John M. Letts, *California Illustrated; Including a Description of the Panama and Nicaragua Routes* (New York: R.T. Young, 1853), 134.

41. Joseph Warren Revere, *Keel and Saddle* (Boston: James R. Osgood & Co., 1872), 160; Franklin Buck, *A Yankee Trader in the Gold Rush* (Boston: Houghton Mifflin Co., 1930), 56.

42. Peter R. Decker, *Fortunes and Failures: White-Collar Mobility in Nineteenth-Century San Francisco* (Cambridge, MA: Harvard University Press, 1978), 37.

43. Reid, Diary of a Voyage to California in the Bark *Velasco*," Sunday October 7, 1849, Bancroft Library, University of California.

44. Abraham P. Nasatir, *A French Journalist in the California Gold Rush: The Letters of Etienne Derbec* (Georgetown, CA: The Talisman Press, 1964), 208 n53.

45. "U.S. Customs House, San Francisco—Records. 1849-1897," box 1 1849-1850 (A-Gen) and box 2 1849-1850 (Geo-Z), Bancroft Library, University of California.

46. J. G. Player-Frowd, *Six Months in California* (London: Longmans, Green, & Co., 1872), 130.

47. John. O. Earll, "Statement of John O. Earll, A Pioneer of 1849—Bancroft Library, 1877," 2, Bancroft Library, University of California.

48. Ibid., 7-8.

49. "The Wonders of California," *New York Daily Times*, November 3, 1851.

50. James Douglas Jr., "Chile. Its Geography, People and Institutions," *Journal of the American Geographical Society of New York* 13 (1881): 91.

51. Henry Clay Evans Jr., *Chile and Its Relations with the United States* (Durham, NC: Duke University Press, 1927), 75.

52. Paul W. Gates, *California Ranchos and Farms, 1846-1862* (Madison: The State Historical Society of Wisconsin, 1967), 51.

53. Horace Davis, "California Breadstuffs," *Journal of Political Economy* 2 (March 1894): 525.

54. Albert Williams, *A Pioneer Pastorate and Times, Embodying Contemporary Local Transactions and Events* (San Francisco: Wallace & Hassett, Printers, 1879), 212-13.

55. Reynold M.Wik, *Steam Power on the American Farm* (Philadelphia: University of Pennsylvania Press, 1953), 51-52.

56. Nancy S. Seasholes has studied the urban growth of Boston's topography through outward expansion of its shoreline in *Gaining Ground: A History of Landmaking in Boston* (Cambridge, MA: MIT Press, 2003); for a history of municipal property law with a focus on New York's water lots, see Hendrik Hartog, *Public Property and Private Power: The Corporation of the City of New York in American Law, 1730-1870* (Chapel Hill: University of North Carolina Press, 1983).

57. Thaddeus S. Kenderdine, *California Revisited, 1858-1897* (Doylestown, PA: Doylestown Pub. Co., Printers, 1898), 87-90.

58. Robert Grossinger, "Documenting Local Landscape Change: The San Francisco Bay Area Historical Ecology Project," in Dave Egan and Evelyn A. Howell, ed., *The Historical Ecology Handbook: A Restorationist's Guide to Reference Ecosystems* (Washington, DC: Island Press, 2001), 425-42.

59. Matthew Morse Booker, "Oyster Growers and Oyster Pirates in San Francisco Bay," *Pacific Historical* Review 75 (February 2006): 65.

60. James Gerber, "Gold Rushes and the Trans-Pacific Wheat Trade: California and Australia, 1848-57," in. Dennis O. Flynn, Lionel Frost, and A. J. Latham, ed., *Pacific Centuries: Pacific and Pacific Rim History Since the Sixteenth Century* (London: Routledge, 1999), 130.

61. Frank Soulé, John H. Gihon, and James Nisbet, *The Annals of San Francisco*, comp. Dorothy Higgins, rev ed. (1855; Palo Alto, CA: Lewis Osborne, 1966), 291-92; Bancroft, *History of California*, 6: 177-78.

62. Frank Lecouvreur, *From East Prussia to the Golden Gate*, ed. Josephine Rosana Lecouvreur, trans. Julius C. Behnke (Los Angeles: Angelina Book Concern, 1906), 178.

63. Carrie Casey, "Oakland's Redwood Retreat," *American Forests* 97 (November-December, 1991): 55-57; Andrew C. Isenberg, *Mining California: An Ecological History* (New York: Hill & Wang, 2005), 8.

64. Peter Linebaugh and Marcus Rediker, *The Many-Headed Hydra: Sailors, Slaves, Commoners, and the Hidden History of the Revolutionary Atlantic* (Boston: Beacon Press, 2000), 43.

65. Soulé, Gihon, and Nisbet, *Annals of San Francisco*, 282.

66. *San Francisco Daily Evening Picayune*, May 5, 1851.

67. Benjamin I. Hayes, *Pioneer Notes from the Diaries of Judge Benjamin Hayes, 1849-1875* (Los Angeles: Privately Printed, 1929), 152.

68. Albert Williams, *A Pioneer Pastorate and Times, Embodying Contemporary Local Transactions and Events* (San Francisco: Wallace & Hassett, Printers, 1879), 48.

69. Ira B. Cross, *Financing an Empire: History of Banking in California,* 4 vols. (Chicago: S.J. Clarke Publishing Co., 1927), 1: 149; Roger Lochin, *San Francisco*, 18.

70. William Deverell, *Whitewashed Adobe: The Rise of Los Angeles and the Remaking of Its Mexican* Past (Berkeley: University of California Press, 2004), 131.

71. Leonard Pitt, *The Decline of the Californios: A Social History of the Spanish-Speaking Californians, 1846-1890* (Berkeley: University of California Press, 1970), 53.

72. William M'Collum, *California as I Saw It* (Buffalo, NY: George H. Derby & Co., 1850), 36.

73. Ryan, *Personal Adventures in Upper and Lower California, in 1848-9*, 1: 406; Harold Kirker, "El Dorado Gothic," *California Historical Society Quarterly* 38, no. 1 (1959): 35.

74. Samuel C. Upham, *Notes of A Voyage to California* (Philadelphia: Author, 1878), 161.

75. Othero Weston, *Mother Lode Album* (Stanford: Stanford University Press, 1948), 134.

76. Charles B. Turrill, *California Notes* (San Francisco: E. Bosqui & Co., 1876), 61; Charles B. Turrill, "A City Within a City," *San Francisco News Letter and California Advertiser*, May 27, 1876.

77. Philip J. Ethington, *The Public City: The Political Construction of Urban Life in San Francisco, 1850-1900*, 2nd ed. (Berkeley: University of California Press, 2001), 259.

78. Felix Paul Wierzbicki, *California As It Is & As It May Be; Or, A Guide to the Gold Region* (reprint; San Francisco, The Grabhorn Press, 1933), 65.

79. *San Francisco Alta California*, August 2, 1849; on the role of gender in the shaping of San Francisco during the decades following the Mexican War, see Michelle E. Jolly, "Inventing the City: Gender and the Politics of Everyday Life in Gold-Rush San Francisco, 1848-1869," Ph.D. diss., University of California, San Diego, 1998.

80. Carlos López Urrutia, *Chilenos in California: A Study of the 1850, 1852, and 1860 Censuses* (San Francisco: R and E Research Associates, 1973), xxi.

81. Nell Kimball, *Nell Kimball: Her Life as an American Madam, by Herself*, ed. Stephen Longstreet (New York: Macmillan, 1970), 217-18.

82. Patricia Nelson Limerick, *The Legacy of Conquest: The Unbroken Past of the American West* (New York: W.W. Norton, 1987), 49.

83. I am borrowing here from David Roediger's brilliant formulation of a "wage of whiteness." Roediger demonstrates the ways in which the public and psychological benefits of whiteness have helped to placate Anglo workers as they are alienated and exploited by an expanding system of capitalist wage-labor, see David R. Roediger, *The Wages of Whiteness: Race and the Making of the American Working Class*, 2nd ed. (London: Verso, 1991), 12-13.

84. Timothy Coffin Osborn, Journal, transcript, 162, Bancroft Library, University of California.

85. Robert J. Chandler, *California Gold Rush Camps: A Keepsake in Fourteen Parts* (San Francisco: Book Club of California, 1998), sect. 1: 2.

86. Mary Jane Megquier, *Apron of Gold: The Letters of Mary Jane Megquier from San Francisco, 1849-1856*, ed. Robert Glass Cleland (San Marino, CA: The Huntington Library, 1949), 59 [italics added].

87. The quote is from Jacqueline Baker Barnhart, *The Fair But Frail: Prostitution in San Francisco, 1849-1900* (Reno: University of Nevada Press, 1986), 20.

88. Enos Christman, *One Man's Gold; The Letters & Journal of a Forty-Niner*, ed. Florence Morrow Christman (New York: Whittlesey House, McGraw-Hill Book Co., Inc., 1930), 198.

89. James W. Buel, *Metropolitan Life Unveiled, or the Mysteries and Miseries of America's Greatest Cities* (St. Louis, MO: Historical Publishing Co., 1882), 254.

90. Gordon Young, *Days of '49* (New York: George H. Doran Co., 1925), 41.

91. *San Francisco Daily Alta California*, November 22, 1857.

92. Albert L. Hurtado, *Intimate Frontiers: Sex, Gender, and Culture in Old California* (Albuquerque: University of New Mexico Press, 1999), 16.

93. Richard Henry Dana Jr., *Two Years Before the Mast: A Personal Narrative (with a supplement by the author and introduction and additional chapter by his son)* (1840; expanded edition, Boston and New York: Houghton Mifflin, 1911), 215.

94. George Coffin, *A Pioneer Voyage to California and Round the World, 1849 to 1852* (Chicago: Gorham B. Coffin, 1908), 57.

95. Herbert Asbury, *The Barbary Coast: An Informal History of the San Francisco Underworld* (New York: Alfred A. Knopf, 1933), 34-35.

96. Elisha Oscar Crosby, *Memoirs of Elisha Oscar Crosby, Reminiscences of California and Guatemala from 1849 to 1864*, ed. Charles Albro Baker (San Marino, CA: The Huntington Library, 1945), 109.

97. John W. Palmer, *The New and the Old; Or, California and India in Romantic Aspects* (New York: Rudd & Carleton, 1859), 34-35.

98. Pérez Rosales, *Times Gone By*, 218.

99. Ibid., 228; Rosario Améstica reappears in Eduardo Galeano's poetic history of Latin America, *Faces and Masks*, trans. Cedric Belfrage (New York: W.W. Norton, 1987), 167.

100. Mark Twain [Samuel Langhorn Clemens, pseudo.] *Mark Twain's Notebooks & Journals*, ed. Frederick Anderson, Michael B. Frank, and Kenneth M. Sanderson, 3 vols. (Berkeley: University of California Press, 1975) 3: Notebook 42 (1898); Mark Twain, *Roughing It* (Hartford, CT: American Publishing Co., 1872).

101. Benjamín Vicuña Mackenna, as quoted in Beilharz and and López, trans. and ed., *We Were 49ers!: Chilean Accounts of the California Gold Rush* (Pasadena, CA: Ward Ritchie Press, 1976), 200.

102. *Los Angeles Times*, November 12, 1993.

103. Dana, *Two Years Before the Mast*, 465.

104. Carey McWilliams, "Cultural Arts in California," in *The Cultural Arts; Conference Number 2, University of California, Los Angeles, April 5-7, 1963* (Berkeley: University of California Press, 1964), 79.

105. Some adventurous souls chose to traverse the Isthmus of Panama, but the prevalence of tropical diseases, swarms of insects, and bands of ruthless brigands served as disincentives to forty-niners contemplating this route. This changed with the opening of a trans-Isthmus railroad in 1855, which shuttled passengers from the Atlantic to the Pacific in under five hours.

106. James P. Delgado, *To California by Sea: A Maritime History of the California Gold Rush* (Columbia: University South Carolina Press, 1990), ix.

107. Ramón Gil Navarro, *The Gold Rush Diary of Ramón Gil Navarro*, ed. and trans. María del Carmen Ferreyra and David S. Reher (Lincoln: University of Nebraska Press, 2000), 251.

9

1. W. Jeffrey Bolster, "To Feel Like A Man: Black Seamen in the Northern States, 1800-1860," *Journal of American History* 76 (March 1990).

2. James Farr, "A Slow Boat to Nowhere: The Multi-Racial Crews of the American Whaling Industry," *Journal of Negro History* 68, no. 2 (Spring 1983): 159-70.

3. E. Berkeley Tompkins, "Black Ahab: William T. Shorey, Whaling Master," *California Historical Quarterly* 51, no 1 (Spring 1972): 75-84.

4. Delilah Leontium Beasley, *Negro Trailblazers of California* (Los Angeles: Times Mirror Printing and Binding House, 1919), 125.

5. Between 1863 and 1874, Leach commanded a number of whalers that shipped out of that port.

6. Shorey's responsibilities included harpooning the whale from the bow of the 30-foot whaleboat when ordered to do so by the mate, then going aft to steer the boat when the mate came forward to lance the whale to death. Boatsteerers ranked just below the ship's mates, who commanded the whaleboats.

7. *Pacific Commercial Advertiser,* February 25, 1908.

8. *Record of American and Foreign Shipping* (New York: American Bureau of Shipping, 1886), 358.

9. Born in San Francisco on June 10, 1865, Shelton—described as having a wonderful, calm personality—was the daughter of Frank Shelton of Arkansas; the family residence at 4 Gerke Alley was on the slopes of Telegraph Hill.

10. Shorey's voyage netted some 150 barrels of sperm whale oil, 420 barrels of whale oil, and over 5,000 pounds of whalebone, Reginald B. Hegarty, *Returns of Whaling Vessels Sailing from American Ports* (New Bedford: Old Dartmouth Historical Society, 1959), 20. While in Hawai'i, Mrs. Shorey, an amateur

naturalist, wrote several letters about her observations for the *San Francisco Elevator*. The couple had five children, two of whom died within six months of each other in Hawai'i.

11. The *Alexander* was described as "a staunch, seaworthy little vessel. She had no fine lines; there was nothing about her to please a yachtsman's eye— but she was far from being a tub as whaling ships are often pictured." Her crew included a pair of Cape Verdeans, two Swedes, a German, a Norwegian, an Irishman, and assorted ne'er-do-wells, see Walter Noble Burns, *A Year with a Whaler* (New York: Outing Publishing Company, 1919), 21-32.

12. During its first year, the *Alexander* caught four whales, each of which produced some 1,800 pounds of baleen. An additional cargo of oil brought the proceeds to approximately $50,000. Shorey's take was one-sixth, or $8,400, Burns, *A Year with a Whaler*, 247-48. *Lloyd's Register of British and Foreign Shipping.*

13. *San Francisco Examiner*, August 14, 1892. Shorey stated that his crew would have starved to death but for the assistance of an agent of the North American Commercial Crew, "who did all in his power to aid the shipwrecked men." Captain Robert Evans of the *Yorktown* explained his position by stating that he was not there to assist shipwrecked whalers. Captain Michael Healy of the Revenue Cutter *Bear* was likewise unhelpful, stating that he was unable to render assistance to Shorey as he was "on a special mission for reindeer." Evans eventually made arrangements for the men to be transferred from Unalaska to Port Townsend.

14. Burns, *A Year with a Whaler*, 114.

15. Ibid., 182-90.

16. United States Criminal Case #2822, Criminal Register #5, San Francisco, California.

17. This is notable given the decrepit condition of the vessel. Built in 1867, it was described as "might shaky . . . her rigging is in terrible shape, about ready to fall off her. I should not be surprised to see the mainmast go over the side any day," Lloyd C. M. Hare, *Salted Tories: The Story of the Whaling Fleets of San Francisco* (Mystic, CT: Marine Historical Association, 1960), 102.

18. Beasley, *Negro Trailblazers of California,* 126.

19. Affidavit, signed by John C Baird, Department of Justice, Office of U.S. Attorney, District of Hawai'i, March 1901, Federal Records Center, San Francisco.

20. The first typhoon struck on October 13, the second on November 11.

21. *San Francisco Examiner*, November 20, 1907; *San Francisco Chronicle*, November 26, 1907*; Pacific Commercial Advertiser,* February 2, 1908.

22. Shorey had five children: Zenobia, born in 1888; Elvira, 1891; Hazel, 1893; Victoria, 1898; and William Thomas, Junior, 1902. Elvira passed away in 1893, Hazel in 1894, and Zenobia in 1908.

23. The Shoreys resided at 1174 Division Street, and there is currently a movement to have this edifice declared a historic landmark.

24. Additionally, he was a member of the International Order of Odd Fellows (Golden Gate Lodge 2007) and the Ancient Order of the Forest (Lodge 7804).

25. Crew list of the *Andrew Hicks*, 1900, Federal Records Center, San Francisco.

26. *San Francisco Chronicle*, October 31, 1901.

27. Bill Pickelhaupt, *Shanghaied in San Francisco* (1996; reprint, Mystic, CT: Mystic Seaport, 2007).

28. Including in those 64 offenses were 14 murders.

29. *San Francisco Chronicle*, November 20, 1907.

10

1. Iris Chang, *The Chinese in America: A Narrative History* (New York: Viking, 2003) is a fine starting point for the non-specialist interested in the Chinese-American community.

2. For an important consideration of the "model minority" idea, see Frank H. Wu, *Yellow: Race in America Beyond Black and White* (New York: Basic Books, 2002), ch. 2, "The Model Minority: Asian American 'Success' as a Race Relations Failure," 39-77.

3. See Wu, *Yellow*, ch. 3, "The Perpetual Foreigner: Yellow Peril in the Pacific Century," 79-129.

4. Frank G. Carpenter, *North America* (New York: American Book Company, 1898; 2nd ed., 1910), 308-11.

5. *Annual Report of the Commissioner of Navigation for the Fiscal Year Ended June 30, 1902* (Washington, DC: U. S. Government Printing Office, 1902), 46.

6. Robert Barde, "The Scandalous Ship *Mongolia*," *Steamboat Bill* no. 250 (Summer 2004): 114.

7. For Frank Besse's journals, see William H. Bunting, *Sea Struck* (Gardiner, ME: Tilbury House Publishers, 2004), 111-19; another interesting account is in *Steamboat Bill.*

8. Wu, *Yellow*, 39-77 passim.

9. Robert A. Nash, "The 'China Gangs' in the Alaska Packers Association Canneries, 1892-1935," in Thomas W. Chinn, ed., *The Life, Influence and the Role of the Chinese in the United States, 1776-1960* (San Francisco: Chinese Historical Society of America, 1976), 257-83.

10. Ronald Takaki, *Strangers from a Different Shore: A History of Asian Americans* (Boston: Little, Brown and Company, 1989), 65-75, 316-18; see also Thomas W. Chinn, H. Mark Lai, and Philip P. Choy, eds., *A History of the Chinese in California: A Syllabus* (San Francisco: Chinese Historical Society of America, 1969; 4th printing, 1973); while there are five units dedicated to fisheries, there are none dedicated to commercial seafaring.

11. A local study of Chinese fishermen is Arthur F. McEvoy, "In Places Men Reject: Chinese Fishermen at San Diego, 1870-1893," *The Journal of San Diego History* 23, no. 4 (Fall 1977), available at http://www.sandiegohistory.org/journal/77fall/chinese.htm (accessed September 21, 2006); see also Robert F. Walsh, "Chinese and the Fisheries in California," *The California Illustrated Magazine* 4 (November 1893): 834.

12. Smithsonian National Museum of History Web site, "David Starr Jordan," http://www.mnh.si.edu/vert/fishes/baird/jordan.html (accessed September 6, 2006); for Stanford's racial problems, see "Asian Americans debate use of race," *The Stanford Daily* (Online version), April 3, 2003, http://daily.stanford.edu/article/2003/4/3/asianAmericansDebateUseOfRace (accessed September 6, 2006).

13. George Brown Goode and Joseph W. Collins, *The Fisheries and Fishery Industries of the United States, Sect. 4: The Fishermen of the United States* (Washington, DC: U.S. Government Printing Office, 1887), 37-42.

14. Arthur F. McEvoy, *The Fisherman's Problem: Ecology and Law in the California Fisheries, 1850-1980* (Cambridge: Cambridge University Press, 1986), 113-14.

15. Jack London, "Yellow and White," in *Tales of the Fish Patrol* (New York: Macmillan Co., 1905).

16. Goode, *Fisheries*, sect., 5, vol. 1, 748.

17. Rudyard Kipling, *From Sea to Sea: Letters of Travel*, vol. 2 (New York: Doubleday & McClure Company, 1899), 34-35.

18. Chris Friday, *Organizing Asian American Labor: The Pacific Coast Canned Salmon Industry, 1870-1942* (Philadelphia: Temple University Press, 1994), 84-85.

19. United States. Congress. Senate. *Alaska Fisheries: Hearings Before the Subcommittee of the Committee on Fisheries* (Washington, DC: U. S. Government Printing Office, 1912), 135.

20. Ibid., 154.

21. Ibid., 160, 264.

22. Friday, *Organizing Asian American Labor*, 83.

23. Alexander Saxton, *The Indispensable Enemy: Labor and the Anti-Chinese Movement in California* (Berkeley: University of California Press, 1971).

24. Ibid., 222, quoting *Daily Report*, December 3, 1885.

25. Winfield J. Davis, ed., *History of Political Conventions in California, 1849-1892* (Sacramento: California State Library, 1893), 327.

26. United States. Merchant Marine Commission. *Report of the Merchant Marine Commission: vol. 2, Hearings on the Great Lakes and Pacific Coast* (Washington, DC: U.S. Government Printing Office, 1905), 1086 (hereafter cited as *Merchant Marine Commission*).

27. Ibid., 1249.

28. Saxton, *Indispensable Enemy*, 223.

29. Stuart B. Kaufman, Peter J. Albert, and Grace Palladino, eds., *Samuel Gompers Papers volume 5: An Expanding Movement at the Turn of the Century, 1898-1902* (Urbana: University of Illinois, 1996), 15n.

30. "An American Marine," *The World's Work: A History of Our Time* 29 (November-April 1915): 154.

31. United States. Industrial Commission. *Report of the Industrial Commission on Transportation*, vol. 4 (Washington, DC: U.S. Government Printing Office, 1900), 708.

32. *Report of the Merchant Marine Commission*, 1249.

33. Andrew Furuseth, "Give American Seamen a Chance," *Fort Wayne (IN) Sentine*l, October 30, 1912.

34. United States. Congress. Committee on Merchant Marine and Fisheries. *Creating a Shipping Board, a Naval Auxiliary, and a Merchant Marine: Hearings Before the Committee on the Merchant Marine and Fisheries,* H.R. 10500, 64th Congress, 1st Session, February 10-16, 1916, 27, 36-37.

35. *Report of the Merchant Marine Commission*, 1341.

36. Ibid., 1249.

37. Ibid., 1087, 1346.

38. Ibid., 1344-45.

39. Ibid., 1252.

40. Ibid., 1250-51.

41. United States. Congress. House. *Hearings Before the Select Committee to Inquire into the Operations, Policies, and Affairs of the United States Shipping Board and the Emergency Fleet Corporation* (Washington, DC: U.S. Government Printing Office, 1925), 4125-27.

42. Ibid., 102-04; the actual ability of the officers to speak Chinese is somewhat suspect in this instance.

43. See United States. Congress. House. Committee on Immigration and Naturalization, *Deportation of Alien Seamen Hearings Before the United States House Committee on Immigration and Naturalization, Seventy-First Congress, Third Session, on Feb. 24-28, 1931* (Washington, DC: U.S. Government Printing Office, 1931); Sucheng Chan, *Asian Americans: An Interpretive History* (Boston: Twayne, 1991), 90.

44. United States. Congress. House. *To Develop and American Merchant Marine: Hearings before the Committee on Merchant Marine and Fisheries* (Washington, DC: U.S. Government Printing Office, 1935), 822-23; see also Marshall P. Wilder, *Smiling 'round the World* (New York: Funk & Wagnalls Co., 1908), 42, 46; Thomas W. Hinchcliff, *Over the Sea and Far Away* (New York: Longmans, Green & Co., 1876), 312.

45. Percy Stickney Grant, *Observations in Asia* (New York: Brentano's, 1908), 13-14; Thomas Stewart Blair, *Public Hygiene,* vol. 1 (Boston: R.G. Badger, 1911), 587.

46. Wilbur J. and Georgia Louise Chamberlin, *Ordered to China; Letters of Wilbur J. Chamberlin Written from China While Under Commission from the New York Sun During the Boxer Uprising of 1900 and the International Complications Which Followed* (New York: F.A. Stokes Co., 1903).

47. Ibid., 8-9, 11.

48. Ibid., 16.

49. Chan, *Asian Americans*, 89.

11

1. Woman's Club of Gulfport, Federal Writer's Project in Mississippi Works Progress Administration, *Mississippi Gulf Coast: Yesterday 1600 and Today 1939* (Gulfport: Gulfport Printing Co., 1939), 39; Colleen C. Scholtes and L. J. Scholtes, *Biloxi and the Mississippi Gulf Coast, A Pictorial History* (Norfolk, VA: The Donning Company Publishers, 1986), 46; Mississippi Land Deed Book, 5, Jackson County Courthouse, Pascagoula, MS., 299. As a result of expanded railroad service and the invention of dry ice, the first shrimp cannery along the Mississippi Gulf Coast was established at Pascagoula in 1880. Joseph T. Maybury was president of the Mexican Gulf Canning Company, an enterprise chartered in Mobile, Alabama. Maybury also established a cannery in Mississippi. When the business opened, it advertised for "75 Women, Boys and Girls, above 12 years old . . . to shuck steamed oysters, fill cans, paste labels, pick and clean crabs and shrimp, and do other light work." The cannery also offered employment for "FIFTY MEN to man our oyster skiffs, unload oysters, etc.," see *Pascagoula Democrat-Star*, November 19, 1880.

2. Charles L. Sullivan and Murella Hebert Powell, *The Mississippi Gulf Coast: Portrait of a People* (Northridge, CA.: Windsor Publications, 1985), 116-19; Aimee Schmidt, "Down Around Biloxi: Culture and Identity in the Biloxi Seafood Industry," *Mississippi Folklife* 28 (1995): 3-6.

3. Margaret Filipich Soper, Oral History Interview by author, October 17, 2006. Soper began working in the seafood industry at age 13 and retired when she was 62. She has lived in Biloxi all of her life and can fluently speak Croatian, her father's language. She worked at the following factories, either in shrimp, oysters, or crabs: Anticich, Mavar's, DeJean, G. B. Mavar, Mlandinich's, Wentzell Brothers, Dubaz Brothers, Kuljis Brothers, Cvitanovich, Gulf Central, Cruso's Cannery, Sea Coast, Southern Shell, Gulf Central, and Mike Sekul's factory. Today, she lives in West Biloxi close to her daughter but still misses life on Point Cadet in East Biloxi. She is saddened that the Point of Biloxi no longer exists as a cultural enclave or an architectural district because of Hurricane Katrina's destruction and that the seafood industry is also struggling to recover as a result of the storm.

4. *Biloxi Daily Herald*, January 11, 1890; Murella Hebert Powell, "Biloxi, Queen City of the Gulf Coast," *Marine Resources and History of the Mississippi Gulf Coast: History, Art, and Culture of the Mississippi Gulf Coast* I (Jackson: Mississippi Department of Marine Resources: 1998), 142-43; Amelia "Sis" Eleuteris, Oral History Interview, June 1975, Biloxi Public Library Collection, Biloxi, Mississippi; C. Paige Gutierrez, *The Mississippi Coast and Its People: A History for Students* (Biloxi: Bureau of Marine Resources, Marine Discovery Series, 1987), 9-10; Eleuteris began working in Ernest Desporte's Seafood Factory at the age of 12 and has lived in Biloxi her entire life; the Biloxi Oral History Collection, however, housed at the Biloxi Public Library, sustained extensive damage along with everything else in the library as a result of Hurricane Katrina. Currently, the collection is under restoration.

5. Sister Mary Adrienne Curet, Oral History Interview by C. Paige Guiterrez, July 16, 1975, Biloxi Public Library Collection.

6. Lucretia Buzalich Lee, Oral History Interview, September 4, 1990, Biloxi Public Library Collection.

7. David A. Sheffield and Darnell L. Nicovich, *When Biloxi was the Seafood Capital of the World,* ed. Julia Cook Guice (Biloxi: City of Biloxi, 1979), 26, 67.

8. Schmidt, "Down Around Biloxi," 4; *Polk's Biloxi City Directory*, comp. W. W. A. Smith (Memphis, TN: R. L. Polk & Co., 1905), 37.

9. *Biloxi City Directory*, 1905, 18, 44, 105. The "Bohemian Camps" existed for the five canneries in the city at that time: the Barataria Canning Company, Gorenflo's Canning Company, E. C. Joullian Packing Company, Biloxi Canning Company, and Lopez & Dukate Company. However, more oyster dealers and houses existed in the city besides the large canneries. Listed are the following: Biloxi Fish & Oyster Company, Biloxi Oyster House with T. L. McCabe as Proprietor, Euceniat Matio, J. A. Broadus, Clark's Oyster House, P. W. Desporte, Ulysses Desporte, Lamas Brothers, and Jas. McCabe.

10. Stephan Thernstrom, ed., *Harvard Encyclopedia of American Ethnic Groups* (Cambridge, MA: Harvard University Press, 1980), 249.

11. United States Bureau of the Census. 1910 (Washington, D. C.: U.S. Government Printing Office).

12. C. Paige Gutierrez, *The Cultural Legacy of Biloxi's Seafood Industry* (Biloxi: 1984). In Biloxi, locals use the term Slavonian to denote anyone of Croatian, Serbian, or Slavonian descent. The majority of immigrants from the Dalmatian Coast in the Biloxi region are Croatian.

13. Soper Interview, October 17, 2006.

14. Ibid.

15. Ibid.

16. *Polk's Biloxi City Directory* (Memphis, TN.: R. L. Polk & Co., 1922), 26.

17. Soper Interview, October 17, 2006.

18. Murella Hebert Powell Oral History Interview by author, October 25, 2006, personal oral history collection of author.

19. Soper Interview, Oct. 17, 2006.

20. Ibid.

21. In 1888 Biloxi established a separate school district and began constructing public schools. That same year Frank Turner Howard and Harry Turner Howard donated land and buildings for the public schools. In 1896 Lazaro Lopez Sr. also donated the grounds and Point Cadet School on the corner of Oak and First Streets. Two years later, W. K. M. Dukate and William F. Gorenflo also donated land and buildings to the city for schools. These families were either founders of the seafood industry in Biloxi or heavily invested in it by the time of their donations. By 1902 a free night school established by Reverend H. S. VanHook also accommodated those young men and women who worked during the day and could not attend day school. Central High School was constructed in 1912, and in 1920 a Naturalization School on Point Cadet provided basic courses needed by the Slavonians in the neighborhood who needed to pass the naturalization test and become United States citizens.

22. Soper Interview, October 17, 2006.

23. Katie Kovacivich, Oral History Interview by Aimee Schmidt, January 2, 1993.

24. Lucretia Buzalich Lee, Oral History Interview, September 4, 1990.

25. Grace Gaudet Hebert, Oral History Interview by Murella Hebert Powell, August 11, 1992, personal collection of Powell.

26. Addie Blanchard Leduc, Oral History Interview by Murella Hebert Powell, n.d., personal collection of Powell.

27. Leduc Interview, August 11, 1992, and Powell Interview, October 25, 2006.

28. Powell Interview, October 25, 2006.

29. Soper Interview, October 17, 2006.

30. Ibid.

31. Powell Interview, October 25, 2006.

32. Ibid.

33. Hebert Interview, August 11, 1992.

12

1. Teruyo Hamaguchi, Junior Outing Club Minutes (1936-1942), Terminal Island, March 7, 1941, Hirasaki National Resource Center, Japanese American National Museum, 94.91.1 (hereafter cited as Minutes).

2. Donna R. Gabaccia and Vicki L. Ruiz, "Introduction," in *American Dreaming, Global Realities: Rethinking U.S. Immigration History* (Urbana: University of Illinois Press, 2006), 1-8.

3. Brian Niiya, "More Than a Game: Sport in the Japanese American

Community—An Introduction," in Brian Niiya, ed., *More Than a Game: Sport in the Japanese American Community* (Los Angeles: Japanese American National Museum, 2000), 14.

4. Valerie Matsumoto, *Farming the Home Place: A Japanese American Community in California, 1919-1982* (Ithaca, NY: Cornell University Press, 1993), 54.

5. Matsumoto, *Farming*, 24, 25; see also Dorothy Fujita-Rony, "Water and Land: Asian Americans and the U.S. West," *Pacific Historical Review* 76, no. 4 (November 2007): 564-74; David Igler, "Commentary: Re-Orienting Asian American History through Transnational and International Scales," *Pacific Historical Review* 76, no. 4 (November 2007): 611-14; and Rainer F. Buschmann, "Oceans of World History: Delineating Aquacentric Notions in the Global Past," *History Compass* 2, no. 1 (March 2004).

6. John Modell, *The Economics and Politics of Racial Accommodation: The Japanese of Los Angeles, 1900-1942* (Urbana: University of Illinois Press, 1977), 20, and Leonard Broom and Ruth Riemer, *Removal and Return: The Socio-Economic Effects of the War on Japanese Americans*, vol. 4 (Los Angeles: University of California Press, 1949), 7.

7. Modell, *Economics and Politics of Racial Accommodation*, 32.

8. George J. Sanchez, *Becoming Mexican American: Ethnicity, Culture, and Identity in Chicano Los Angeles, 1990-1945* (New York: Oxford University Press, 1993), 97.

9. Edwin Fitton Bamford, "Social Aspects of the Fishing Industry at Los Angeles Harbor," M.A. thesis, University of Southern California, 1921, 25, 26.

10. Kanichi Kawasaki, "The Japanese Community of East San Pedro, Terminal Island, California," M.A. thesis, University of Southern California, 1931, 1.

11. Ibid., quoting Bogardus, 179.

12. Ibid., 180.

13. David K. Yoo, *Growing Up Nisei: Race, Generation, and Culture among Japanese Americans of California, 1924-49* (Urbana: University of Illinois Press, 2000), 6-8.

14. Kanshi Stanley Yamashita, "Terminal Island: Ethnography of an Ethnic Community: Its Dissolution and Reorganization to a Non-Spatial Community," Ph.D. diss., University of California, Irvine, 1985, 12. For an interview with Yamashita and a study influenced by his approach, see The Terminal Islanders and Rob Fukuzaki, narrator, *Furusato: The Lost Village of Terminal Island*, special ed. DVD, Directed by David Metzler (Culver City, CA: Our Stories, 2007). I thank David Metzler for the opportunity to view the pre-release version for this paper.

15. Yamashita, "Terminal Island," viii.

16. Historiography on the commercial fishing industry of the Pacific's eastern littoral contributes to several fields. Recent scholarship includes Carol Lynn McKibben, *Beyond Cannery Row: Sicilian Women, Immigration, and*

Community in Monterey, California, 1915-99 (Urbana: University of Illinois Press, 2006); Lissa Wadewitz, "Pirates of the Salish Sea: Labor, Mobility, and Environment in the Transnational West," *Pacific Historical Review* 74, no. 4 (November 2006): 587-627; Connie Y. Chiang, "Monterey-by-the-Smell: Odors and Social Conflict on the California Coastline," *Pacific Historical Review* 73, no. 2 (2004): 183-214; Ann M. Peterson, "Recollections of Andrea Gómez: Terminal Island Fish Cannery Employee and Union Organizer, 1924-1965," M.A. thesis, California State University Long Beach, 2005; Chris Friday, *Organizing Asian American Labor: the Pacific Coast Canned-Salmon Industry, 1870-1942* (Philadelphia: Temple University Press, 1994); and Linda Bentz and Robert Schwemmer, "The Rise and Fall of the Chinese Fisheries in California," in Susie Lan Cassel, ed., *The Chinese in America: A History from Gold Mountain to the New Millennium* (Walnut Creek, CA: AltaMira Press, 2002), 140-55.

17. Vicki L. Ruiz and Ellen Carol DuBois, "Introduction to the Third Edition," in *Unequal Sisters: A Multicultural Reader in U.S. Women's History* (New York: Routledge, 2000), xii, xiii; and Nancy A. Hewitt, "Beyond the Search for Sisterhood: American Women's History in the 1990s," in *Unequal Sisters*, 2; and Shirley Hune, "Introduction, Through 'Our' Eyes: Asian/Pacific Islander American Women's History," in Shirley Hune and Gail M. Nomura, eds., *Asian/Pacific Islander American Women: A Historical Anthology* (New York: New York University Press, 2003), 1.

18. Valerie J. Matsumoto, "Japanese American Girls' Clubs in Los Angeles During the 1920s and 1930s," in *Asian/Pacific Islander American Women*, 172.

19. Shirley Jennifer Lim, *A Feeling of Belonging: Asian American Women's Public Culture, 1930-1960* (New York: New York University Press, 2006), 1, 36.

20. Lisa Norling, Daniel Vickers, et. al., "Roundtable: Review of Daniel Vickers with Vince Walsh, *Young Men and the Sea: Yankee Seafarers in the Age of Sail* with a Response by Daniel Vickers," *International Journal of Maritime History* 17, no. 2 (December 2005): 329-30, 363.

21. Yamashita, "Terminal Island," 82; Arthur F. McEvoy, *The Fisherman's Problem: Ecology and Law in the California Fisheries, 1850-1980* (New York: Cambridge University Press, 1986), 130.

22. Estimates vary, Terminal Islander oral histories and Yamashita, "Terminal Island," 56.

23. Oral histories in Orie Mio, *Terminal Island: An Island in Time, Collection of Personal Histories of Former Islanders, 1994-1995* ([Los Angeles, CA]: [Terminal Islanders], 1995), 261, 262 (hereafter cited as *Terminal Island*); David Igler, "Diseased Goods: Global Exchanges in the Eastern Pacific Basin, 1770-1850," *American Historical Review* 109, no. 3 (November 2004): 693-719.

24. Yamashita, "Terminal Island," 75; and Richard R. Perkins, "The Terminal Island Japanese, Preservation of a Lost Community," M.A. thesis, California State University Dominguez Hills, 1992, 62-70.

25. Henry P. Silka, Irene M. Almeida, et al., picture captions, assisted by Arthur A.

Almeida, Samuel Botwin, *San Pedro: A Pictorial History* (San Pedro, CA: San Pedro Bay Historical Society, 1984); and Charles F. Queenan, *The Port of Los Angeles: From Wilderness to World Port* (Los Angeles: Los Angeles Harbor Department, 1983).

26. Clifford M. Zierer, "The Los Angeles Harbor Fishing Center," *Economic Geography* 10, no. 4 (October 1934): 416.

27. Waldo Drake, "Shipping News ... Noted Liner Drops Flag," *Los Angeles Times*, December 20, 1934, 7.

28. S. H. Dado, California Division of Fish and Game, "Sardine Plants Report Season 1937-1938," *Statistical Report on Fresh and Canned Fishery Products 1937,* Circular No. 12 (May 1938), 6; also see "Caught, Canned, and Eaten: The History of San Pedro's Fishing and Canning Industries," a permanent exhibit at the Los Angeles Maritime Museum; and Zierer, "Los Angeles Harbor Fishing Center," 402-18.

29. Chotoku Toyama, "The Japanese Community in Los Angeles," M.A. thesis, Columbia University, 1926, 17; and Yamashita, "Terminal Island," 93.

30. "California Tuna Vessels," *Pacific Fisherman: 1938 Year Book Number* 36, no. 2 (January 1938): 149; and "Japanese Fishing Boats and Fishermen, October 1940-October 1941," Southern California Japanese Fishermen's Association, Hirasaki National Resource Center, Japanese American National Museum, 94.141.1.

31. Southern California Japanese Fishermen's Association, 94.141.1, and Kanshi Stanley Yamashita, "Kiyoo Yamashita," *Terminal Island*, 419-39. Kiyoo Yamashita was the father of ethnographer Kanshi Stanley Yamashita.

32. Lois [J. Weinman] Roberts and E. Gary Stickel, *The Los Angeles-Long Beach Harbor Areas Cultural Resource Survey, Prepared for U.S. Army Engineer District, Los Angeles, CA; Submitted by Lois J. Weinman and E. Gary Stickel* (Los Angeles: Army Corps of Engineers, 1978), 104.

33. See also Peterson, "Recollections of Andrea Gómez."

34. "Badge, ca. 1940, Standard Object Report," Hirasaki National Resource Center, Japanese American National Museum, 94.98.13.

35. Southern California Japanese Fishermen's Association, 94.141.1.

36. *Terminal Island*, 261, 262.

37. Yamashita, "Terminal Island"; see also Vicki L. Ruiz, *Cannery Women, Cannery Lives: Mexican Women, Unionization, and the California Food Processing Industry, 1930-1950* (Albuquerque: University of New Mexico Press, 1987).

38. Yukio Tatsumi, "Preface," *Terminal Island,* [n.p.].

39. Yamashita, "Terminal Island," 45, 46.

40. Leonard Broom and Ruth Riemer, *Removal and Return: The Socio-Economic Effects of the War on Japanese Americans*, vol. 4 (Los Angeles: University of California Press, 1949), 7; and John Modell, *Economics and Politics of Racial Accommodation*, 20.

41. Yamashita, "Terminal Island," 9-12; James R. McGoodwin, *Crisis in the World's Fisheries: People, Problems, and Policies* (Stanford, CA: Stanford University Press, 1990), 27

42. For instance, see Joan F. Broomfield, "The Fishery Industry of Southern California," Ph.D. diss., University of California at Los Angeles, 1949, map at 24-25.

43. Frank Koo Endo, written by Frank Koo Endo, *Terminal Island*, 2.

44. Toshiro Izumi, *Terminal Island*, 145.

45. Orie Mio, *Terminal Island*, 261.

46. Vicki L. Ruiz, *From Out of the Shadows: Mexican Women in Twentieth-Century America* (New York: Oxford University Press, 1998), 50.

47. Yukio Tatsumi, "Preface," *Terminal Island*, [n.p.], and William Olesen, "Terminal Island: A Sandspit Grows Up," *Channel Crossings: Newsletter of the Los Angeles Maritime Museum, San Pedro, California* 2, no. 2 (Autumn 2005): 4, 5, 7.

48. Frank Koo Endo, *Terminal Island*, 4.

49. Yamashita, "Terminal Island," 121. The only reference to the YWCA Girls' Reserve in the Junior Outing Club Minutes was by Masako Terada on November 26, 1941: "Miss Hills and Mrs. Moth from YWCA came and explained to us about organizing a club of Girl[s']Reserve. Everybody was asked to tell their mother about it."

50. *Terminal Island*; Yamashita, "Terminal Island," 123, 126, 127; and Masako Terada, Minutes, November 26, 1941.

51. Kawasaki, "Japanese Community of East San Pedro," 47; and Yamashita, "Terminal Island," 117-21.

52. Valerie Matsumoto, "Desperately Seeking 'Deirdre': Gender Roles, Multicultural Relations, and Nisei Women Writers of the 1930s," *Frontiers: A Journal of Women Studies* 12, no. 1 (1991): 19-32; and Valerie Matsumoto, "Redefining Expectations, Nisei Women in the 1930s," *California History* 73, no. 1 (Spring 1994): 45-53.

53. Matsumoto, "Japanese American Girls' Clubs in Los Angeles during the 1920s and 1930s," 172, 182-83.

54. "Big Pines Outing Planned for Bussei," *Rafu Shimpo*, no. 10,795, Tuesday, January 12, 1937, 6; and "Mariners Invite Friends to Skate," *Rafu Shimpo*, no. 10,793, Sunday, January 10, 1937, 2; and "Girls Give Program At Children's Home," *Rafu Shimpo*, no. 10,793, Sunday, January 10, 1937, 1.

55. Matsumoto, "Japanese American Girls' Clubs in Los Angeles during the 1920s and 1930s," 175.

56. Fumi Shirokawa, Minutes, September 25, 1936, and passim; and U.S. Bureau of the Census, 1930, Long Beach, Los Angeles, California, Roll 130, Page, 12A,

Enumeration District 1140, Image 1110.0, www.ancestry.com (accessed May 22, 2006).

57. Kazuye Shibata Kushi, *Terminal Island*, 332.

58. Teruko Miyoshi Okimoto, *Terminal Island*, 315, 316.

59. Teruko Miyoshi Okimoto, *Terminal Island*, 318; and Minutes.

60. Chikao Robert Ryono, *Although Patriotic, We Were Drydocked* (Los Angeles: [Terminal Islanders], [1994]), 29.

61. Irving Hendrick, *The Education of Non-Whites in California, 1849-1970* (San Francisco: R & E Research Associates, Inc., 1977), 89.

62. Ibid., 89.

63. Yamashita, "Terminal Island," 123.

64. Ryono, *Although Patriotic*, 28, 29; see also Maggie Shelton, *The Red Lacquer Bridge* (Bloomington, IN: AuthorHouse, 2007).

65. Hideyo Ono, Minutes, January 14, 1938.

66. Hideyo Ono, Minutes, March 25, 1938.

67. Fumi Shirokawa, Minutes, January 22, 1937.

68. Yamashita, "Terminal Island," 120.

69. Hideyo Ono, Minutes, September 24, 1937.

70. Minutes, October, 9, 1936, January 8, 1937, September 24, 1937, November 12, 1937, February 14, 1938 (Mr. Yokozeki), February 25, 1938, November 10, 1938, May 26, 1939, and June 8, 1939. Other Issei women by name or as mother sponsors: September 24, 1937, November 12, 1937, January 14, 1938, March 24, 1939, June 8, 1939, January 12, 1940, February 9, 1940, and March 8, 1940. References to mothers as a group: February 26, 1937, March 12, 1937, April 8, 1938, April 22, 1938, March 10, 1939, April 14, 1939.

71. Ryono, *Although Patriotic*, 29, 38, and *San Pedro and Wilmington (California) City Directory* ([Los Angeles]: Los Angeles Directory Co., 1932), 333.

72. *City Directory*, 163; and U.S. Census, 1930, Los Angeles, California, Roll 156, Page 9B, Enumeration District 601, Image 242.0, www.ancestry.com (accessed June 11, 2006).

73. Fumi Shirokawa, Minutes, January 22, 1937, and Aiko Tani, Minutes, September 2, 1939.

74. Ryono, *Although Patriotic*, 31, 47.

75. Yamashita, "Terminal Island," 101.

76. Yuji Ichioka, *The Issei: The World of the First Generation Japanese Immigrants, 1885-1924* (New York: The Free Press, 1988), 164-75; *Terminal Island;* and McKibben, *Beyond Cannery Row*, 11, 12.

77. Yamashita, "Terminal Island," 101, 102.

78. “Constitution,” Minutes [tipped in].

79. Lim, *A Feeling of Belonging,* 36.

80. Shizuka Ishikawa, Minutes, November 10, 1938 and Emiko Kohigashi, December 9, 1938.

81. Matsumoto, “Japanese American Girls’ Clubs in Los Angeles during the 1920s and 1930s,” 184.

82. Fumi Shirokawa, Minutes, April 9, 1937.

83. Fumi Shirokawa, Minutes, November 12, 1936; Shizuka Ishikawa, Minutes, March 10, 1939; and Masako Terada, Minutes, November 26, 1941; also see Brian Niiya, “More Than a Game: Sport in the Japanese American Community—An Introduction,” *More Than a Game,* 16, 17.

84. “Constitution,” Minutes [tipped in].

85. Yamashita, “Terminal Island,” 112-17.

86. Toshiro Izumi, “Charlie O. Hamasaki,” transcribed by Mary Tamura, *Terminal Island*, 40, 41.

87. Shizuka Ishikawa, Minutes, March 24, 1939.

88. Teruyo Hamaguchi, Minutes, March 7, 1941. This is the quote appearing at the beginning of this chapter.

89. Orie Mio, *Terminal Island*, 261; and Frank Koo Endo, *Terminal Island*, 3.

90. “Constitution,” Minutes [tipped in].

91. Fumi Shirokawa, Minutes, May 14, 1937; Hideyo Ono, Minutes, May 27, 1938; Shizuka Ishikawa, Minutes, May 26, 1939; and “Constitution,” Minutes [tipped in].

92. Shizuka Ishikawa, Minutes, February 9, 1939; and Teruyo Hamaguchi, Minutes, March 7, 1941.

93. Fumi Shirokawa, Minutes, January 22, 1937; Shizuka Ishikawa, Minutes, November 10, 1938; and Teruyo Hamaguchi, Minutes, February 28, 1941.

94. Ford H. Kuramoto, *A History of the Shonien 1914-1972: An Account of a Program of Institutional Care of Japanese Children in Los Angeles* (San Francisco: R and E Research Associates, 1976), 24; Fumi Shirokawa, Minutes, September 25, 1936; and Hideyo Ono, Minutes, November 12, 1937.

95. Modell, *Economics and Politics of Racial Accommodation,* 167, 168.

96. Fumi Shirokawa, Minutes, February 26, 1937.

97. Hideyo Ono, Minutes, undated. The sequence of the diary indicates that it was made between November 12, 1937, and January 14, 1938.

98. Hideyo Ono, Minutes, April 8, 1938, April 22, 1938, and May 13, 1938.

99. Masako Terada, Minutes, October 17, 1941.

100. Hideyo Ono, Minutes, February 25, 1938.

101. Teruko Miyoshi Okimoto, *Terminal Island*, 316.

102. Orie Mio, *Terminal Island*, 262.

103. [Junior Class], "Japanese Program," *Black and Gold*, vol. 17 (San Pedro, CA: San Pedro High School Printing Department, 1927), 88; Hirasaki National Resource Center, Japanese American National Museum, 94.71.1. The East San Pedro School was the elementary school in the Terminal Island fishing community.

104. Matsumoto, "Japanese American Girls' Clubs in Los Angeles during the 1920s and 1930s," 172, 182-84.

105. Fumi Shirokawa, Minutes, May 14, 1937.

106. Teruyo Hamaguchi, Minutes, February 7, 1941.

107. Brian Niiya, "More Than a Game: Sport in the Japanese American Community—An Introduction," *More Than a Game,* 16, 17.

108. Matsumoto, "Japanese American Girls' Clubs in Los Angeles during the 1920s and 1930s," 179.

109. Fumi Shirokawa, Minutes, May 14, 1937; Kyo Mio, Minutes, February 21, 1940; Teruya Hanaguchi, Minutes, February 7, 1941; and Kazuye Shibata Kushi, *Terminal Island*, 333.

110. Aiko Tani, Minutes, January 12, 1940.

111. Kyo Mio, Minutes, June 12, 1940. I added commas between list items.

112. Kyo Mio, Minutes, February 21, 1940.

113. Teruyo Hamaguchi, Minutes, April 4, 1941.

114. Mas Tanibata, transcribed by Mary Tamura, March 4, [1994], *Terminal Island*, 342, 343.

115. Kazuye Shibata Kushi, *Terminal Island*, 333.

116. Mas Tanibata, *Terminal Island*, 342, 343, 344. The Junior Outing Club's minutes indicate that the Junior and Senior Outing Clubs sometimes practiced together.

117. Kyo Mio, Minutes, February 21, 1940.

118. Kazuye Shibata Kushi, *Terminal Island*, 332; and Katsuyemon Shibata, written by Kazuye Shibata Kushi, November, 1994, *Terminal Island*, 326.

119. Ryono, *Although Patriotic*, 76.

120. Lim, *A Feeling of Belonging*, 11-46; and Yuri Nakahara Kochiyama, *Passing It On - A Memoir* (Los Angeles: UCLA Asian American Studies Center Press, 2004), 11; *Terminal Island.*

121. Kazuye Shibata Kushi, *Terminal Island*, 332.

122. Bessie Shibata, Minutes, November 7, 1941.

123. Kyo Mio, Minutes, April 12, 1940; letter from Leon L. Dwight, Chairman, San Pedro Boy's Club, Inc., May 16, 1941 [tipped-in]; *City Directory*, 279.

124. Teruyo Hamaguchi, Minutes, March 21, 1941.

125. Masako Terada, Minutes, October 3, 1941, and October 17, 1941.

126. Bessie Shibata, Minutes, December 5, 1941.

127. Brian Niiya, ed., *Japanese American History: An A-to-Z Reference from 1868 to the Present* (Los Angeles: The Japanese American National Museum, 1993), 327.

128. Yamashita, "Terminal Island," 148.

129. Kuichi Izumi, Narrated by Son, Toshiro Izumi, February 6, 1994, transcribed by Mary Tamura, *Terminal Island*, 105, 106.

130. Fusaye Hashimoto, *Terminal Island*, 67, 69, 74.

131. Masako Terada, Minutes, January 23, 1942.

132. Fusaye Hashimoto, *Terminal Island*, 73; Niiya, *Japanese American History*, 327.

133. Niiya, *Japanese American History*, 55.

134. Rasa Gustaitis, *Back in Time: A Historic Cove Comes Back to Life* (Oakland, CA: California State Coastal Conservancy, Summer 1997) http://www.coastalconservancy.ca.gov/coast&ocean/suchive/TCSUM.HTM (accessed September 3, 2005).

135. Fusaye Hashimoto, *Terminal Island*, 76; see also Broom and Riemer, *Removal and Return*.

136. Fusaye Hashimoto, *Terminal Island*, 80; Niiya, *Japanese American History*, 327.

137. Yamashita, "Terminal Island," 148; Manzanar High School, *Our World, 1943-44, Manzanar High*, [Edited by new edition editor Diane Yotsuya Honda] (Logan, UT: Herff Jones Yearbook Co., 1998, [n.p.]). For instance, see senior portraits of Misuko Ryono and Masako Terada.

138. Ryono, *Although Patriotic*, 79.

139. Yamashita, "Terminal Island," viii and passim; *Furusato* DVD.

140. Ryono, *Although Patriotic*, 27.

Index

I

J

K

L

U

V

W

Y

Z